EUROPEAN STAMP ISSUES AND THE FIRST WORLD WAR

Fall of Empires, Rise of Nations

EUROPEAN STAMP ISSUES AND THE FIRST WORLD WAR

Fall of Empires, Rise of Nations

DAVID PARKER

HALSGROVE

First published in Great Britain in 2018

Copyright © 2018 David Parker

All rights reserved. No part of this publication may be reproduced,
stored in a retrieval system, or transmitted in any form or by any
means without the prior permission of the copyright holder.

British Library Cataloguing-in-Publication Data
A CIP record for this title is available from the British Library

ISBN 978 0 85704 330 6

HALSGROVE
Halsgrove House, Ryelands Business Park,
Bagley Road, Wellington, Somerset TA21 9PZ
Tel: 01823 653777   Fax: 01823 216796
email: sales@halsgrove.com

Part of the Halsgrove group of companies
Information on all Halsgrove titles is available at: www.halsgrove.com

Printed and bound by Parksons Graphics, India

Contents

Introduction and Explanatory Notes 6

Chapter 1   Imperial Germany and the 'Weimar' Republic 8
Map Germany 1815-1914
Map Europe according to the peace treaties 1919-22

Chapter 2   Belgium 29

Chapter 3   Luxembourg 38

Chapter 4   France 42

Chapter 5   Poland 51
Map Poland 1815-1914

Chapter 6   Imperial Russia and the Soviet Union 62

Chapter 7   The Baltic States: Estonia, Latvia and Lithuania 74

Chapter 8   The Austro-Hungarian Empire, Austrian Republic and Regency Hungary 84
Map Austria-Hungary 1815-1914

Chapter 9   Czechoslovakia 106

Chapter 10 Italy 113
Map Italy 1815-1914

Chapter 11 Serbia, Montenegro and the Kingdom of the Serbs, Croats and Slovenes 127

Chapter 12 Romania 136

Chapter 13 Bulgaria 143

Chapter 14 Albania 151

Chapter 15 Greece 157

Bibliography 166

Index 166

Introduction

Stamps are far more than the universal sign that postal charges have been paid. Very often they are skillfully designed works of art calculated to impart particular messages to the user. Certainly this was true a century or more ago. From the last decades of the nineteenth century most governments, whether of great empires, newly independent nations or short-lived breakaway states, fully exploited the great additional value of postage stamps as visual propaganda promoting dynasties, celebrating territorial acquisitions, and strengthening national identities through the commemoration of past as well as present military and cultural achievements. These small pieces of paper were often adorned with eye-catching images of people and places, allegories and cultural icons, whose carefully contrived and executed designs far exceeded the mundane need to record the fee for a postcard, letter or parcel.

Only the United Kingdom abstained from this policy, viewing the monarch's head as sufficient publicity and the country in no need of philatelic promotion. The sole exceptions were the 1924 and 1925 images of a determined looking lion alongside the head of King George V in the pairs of stamps that marked the Empire Exhibition in Wembley. Every other European country thought very differently and deemed it well worth while, whatever the distractions and pressures, to promote its version of national affairs through the tiny images that permeated every town and village. In addition they carried their messages abroad either affixed to mail or in the hands of the host of avid collectors. International stamp exhibitions were popular events, and nations welcomed hosting them. A century ago, as now, many cash-strapped states welcomed the profits from commemoration sets, and often sets were used to raise funds for special events, including the Olympic Games, and, of course, major war memorials.

As the following chapters recall, the assassination of Archduke Franz Ferdinand, the heir of Franz Joseph, Emperor of Austria and King of Hungary, in Sarajevo, the capital of the province of Bosnia, on 28 June 1914 brought to a head decades of European territorial disputes, commercial rivalry and violent nationalism. Like falling dominoes Austria-Hungary and Serbia, Germany and Russia, France, Belgium and Great Britain were swiftly drawn into war, and many other countries, notably Italy, Bulgaria and Romania, were to follow.

The battles raged across swathes of Europe from eastern France to the Balkans, and into Russia, the Near and Middle East, and across the oceans of the world and in various African colonies, and by and large stalemate ensued until the Russian Empire collapsed in 1917 and was followed by the disintegration of the Austro-Hungarian Empire and the exhaustion of the German Empire the following year. And all the while numerous sets of new or overprinted stamps marked the occupation of enemy territory and sought funds for the care of the wounded, sick, homeless and starving,

Although a few prescient statesmen and generals prophesied a long-drawn out war of attrition most were bewildered by the consistent lack of success of huge offensives that began with vast bombardments from heavy artillery and then ground to bloody halts amidst hails of machine gun bullets slaughtering thousands of men. Few had any satisfactory alternative strategies

Death on such a scale, and the misery of the destruction of hundreds of towns, and thousands of villages, factories and farms, created deep disenchantment with the politicians and generals who failed to achieve victory and peace. And this in turn intensified the atmosphere in which pre-war thoughts of revolution and the creation of new societies based on self-determination and greater social equality could be turned into action – and, if necessary, violent action borne of frustration and desperation. Thus the Czechs and Slovaks broke from Austrian and Hungarian authority to form the fragile state of Czechoslovakia, Poland was recreated from its historic regions that had been annexed by Austria, Prussia and Russia in the late eighteenth century, and Estonia, Latvia and Lithuania wrestled themselves free from Russian control. And numerous stamp issues traced the downfall of dynasties and the dramatic, often bloodstained, emergence of fragile new states, some destined to survive and others quickly suppressed.

For several years after 1918 many international borders were bitterly contested, with Allied Peace Conference members and International Commissions striving to stop the intermittent warfare and impose plebiscites where no obvious solutions were available to them. Undoubtedly the post-war settlements, many of which sought to be fair to the ethnic groups that had lived within the German and Austro-Hungarian

Empires, sowed the seeds of the Second World War. Germany resented the loss of Alsace-Lorraine to France and swathes of eastern territory to Poland, and the Soviet Union never lost its interest in Poland and the Baltic States, and ensured the independence of the Ukraine, Armenia and Georgia was short-lived. Across the battle-scarred Balkans, once the proud domain of the Ottoman Turks, Hungary, Romania, Bulgaria, Albania and Greece remained dissatisfied with their borders and constantly at odds with each other – a factor waiting to be exploited by Mussolini and Hitler. And all the while nations traumatised by the war, and notably France, sought to ensure Germany could never rise to prominence again, while Italy nursed its resentment towards its old Allies at the lack of territory around the Adriatic it was awarded at the Paris Peace Conference.

This book explores the identity, anxieties and aspirations pervading each empire and country prior to its engagement in the war, and reveals the successes and failures of its military campaigns and the impact of these upon its people and rulers. It looks, too, at the processes of decay and disintegration of the three great empires of Russia, Austria-Hungary and Germany and the emergence of new countries or recreated ancient ones that arose out of their ashes. And it examines the interests and ambitions of each country, and the perils it faced, during the early post-war years. Every nation, whether old or new, and whether some form of monarchy or republic, sought to stabilize itself throughout the 1920s, and major contributors to this vital task were the sets of stamps that promoted national pride, purpose, and unity through their portrayal of celebrated figures, past achievements, historic sites, evocative landscapes, and poets, painters and writers who strove to promote the national identity. These tiny pieces of paper reveal much about their countries of origin and their view of themselves.

A NOTE ON CAPTIONS

Exact dates of issues are not always known and the captions give the best information available from Michel, Scott and Stanley Gibbons catalogues. Sometimes the month and year only are known, and occasionally only the year.

If an illustration is of an issue comprising a single stamp it is noted as, for example, *(1 January 1919)*.

If selected examples from a set are shown it is noted as *(from set 8 October 1915)*.

If the issuing of a set ranged over a lengthy period it is noted as *(from set 23 March 1917+)*.

If all the stamps in a set are shown it is noted as *(set 12 May 1932)* or *(set 7 April 1916+)*.

If a set includes a variety of papers, perforations and colour changes, as well as dates of issue, it is noted as *(from series 9 August 1913+)*. Sometimes overprints were applied in wartime, or in the ensuing chaos, to residual stocks of any stamps that could be found, and they are similarly captioned.

Where a capital 'E' appears by a stamp or set of stamps it means they have been enlarged to highlight/clarify the central images within them.

ACKNOWLEDGEMENTS

My thanks are given to Mark Ware for his skilled work on the design of the front cover based on a striking Belgian stamp of 1932.

CHAPTER 1
Imperial Germany and the 'Weimar' Republic

King Wilhelm I of Prussia was proclaimed German Emperor in the Hall of Mirrors at the Palace of Versailles in France on 18 January 1871. The ceremony was the fulfillment of the vision of his Chancellor, Otto von Bismarck, who had masterminded the progress of unifying numerous hitherto independent German states while ensuring the dominance of Prussia. A succession of brief but highly successful wars against Denmark in 1864, Hapsburg Austria in 1866 and France in 1870-71 had contributed much to both German pride and Prussian dominance – and indeed to wider European anxiety. Denmark had lost Schleswig-Holstein, France Alsace-Lorraine, and the Hapsburgs all influence in German affairs.

Officially the Empire was a federation of equals, and the states retained their rulers and internal administrations. The stamp issues of most individual states lapsed around 1871, but Bavaria kept its own issues until 1920, after the collapse of the German Empire, and although Wurttemberg used Imperial German sets from 1902 it retained its own Official and Municipal Service stamps until 1923.

GERMANY UNDER KAISER WILHELM II

One of the great 'What ifs' of History is how Germany and indeed Europe would have evolved if Wilhelm I's genuinely liberal minded son Frederick III had ruled far longer than 99 days in 1888 before throat cancer killed him. In the event it was his son, Wilhelm II, who turned the empire into a personal vision of an armed camp ready to challenge the fleets, overseas empires and trade monopolies of the other Great Powers, and notably Great Britain. Arrogant and yet emotional by nature, the new Kaiser dismissed Bismarck in March 1890 along with his policy of keeping Germany's mighty neighbours France and Russia from sealing an encircling alliance. Wilhelm became notorious for his aggressive speeches on foreign policy and ill-concealed jealousy of Britain's pre-eminent world position. He encouraged African and Asiatic colonialism, courting serious if short-lived diplomatic scares with both France and Great Britain when their interests clashed, and while Wilhelm's ambitious plans for a Grand Fleet were unlikely to threaten the Royal Navy's global supremacy they did cause enough anxiety to spark an immensely costly naval race. Fears of a major war rarely went away in the first decade of the twentieth century.

Not surprisingly these fears heightened each nation's search for allies, and in doing so paved the way for the First World War. In 1882 Germany, Austria-Hungary and Italy had formed a Triple Alliance that was periodically renewed up to 1914. Germany and Austria-Hungary promised mutual support in a war, although Italy only committed itself to neutrality except if France attacked Germany. The fatal moment for Germany, however, was Wilhelm II's decision to let Germany's 'Reinsurance Treaty' with Russia lapse when it expired in 1890. This had guaranteed German neutrality if Russia was at war with anyone except Austria-Hungary, and Russian neutrality if Germany was at war with anyone except France. Soon afterwards Germany found itself faced with the possibility of a war on two fronts as between 1891 and 1893 Russia and France signed several political and military agreements that ensured they provided mutual aid if one of them was attacked by Germany. And in 1904 Germany's hopes that centuries of Anglo-French antagonism would continue were largely dashed by the celebrated Entente Cordiale that settled several colonial disputes and drew the two nations together, although it fell short of a military alliance. Notwithstanding all the limitations written into some of the treaties, Europe was effectively divided into two mutually suspicious armed camps. Indeed, for much of 1905 and 1906 Europe held its breath when Germany deliberately challenged France's growing influence over Morocco. As a result French and German troops were placed on the alert in Alsace and Lorraine, and Germany only reluctantly backed down in the face of united French, British and American opposition.

Imperial Germany's stamps reflected its self-image. From 1872 some stamps featured the medieval Holy Roman Empire's single headed eagle with outstretched wings, while others incorporated the crown above a value tablet and a decorative surround.(1.1/1.2)

They changed, though, in 1899 and 1900 when a lengthy set with five designs reflected the Empire's growing might and Wilhelm II's soaring confidence. An actress named Anna Fuhring attained lasting fame by

IMPERIAL GERMANY AND THE 'WEIMAR' REPUBLIC

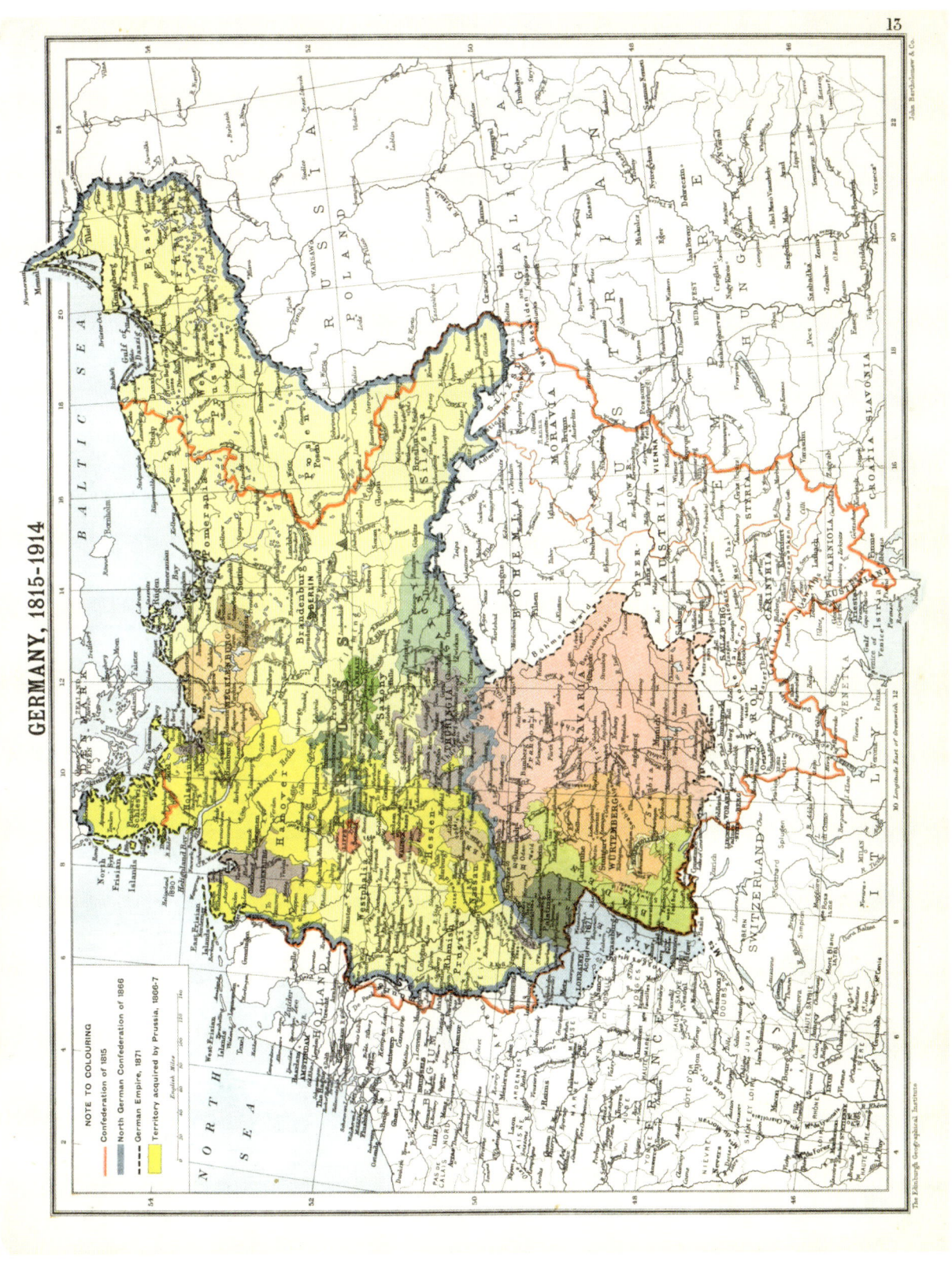

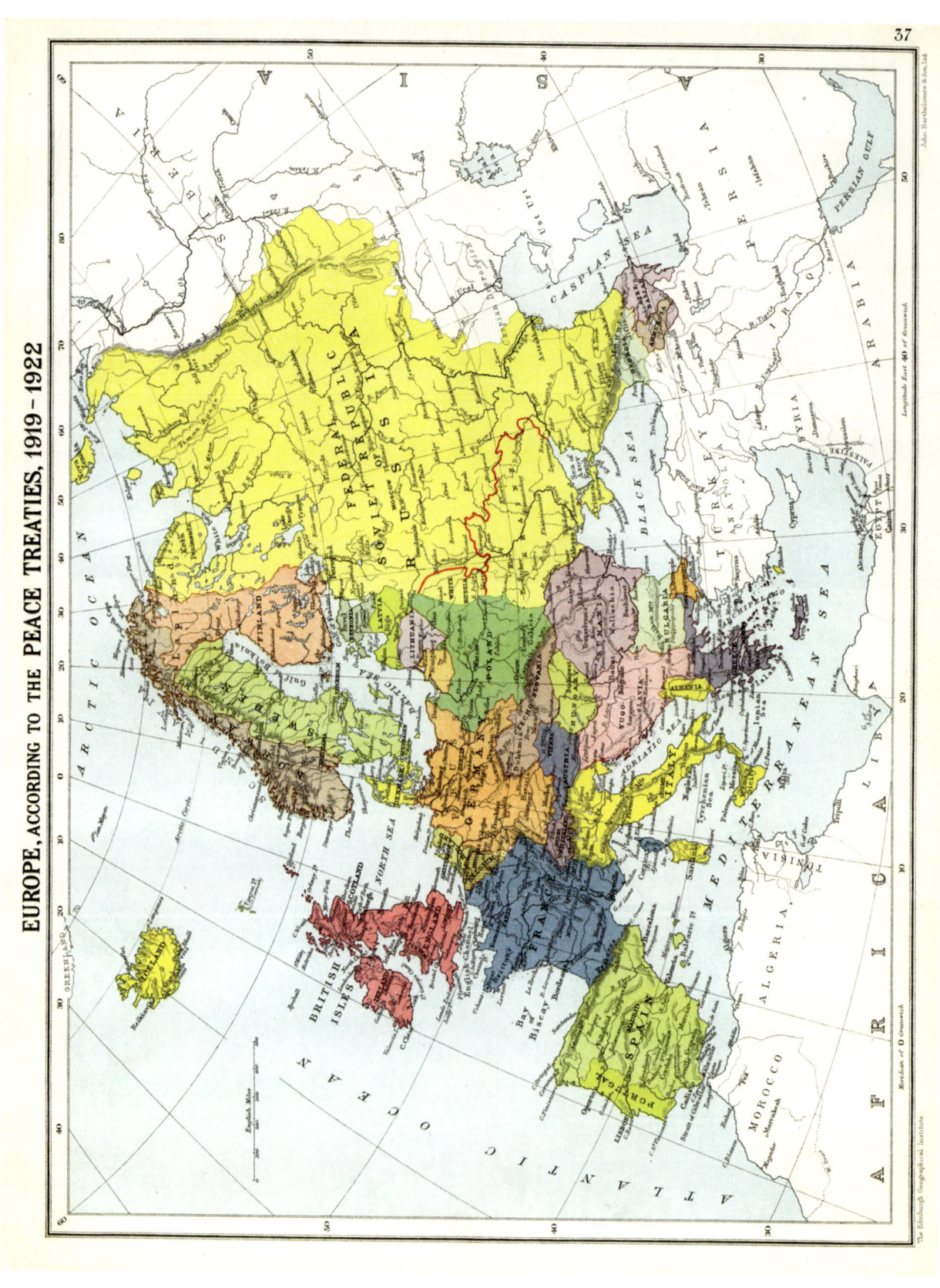

IMPERIAL GERMANY AND THE 'WEIMAR' REPUBLIC

1.1 3pf crown above wreath and value tablet (from set November 1889+)

1.2 20pf crown above Imperial eagle (from set November 1889+)

1.3 20pf single colour and 80pf twin colour Germania values (from set December 1899+)

sitting for the allegorical figure of *Germania* that first appeared on ten lower values in this commemorative set.(1.3) The unity of the Empire was further emphasized in a second allegorical stamp featuring a winged female figure bringing together warriors from northern and southern Germany. A third stamp pictured the unveiling of the massive equestrian statue of Kaiser Wilhelm I in Berlin with Wilhelm II conspicuous on his horse. A fourth featured Wilhelm II giving his address to mark the 25th anniversary of the Empire. The least dramatic stamp in the set featured Berlin's General Post Office. However it, too, symbolized national unity as the Imperial postal service was touching many, if not yet all, parts of Empire – and the image also enhanced the importance of the new capital city.(1.4) The designs of the 2m, 3m and 5m had been taken from huge paintings undertaken in the exuberant heroic style so fashionable across central Europe at this time.

It was on 27 July 1900, at the time this set was appearing, that Wilhelm II addressed the troops about to leave Bremerhaven to help suppress the Boxer Rebellion in China where European interests and lives were under threat, and famously asserted *Just as a thousand years ago the Huns under their King Attila made a name for themselves, one that today makes them seem mighty in history and legend, may the name German be affirmed by you in such a way in China that no Chinese will ever again dare to gaze cross-eyed at a German.* The rest of the world was soon to make much of his embarrassing analogy. The set was reprinted in 1902 with the

1.4 (E) 1m General Post Office Berlin, 2m Allegory of the Union of North & South Germany, 3m Unveiling of the Memorial to Wilhelm I in Berlin, and 5m Address by Wilhelm II on the 25th Anniversary of the German Empire (from set December 1899+)

title *Deutsches Reich* (German Empire) replacing *Reichpost* (Imperial Post) and again in 1905, and as we shall see two higher value designs reappeared as late as 1920. The stamps appeared in many guises – recess or typographical printed, in different shades, and with different perforation sizes.

In 1905 *Germania* was chosen for a new definitive set, and with slight variations in lettering and shading it was to be the main German stamp during the war and the final printing of two values was as late as 1922. With its many wartime Gothic overprints, it became the potent and hated symbol of German rule in occupied territories, and reappears in several other chapters of this book. The 1916 issue was slightly different to the others as the background to the portrait was left unshaded.

GERMANY AT WAR

Historians have fought many battles over the reasons why Germany engaged in war in 1914. The Kaiser and many, but far from all, of his advisers glorified the memory of distant and recent Prussian victories, and yet while they thought the German army unbeatable they were beset by nagging fears of French and Russian encirclement and possessed an abiding jealousy of British naval and colonial supremacy. With justification they believed Italy to be a weak and uncertain ally, and again with justification they saw Austria-Hungary, their only true ally, as hardly an equal in wealth and military might. Austria-Hungary was, though, a bastion against Russian ambitions in the Balkans, and here lay the touch paper that Germany encouraged Austria-Hungary to light in July 1914.

In addition, within the German elite there was a strange contradictory mix of glorification and fatalism about events, not far from Nordic mythology's *Gotterdammerung* – the Twilight of the Gods – where a prophesied war brings fire, flood and destruction but also the renewal of the world. Typical of the period was a 1913 pre-paid postcard celebrating Wilhelm II's 25 years as Kaiser with his portrait surrounded by a menacing German eagle and his armed forces seemingly poised for action.(1.5)

There was a sense that if Franz Ferdinand's assassination on a visit to Bosnia on 28 June exploded into a general European war, as some foretold, then at least all the German Empire's anxieties and ambitions might be settled one way or the other. Indeed, for many years the German High Command had laid down detailed plans to guide its armies in campaigns against both France and Russia. And Russia and France, knowing this, had their own plans of attack.

Soon after 'the Sarajevo incident' the Kaiser offered the Emperor Franz Joseph full support for whatever action he took against Serbia, the suspected centre of the assassination plot. On top of this alarming ' blank cheque' Wilhelm repeatedly chivvied Franz Joseph into military action although Austria-Hungary needed little encouragement to deal harshly with Serbia even though at this stage there was little hard evidence of its guilt. But then Russia entered the fray and reassured Serbia that it would protect its independence. Suitably encouraged, Serbia rejected the clauses in Austria-Hungary's humiliating ultimatum that demanded detailed intervention in its internal affairs, and war was declared on 25 July. Tsar Nicholas II, convinced by senior officers that his army and navy were well prepared,

1.5 1913 pre-paid postcard celebrating the 25th anniversary of Wilhelm II's accession.

ordered full mobilization with a likely war against Germany as well as Austria-Hungary in mind. Germany warned Russia that unless its mobilization halted Germany would mobilise too, and it did so on 31 July when no reply was received.

Russia's western allies were fully aware of the implications. The Belgians, too, were conscious of their perilous situation if Germany attacked France, and the French were equally aware of the danger stretching from Belgium down through Alsace and Lorraine. On 1 August Germany declared war on Russia, six days before Austria-Hungary did the same, and on 3 August Germany declared war on France. However on 2 August German troops had entered the tiny Duchy of Luxembourg despite the general historic guarantees, including by Germany, of its neutrality. Germany's long planned great sweeping curve through the duchy and Belgium towards Paris and the encircling and crushing of French forces along the Franco-German borders had begun. Belgium's refusal to permit German troops across its territory was ignored, but to German surprise and anger Belgian troops offered resistance and slowed the advance down. For Germany everything hinged on a quick defeat of France, and on Russia taking several weeks to fully mobilise fully. It was a high risk strategy, and failed on both counts.

The Belgians paid dearly for their opposition, notably in their great fortress cities of Liege, Namur and Antwerp. There were many military casualties and the Germans vented their frustration by executing civilians and unnecessarily bombarding unfortified towns. On 14 October 1914 the Belgians halted the Germans along the River Yser in the north-west, and the British and French held them at the River Marne and rendered Paris safe. Other than a small area protected by the Yser and held by the Belgian King Albert I with the remains of his army, the Germans turned occupied Belgium along with the French border area into three different occupied zones. The far west near the front line was the 'Operations Zone', and then came the 'Staging Zone' including the Belgian provinces of East and West Flanders, Hainault and Luxembourg (outside the independent Duchy). These were subject to direct, and harsh, military rule, and thousands of Belgians became forced labourers. The rest of Belgium (outside Yser) along with France's Givet and Furnay became the 'General Government' overseen by a German general whose role included levying forced war contributions, transporting workers and seizing machinery for use in Germany. On 1 October 1914 seven *Germania* stamps, the 1m Berlin Post Office and the 2m North-South Union stamps from the later 1902 set were introduced across Belgium overprinted *Belgien* and centime and franc values in Gothic script.(1.6)

From 1916 onwards further early *Germania* values and

1.6 1911 60pf Germania overprinted Belgien 75 Centimes, and 1906 1m Berlin GPO overprinted Belgien 1Fr. 25C (from set 1 October 1914)

1.7 20pf Germania overprinted Belgien 25 cent., and 1m Berlin GPO stamp overprinted Belgien 1F.25Cent. (from set 1916+)

1.8 15pf Germania overprinted 15 Cent. (from set 1 December 1916)

the 5m featuring Wilhelm's 25th anniversary speech were added, and three new values – 2pf, 7½pf and 15pf - featured the unshaded *Germania* issue from 1916. All the 1916-18 occupation issues contained the word 'Cent' rather than 'Centimes', and the higher values were written as '1F.25 Cent.' rather than the earlier '1Fr.25C'.(1.7)

Until December 1916 these stamps were used across much of German occupied France including the Departments of Pas de Calais, Nord, Somme, Oise, Aisne, Marne, Ardennes, Meuse and Meurthe et Moselle. From then on the German stamps used in French Departments were merely overprinted with the French values.(1.8)

By then both sides had dug hundreds of miles of trenches, and the long war of grim attrition was well underway. German attempts to break through at the battles around Ypres, similar Allied attempts at the Somme, and the avowed intention of Germany to drain France of its morale and manpower at Verdun all failed at the cost of hundreds of thousands of casualties.

Germany had greater success on the Eastern Front that soon stretched from the Gulf of Finland to the Black Sea. As early as 17 August 1914 Russian armies invaded East Prussia where they were halted at the Battle of

Tannenberg, but the Russians had more success in Galicia where four battles against the Austro-Hungarians were won. However German forces were quickly transferred eastwards to form the 9th Army that held the Russians at the River Vistula and Lodz. In 1915 the Germans once again stunted a Russian advance across the Carpathians, and then the combined German and Austro-Hungarian armies pushed the Russians out of Russian Vistula Land (Russian Poland) (see also Poland). From then until the collapse of Imperial Russia in 1917 the frontier was approximately a line from Riga directly south through Lithuania, to Pinsk in western Belorussia and Tarnopol in western Ukraine.

In Russian Vistula Land five 1902 *Germania* stamps were introduced on 12 May 1915 overprinted *Russisch-Polen* (Russian Poland) in Gothic script. (1.9) The German pfennig values remained, as they did on the lengthier set of eleven values succeeding them on 1 August 1916 overprinted *Gen.-Gouv Warschau* (General Government Warsaw) to mark the new territorial administration.(1.10) This set included some values from the shaded 1902 *Germania* design and also the unshaded 2½pf, 7½pf and 15pf stamps from the new 1916 issue. (The 15pf changed from yellow-brown to slate-violet in 1917.) Germany ruled the north-west half of the General Government, and Austria the south-east.

Not quite all Russian Poland was in the General Government. An area north-east of Warsaw remained under the original German Eastern Military Command that encompassed the Russian Baltic Provinces occupied in 1915. The Command included Vilna and much of Lithuania, Courland (western Latvia) and most of historic Livonia (northern Latvia and southern Estonia). From 15 January 1916 the Eastern Command introduced a dozen 1902 and 1905 *Germania* stamps overprinted *Postgebiet Ob.Ost* (Postal Territory of the Commander-in-Chief East) in Gothic script.(1.11) Here, too, the set later included the 1916 unshaded 2½pf, 7½pf and 15pf stamps. The 1m Berlin Post Office stamp was also used.

As in the military command areas of France and Belgium, German rule in the Baltic was harsh with local people viewed little differently than prisoners-of-war – indeed that was the official status afforded them by the Germans.

On 18 August 1916 King Ferdinand of Romania succumbed to Allied promises of the annexation of Hungarian Transylvania, and a few days later his army advanced into it. On 3 September, however, the Germans and Austro-Hungarians retaliated by counter-attacks from the north while the Bulgarians and Turks struck from the south. The large but poorly trained and equipped Romanian armies were overcome, and by early 1917 were pushed back to the River Siret in the east. Later in the year, though, three Romanian victories in short succession stopped the German and Austro-Hungarian advance and successfully kept part of the country free from occupation as well as tying down a million enemy troops. In German territory three 1902 and 1916 *Germania* stamps – the 15pf, 20pf and 30pf values – were introduced in June 1917 overprinted with Romanian bani values in Gothic script and the boxed letters M.V.i.R. for *Militarverwaltung in Rumanien* (Military Administration in Romania).(1.12) These were superseded the following month by the same three stamps together with the 10pf value overprinted with M.V.i.R. unboxed along with the bani values.(1.13) On 1 March 1918 the overprint on the four stamps changed again to *Rumanien* in Gothic script, and a few days later the German's Eastern Command's 9th Army started using the same four values overprinted *Gultig 9. Armee* (Valid 9th Army).(1.14/1.15)

1.9 5pf Germania overprinted Russisch-Polen (from set 12 May 1915)

1.10 7½pf Germania overprinted Gen.-Gouv Warschau (from set 1 August 1916+)

1.11 2½pf Germania overprinted Postgebiet Ob.Ost (from set 15 January 1916+)

1.12 20pf Germania overprinted M.V.i.R. in black and 25 bani (from set 1 June 1917)

1.13 20pf Germania overprinted M.V.i.R and bani in Gothic script (from set 2 July 1917+)

IMPERIAL GERMANY AND THE 'WEIMAR' REPUBLIC

1.14   10f Germania overprinted Rumanien and 10 bani (from set 1 March 1918)

1.15   15pf Germania overprinted Gultig 9. Armee (from set 10 March 1918)

As Imperial Russia dissolved into chaos, partly as a result of the huge war losses for no positive returns, the German armies continued their advance towards Moscow. When Lenin seized power in November 1917 he declared the war would end, but it took until 3 March 1918 for the Treaty of Brest-Litovsk to be agreed with Germany. Under it the Russians vacated and renounced their rights to the Baltic provinces, Russian Poland, the Ukraine and Byelorussia (Belarus). The ecstatic Germans made ambitious plans for a puppet United Baltic Duchy and Kingdom of Poland but they crumbled away alongside German morale a few months later. The Treaty had alarmed the Allies as Germany could concentrate on the Western Front, and indeed some regiments were hastily moved westwards. However the drain in manpower garrisoning and administering their vast eastern territories meant the Germans could never switch a decisive number of troops to counter the massive 1918 Allied summer offensive.

GERMANY IN CHAOS

The endless fighting, huge casualties, lack of reserves, shortages of everything, especially food, due to the Allied blockade, and the spread of revolutionary ideas from Russia, all contributed to a dramatic loss of confidence in the Kaiser and High Command. In October 1918 crews refused to sail from Kiel naval base, and in early November several cities established Workers' Councils on the Bolshevik model. In the face of mounting internal chaos, the disintegration of Austria-Hungary, the Allied advance, and a sullen admission of defeat by the High Command, Wilhelm II and the rulers of all the subordinate state agreed to abdicate, or were forced to do so. On 9 November a Social Democrat Party group in the Reichstag seized the initiative and proclaimed a republic, and two days later secured the Armistice. Many Germans, and particularly servicemen, never dreamed it would be the prelude to the humiliation of the Treaty of Versailles in 1919.

On the same November day that the Reichstag accepted the proclamation of a republic, the leaders of Germany's Communist Spartacist League, Karl Liebknecht and Rosa Luxemburg, proclaimed an alternative 'Free Socialist Republic'. However, Wilhelm's last Chancellor, Prince Max of Baden, made the important, if legally dubious, decision to transfer the chancellorship to the Social Democrat leader Friedrich Ebert. He believed, correctly in the event, that the experienced and conservatively inclined Ebert could attract wide-ranging moderate support for a parliamentary democracy and thereby suppress the Communist threat.

A coalition government called the Council of the People's Deputies embracing moderate and extreme Socialists immediately introduced many welfare reforms including health and unemployment benefits, pensions, freedom of the press and legalizing trades unions in efforts to pacify the country. And despite widespread opposition Ebert asked the army high command (OHL) to crush left wing mutinies and riots – which it did with relish. Many ex-soldiers had joined the independent paramilitary Freikorps that often operated in tacit cooperation with the government and OHL to suppress extremism – especially of the left. Gradually Ebert established control, and in late December 1918 secured a majority for a provisional National Assembly that was tasked with writing a constitution for a specifically parliamentary government and not an extreme socialist republic.

A key move by Ebert was the agreement with General Wilhelm Groener, head of the OHL, that the government would not reform the army as long as the army swore to protect the government. This brought Ebert considerable middle class support although alienating many Socialists and Communists, and also some ultra-Conservatives who thought democracy would keep Germany weak. In January 1919 the Spartacist uprising in Berlin was brutally suppressed by the Freikorps with the covert support of Ebert. Karl Liebknecht and Rosa Luxemburg were shot, and their killers treated leniently by the courts.

With Berlin in uproar the National Assembly met in Weimar, thereby giving an unofficial name to the new republic, and set about compiling the constitution Ebert sought. On 1 July 1919 a set of stamps with suitably optimistic designs and the inscription *Deutsches National Versammlung* (German National Assembly) marked its inauguration. The 10pf pictured a tree in full leaf, the 15pf ears of wheat, and the 25pf and 30pf a trowel and a builder carrying bricks.(1.16) On 11 August 1919 the new constitution became law.

Meanwhile in Munich a Bavarian People's Republic was declared in November 1918. This collapsed early in 1919 but in April the Communists seized control and started to create a hard-line Soviet State. However in

1.16 Official souvenir postcard with the three National Assembly designs and the Weimar first day of issue (1.7.19) cancellation.

May 1919 around 30,000 Freikorps troops and regular army soldiers crushed the revolutionaries in savage street battles during which a thousand people died. After further stand-offs in August 1919 a fragile Socialist alliance agreed a new constitution creating a Bavarian Free State within the Weimar Republic. Munich remained periodically wracked by extremism, both left and right, as Adolf Hitler's failed Munich 'putsch' in 1923 revealed only too clearly.

A sequence of stamp issues tracked events. In March 1919 twenty ex-King Ludwig III Bavarian stamps appeared overprinted *Volksstaat Bayern* (People's State Bavaria).(1.17) In August they were reissued both perforated and imperforate overprinted *Freistaat Bayern* (Free State Bavaria) and joined sixteen *Germania* stamps that were similarly overprinted between May and September.(1.18/1.19) In August during this grim year the common 10pf, 15pf and 20pf King Ludwig III stamps appeared overprinted *5pf fur kriegs-beschadigte Freistaat Bayern* (5pf for the war wounded Free State Bavaria).(1.20)

Early in 1920 the hard-pressed Bavarian Free State introduced a new set of seventeen values featuring five new designs promoting peace, faith and renewed prosperity.(1.21) Three featured a ploughman, a sower and an allegory of water power producing electricity. Significantly in the light of widespread Bolshevik agitation, the fourth portrayed the Madonna and

1.17 75pf (unissued previously) King Ludwig III overprinted Volksstaat Bayern (from set 1 March 1919+)

1.19 1914 1m King Ludwig III overprinted Freistaat Bayern (from set 6 August 1919+)

1.18 1916 7½pf Germania overprinted Freistaat Bayern (from set 17 May 1919+)

1.20 1914 15pf King Ludwig III overprinted Freistaat Bayern and 5pf fur kriegs-beschadigte Freistaat Bayern (from set 25 August 1919)

1.21   5pf ploughman, 20pf allegory of water power, 50pf sower, 2½m Madonna and Child, and 3m Kaulbach mural (from set 1920)

1.22   20pf Municipal Services overprinted Volksstaat Wurttemberg (from set 1919)

1.23   20pf Deer (from set 29 March 1920)

1.24   1m 25 Ellwangen and 3m Stuttgart (from set 29 March 1920)

1.25   10pf Germania overprinted fur kriegs=beschadigte and 5pf surcharge (pair 1 May 1919)

Child with the encircling inscription *PATRONA BAVARIA*, and the fifth stamp one of Wilhelm von Kaulbach's celebrated early nineteenth century civic murals symbolizing the historic spirit of Munich and Bavaria. The selected mural included the ancient Bavarian coat of arms of lions rampant quartered with lozenges. By mutual agreement, in late April 1920 Bavaria's postal services were finally absorbed into that of Germany.

King Wilhelm II of Wurttemberg abdicated on 30 November 1918 and in marked contrast to its neighbour Bavaria the state peacefully transformed itself into a supportive Free State member of the Weimar Republic. After a brief ascendancy of the Social Democrats a stable Conservative coalition ran the ex-kingdom's internal affairs. Wurttemberg used Weimar Republic stamps except for a brief period up to 1 April 1920 during which it continued to print its own Official and Municipal Service issues. These included overprinting earlier abstract design sets with *Volksstaat Wurttemberg* (Free State Wurttemberg) in Gothic script and issuing one new Municipal Services set featuring a deer (a supporter from the state's historic coat of arms) and an Official set with peaceful views across the cities of Ulm, Tubingen, Ellwangen and Stuttgart. (1.22/1.23/1.24)

The Weimar Republic's first stamps were issued on 1 May 1919, and highlighted the lingering horror of the war. Two frequently used *Germania* stamps – the 10pf and 15pf – were issued overprinted with a 5pf surcharge and the legend *fur kriegs=beschadigte* (for victims of the war) in Gothic script.(1.25)

THE LANDS GERMANY LOST

On 28 June 1919 the government signed the Treaty of Versailles admitting guilt for the war, and accepting severe reductions in the armed forces, massive reparation payments, and substantial losses of territory. The recreation of Poland including the province of Posen and the Polish Corridor, the return of Alsace and Lorraine to France, and the ceding of the mainly Belgian speaking regions of Malmedy and Eupen to Belgium, accounted for much of Germany's dramatic 13% reduction in size. Various French commemorative covers with French stamps and postmarks marked the return of Alsace and Lorraine.(1.26) In Malmedy and Eupen Belgian stamps overprinted *Malmedy* or *Eupen*, or both, were used for a time to reinforce the new ownership until ordinary unoverprinted ones took over. (1.27)

Under the terms of the Armistice all German

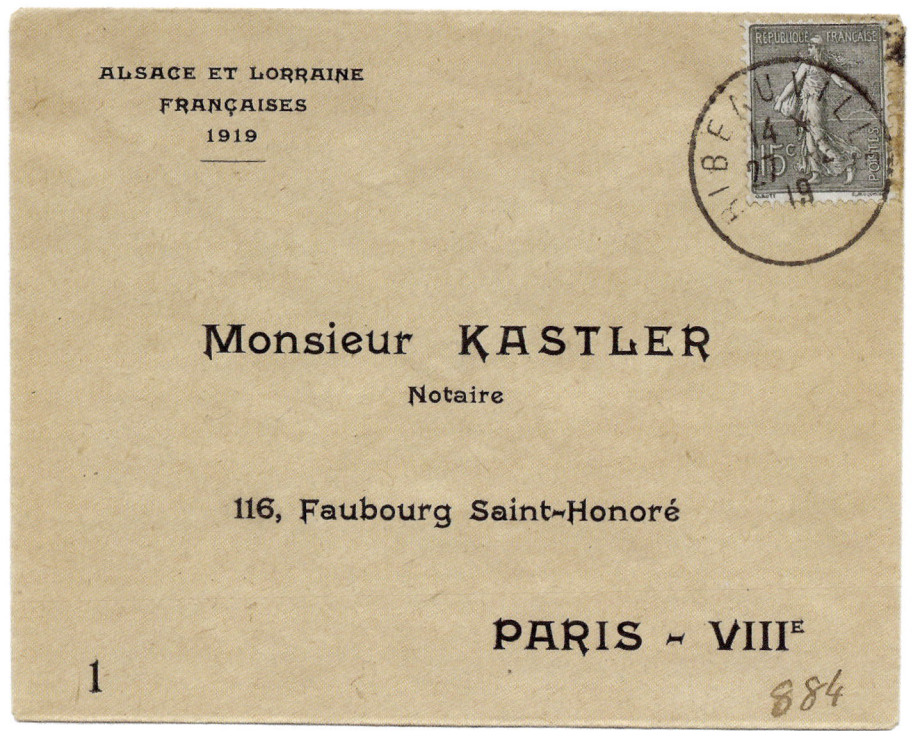

1.28 1919 25c Belgium (featuring Liege's medieval Perron - a column surmounted by an orb and cross symbolizing freedom and autonomy) overprinted ALLEMAGNE and DUITSCHLAND (from set 20 September 1919+)

1.26 1919 commemorative French envelope and 15c Sower postmarked Ribeauville in Alsace.

1.27 1915 1f Belgium (featuring the River Scheldt) overprinted Eupen (from set 20 March 1920+)

territory to the west of the River Rhine up to the borders of the Netherlands, Belgium, Luxembourg and France, and some distance to the east of the river, was occupied by troops from Belgium, France, Great Britain and the USA. The Belgians ensured their northern section was well served with seventeen Belgian King Albert definitive and commemorative issues carefully overprinted *Allemagne* and *Duitschland* without obscuring the images.(1.28) The Rhineland remained under Allied occupation, mainly French, until 1930.

The heavily industrialized Ruhr incorporating conurbations such as Dusseldorf, Dortmund, Essen and Bochum was occupied briefly by the Allies in 1918 and subsequently demilitarized, but in January 1923 French and Belgian troops reoccupied it for two years when they deemed Germany had defaulted on its reparations.

Always deeply anxious about future German aggression, the French secured a League of Nations mandate to administer, and in the event exploit, the coal reserves of the highly industrialised Saar immediately abutting Lorraine. They stayed until a plebiscite in 1935 returned it to Germany.

Numerous sets of stamps were produced for Saar. Initially German stamps from 1905 to 1920, mainly *Germania* stocks, were used overprinted *Sarre* and a heavy bar obliterating *Reichpost* or *Deutsches Reich*. (1.29) They were supplemented by superannuated Bavarian stamps also overprinted *Sarre* or *SARRE* and with three or four lines obliterating *Bayern*.(1.30) In April 1920 the overprint was changed to *SAARGEBIET* (Saar Region).(1.31) There was no hesitation in February 1921 in obliterating the figure of Germania with new values.(1.32)

In February 1921 two *Germania* stamps appeared overprinted with the Saar's Coat of Arms but after that the mandated province regularly produced long sets of its own stamps – almost certainly with collectors uppermost in mind.(1.33) These were interspersed with short sets of surcharged charity issues. The charity stamps usually featured images of orphans, paupers and patients while the commemorative sets concentrated on local scenes.(1.34)

A notable issue was the earliest commemorative set, issued between February and April 1921, whose sixteen stamps realistically portrayed the region's industrial development with, *inter alia*, images of miners, a colliery, slag heap, mill, pottery, railway signal gantry, river traffic and Saarbrucken Town Hall.(1.35) Many of them were reissued with French currency overprints soon afterwards.

Schleswig and Holstein had been ceded to Prussia by Denmark in 1864, and in 1920 the southern province of Holstein was confirmed as German, and so was the southern part of Schleswig. However two plebiscites

1.29 35pf Germania overprinted Sarre with Deutsches Reich obliterated (from set 29 January 1920+)

1.32 75pf Germania with value tablets obliterated, the portrait overprinted with new value, and SAARGEBIET printed over Deutsches Reich (4 February 1921)

1.30 1m King Ludwig III of Bavaria overprinted Sarre with black lines over Bayern (from set 3 March 1920)

1.33 15pf Germania with overprinted new value, SAARGEBIET and Coat of Arms (pair 5 February 1920)

1.34 Welfare Fund 40c+40c patient and nurse (from set 25 October 1926)

1.31 5pf Germania with SAARGEBIET printed over Deutsches Reich (from set 10 April 1920+)

1.35 (E) 25pf river traffic, 40pf slag heap, and 1m 25 colliery (from set 19 February 1921+)

were ordered in central and northern Schleswig (Zones II and I respectively) that resulted in the central Zone staying German and the far larger northern Zone returning to Denmark. Under an International Commission's auspices, in January 1920 ten lower value stamps picturing Schleswig's lion coat of arms and four higher values featuring its landscape, all with the legend SLESVIG PLEBISCIT in Danish, advertised and helped fund the plebiscites.(1.36) After the result, in May 1920 the set was reissued in the Danish northern area overprinted I. ZONE with Danish values. The loss of Zone II caused bitter disappointment in Denmark, but little of the widespread violence between rival ethnic groups that occurred elsewhere.

The former Imperial German port of Danzig became an internationally renowned centre of controversy throughout the inter-war period after the Treaty of Versailles made it a semi-autonomous Free City but with Poland representing it internationally and possessing significant commercial rights within it. It was the outlet to the Baltic Sea that Poland coveted, and stood at the ocean end of the vast new 'Polish Corridor' taken from Imperial Germany that included the province of Posen (Polish Poznan).

1.36 Slesvig Plebiscite 20pf Arms and 10m Landscape (from set 25 January 1920)

1.37 5m 25th Anniversary of German Empire (1916-17 reprint) overprinted Danzig, and cancelled in Danzig on the first day of issue (from set 14 June 1920+)

1.38 20pf Germania overprinted Danzig with hatched bar masking Deutsches Reich (from set 20 August 1920+)

1.39 35pf and 2pf Germania with upward left slanting burele background and overprinted Danzig and mark values (from set 1920)

1.40 Set of Danzig AIR stamps (29 September 1920)

Danzig and its hinterland totaled over 1,950 square kilometres embracing several major towns and hundreds of villages, and 95% of its population, which approached 400,000, were German and generally loathed the Poles. The League of Nations High Commissioner was plagued by controversies as the primarily German local administration sought to oppose every attempt by Poland to develop its trade in and through Danzig. The German Danzigers proved particularly obstructive during the 1919-21 Polish-Russian war (see Poland). In the end the Poles preferred to create their own port on their own territory at nearby Gdynia.

Danzig developed its own postal service. Various *Germania* stamps along with the higher value Berlin Post Office, German Union, the Kaiser Wilhelm I statue, and Kaiser Wilhelm II's 25th Anniversary Speech stamps were reissued between 14 June and 21 December 1920 overprinted *Danzig* in Gothic script.(1.37)   From 20 August that year Danzig belatedly decided, probably reluctantly, to obliterate the title *Deutsches Reich* with a coloured bar.(1.38)

Six *Germania* low values were overprinted in various designs with significantly higher values (from 1-10 marks) in 1920. All appeared in four varieties – with a burele background in grey or lilac, and with the burele points slanting upwards left or downwards right.(1.39) In addition the 40pf *Germania* value became an early AIR stamp after being overprinted with surcharges of 40pf, 60pf and 1m and images of a biplane or winged trumpet.(1.40)

Danzig was forbidden by the League of Nations from calling itself the Hanseatic Port of Danzig. This had been its proud name between the fifteenth and nineteenth centuries as a leading member of the powerful confederation of guilds, cities and ports dominating Baltic trade. However, when Danzig's first specially designed set issued in January 1921 featured a medieval Hanseatic Kogge (a cargo sailing ship) it represented a potent symbol of both past glory and a present protest at its circumscribed position.(1.41)

The considerable length of Danzig's definitive, pictorial, Air and Official sets and the regularity with which they were changed suggests that international collectors were far more in the Free City's mind than ordinary postal users. Throughout the 1920s most designs were variations on Danzig's double cross Coat of Arms, or in the case of Air stamps an aeroplane taking off.(1.42) The 1921 Air stamps featured Hans Seehase's 1918 Sablatnig P111 made from plywood and fabric.(1.43) It had a heated cabin for five or six passengers but an open cockpit for the pilot and also, whether reassuringly or not, for his accompanying mechanic.

The surcharged charity sets possessed distinctive images. St George slaying the dragon appeared on the Anti-TB Week set in October 1921, and the baleful stare of an elderly bearded man marked the 'Poor People's

1.41 5pf Hanse Kogge (from set 31 January 1921+)

1.42 20m Danzig Coat of Arms (from set 1 August 1921+)

1.43 10m Sablatnig P111 taking off over Danzig (from set 3 May 1921+)

1.44 1m 20 (+1m 20) Anti-TB Week (from set 16 October 1921) and 100m+30m from the Poor People's Fund (pair 15 March 1923)

1.45 1924 5pf Danzig Arms definitive with overprint marking the tenth anniversary of its Free City constitution (set 15 November 1930)

1.46 15pf Germania and 1m Berlin GPO (1916-17 reprinting) overprinted PLEBISCITE and OLSZTYN ALLENSTEIN (from set 3 April 1920+)

1.47 1m Berlin GPO with oval Treaty of Versailles and Commission overprint (from set May 1920+)

1.48 (E) 20pf Marienwerder Commission (from set 13 March 1920+)

Fund' issue in March 1923.(1.44)

Perhaps significantly, the tenth anniversary of Danzig's constitution, that had been imposed largely by the League of Nations, evoked no commemorative issue beyond several definitive stamps being overprinted with the briefest possible legend – *1920 15.November 1930*.(1.45)

Plebiscites were held under the Treaty of Versailles on 11 July 1920 to identify the preferences of two Imperial German regions centred on Allenstein (Polish Olsztyn) and Marienwerder (Polish Kwidzyn) for inclusion in either Poland or Germany. Both regions were ethnically mixed and abutted the post-Versailles rump of East Prussia now isolated by the Polish Corridor leading to Danzig.

Prior to the Allenstein plebiscite the overseeing Inter-Allied Commission advertised and subsidized the event with two overlapping issues of overprinted German stamps, mainly *Germania* ones together with the Berlin Post Office, German Union and Kaiser Wilhelm I statue stamps. The first issue dated from 3 April was overprinted *PLEBISCITE* at the top and *OLSZTYN* and *ALLENSTEIN* at the bottom.(1.46) The second issue dated from May was overprinted with the inscription *COMMISSION D'ADMINISTRATION ET DE PLEBISCITE. OLSZTYN. ALLENSTEIN.* around a double oval and its authority *TRAITE DE VERSAILLES art.94 et 95* (Treaty of Versailles articles 94 and 95) in the middle.(1.47) They remained valid within Germany, but not abroad, until the end of October that year.

From 13 March 1920 the Marienwerder Commission issued a set of fourteen special stamps up to five marks featuring a female warrior symbolizing Victory standing on a plinth inscribed *POPULI VOLONTA* (THE PEOPLE'S WILL) and holding the standards of the League of Nations overseeing Council of Ambassadors (Great Britain, France, Italy and Japan) and a fasces. The top and bottom borders were inscribed *COMMISSION INTERALLIEE* and *MARIENWERDER*.(1.48) Between 27 March and 11 May five *Germania* and the 1m Berlin Post Office stamps appeared overprinted *Commission Interalliee* and *Marienwerder* with a hefty 2m surcharge, and from 21 April they were joined by four more *Germania* stamps similarly overprinted but with 1m, 2m, 3m and 5m surcharges. As if they were not

1.49 1m 25 Berlin GPO (1920 printing) overprinted Commission Interalliee Marienwerder (from set 9 July 1920+)

enough, in July three higher value Berlin Post Office and German Union stamps appeared with the overprint. (1.49) All of them ostensibly promoted the plebiscite, while hoping that collectors would help pay for it. No doubt with income primarily in mind, on 11 July, the day of the plebiscite, the Victory set was reissued slightly redesigned with the title *PLEBISCITE* at the top.

In Allenstein 97% of those who voted wanted stay in Germany, as did 92% in Marienwerder. Quite possibly the overwhelming result owed much to anxious voters believing Bolshevik Russia would win the current war with Poland, and quite possibly the widespread stories of German violence towards Polish activists and intimidation of communities possessed some truth. The regions became known as West Prussia. In 1945 all Germans were expelled when it became part of Poland.

The Imperial German port of Memel (later Klaipeda) and its hinterland lay close to Lithuania in northern Prussia and was another ethnically mixed area. Its urban population was mainly German; the countryside predominantly Lithuanian. In 1918 it was placed under League of Nations control until a final decision could be reached and French troops were drafted in to keep the peace. However when nothing was finalized, and while France was preoccupied with the Ruhr, in January 1923 Lithuanian forces disguised as civilians surprised and ejected the French. In 1924 the League's Council of Ambassadors agreed that 'Memmelland' could stay a semi-autonomous region within Lithuania and to the fury of the significant German population it denied citizens a plebiscite. Germany itself made little fuss as it had no expectation of its immediate return, and much preferred this option to Polish occupation. Quite possibly Germany already had thoughts of future repossession.

Memel's stamps reflected the drama. Between 1920 and 1922 French Sower and 'Olivier Merson' stamps were used overprinted *MEMEL* and German values, and with bars obliterating *REPUBLIQUE FRANCAISE*. (1.50/1.51) Alongside them were German *Germania*, Berlin Post Office and German Union issues overprinted *Memel=gebiet* or *Memelgebiet* (Memel region) in Gothic script.(1.52) When inflation bit in 1921 and 1922 many of these French and German stamps were overprinted again with much higher values.(1.53/1.54)

Not surprisingly, a flurry of Lithuanian stamps appeared soon after Lithuanian forces arrived in 1923, and these are discussed in the Baltic States chapter.

Far greater controversy, and bitter fighting, occurred when Germany's eastern territory, notably Posen Province and Upper Silesia, became the focus of Polish ambitions and international debate at the Paris Peace Conference. Around 54,000 square kilometres of Germany were transferred to Poland, but the strong ethnic mix of Poles and Germans in Upper Silesia, and the region's massive coal and mineral reserves, led to a hotly fought plebiscite held by an Interallied Commission in March 1921. Prior to this French, British and Italian troops under a French commander

1.50 1917 20c Sower with REPUBLIQUE FRANCAISE obliterated and overprinted MEMEL and 40 pfennig (from set 7 July 1920+)

1.51 1917 25c Sower with REPUBLIQUE FRANCAISE obliterated and overprinted MEMEL and 1 mark, and further overprinted 25 (marks) in red (26 January 1923)

1.52 1920 10pf Germania overprinted Memel=gebiet (from set 1 August 1920)

1.53 'Olivier Merson' with REPUBLIQUE FRANCAISE and 45c barred and overprinted MEMEL and 1 Mark 50 in red (from set 2 January 1922+)

1.54 'Olivier Merson' overprinted Memel and 2 mark in black and further overprinted 10 (mark) in red (26 January 1923)

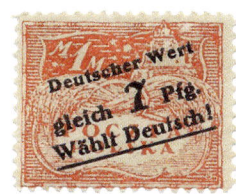

1.55 Forged Polish 1 mark and pro-German overprint Deutscher Wert gleich 7 Pfg Wahlt Deutsch! (German value equal to 7pfg Choose Germany!) (1920-21)

1.56 15pf Commission de Gouvernement Haute Silesie (from set 20 February 1920)

1.57 3m Commission de Gouvernement Haute Silesie (from set 26 March 1920)

1.58 Two 1920 Officials overprinted/mis-overprinted C.G.H.S. (from set 1920)

policed the disputed region but two Polish uprisings in August 1919 and August 1920 attracted a massive intake of German Freikorps units and the inevitable bloodshed. Each side avidly campaigned for votes, with the Germans resorting to transporting back thousands of Silesian migrants to vote and forging Polish stamps with overprinted messages urging a vote in Germany's favour.(1.55)

The Interallied Commission produced a range of postage stamps advertising the plebiscite. The first, in February 1920, comprised a simple oval and ribbon inscribed in French COMMISSION DE GOUVERNEMENT and the region's names HAUTE-SILESIE in French, OBER SCHLESIEN in German, and GORNY SLASK in Polish.(1.56) The second set in March 1920 was more eye-catching featuring, rather optimistically, a dove of peace flying over the Upper Silesian towns and countryside.(1.57) The third, between 1920 and 1922, encompassed several current German stamps overprinted with the Commission's initials C.G.H.S. some within a circle, others not.(1.58) Some old Imperial German stamps also appeared overprinted *Plebiscite 20 mars 1921*, and these may well have had a more partisan source.

Overall Germany won the plebiscite by 59.4% to 40.6% but this hid large and confusing differences between neighbouring districts. After another Polish uprising was suppressed in August 1921 the League of Nations took charge and awarded Germany two-thirds of the region – but the Polish third contained most of the industrial wealth. The dispute was far from over.

THE WEIMAR REPUBLIC ESTABLISHES ITSELF

The Weimar Republic soon started to issue its own stamps. In 1920 it reprinted the 1902 *Germania* set in new colours complete with the title *Deutsches Reich*, and reissued redrawn versions of the pre-war Berlin Post Office and (perhaps poignantly) the German Union stamps – but not the ones featuring the Kaisers.(1.59) The Republic also overprinted *Deutsches Reich* on residual stocks of Bavarian stamps.(1.60) *Deutsches Reich* literally meant 'German Empire', but in the post-war context it was widely, if not universally, assumed to have adopted the alternative meaning of 'German Realm'.

From May 1921 five different designers produced seven images to make up the republic's first definitive set of nineteen stamps. With Imperial Germany

1.59 (E) 1m 25 redrawn GPO (one person stands behind the carriage at the right; in earlier printings three people stood in front of it) and 2m 50 German Union (from set March 1920+)

1.60 Bavarian 1m Madonna and Child, and 10m Kaulbach mural overprinted Deutsches Reich (from set 6 April 1920+)

1.62 1¼m Munich Trade Exhibition (from set 2 April 1922)

1.61 15pf numeral, 60pf blacksmiths, 120pf miners, 160pf reapers, 4m posthorn, 10m rosette and 20m ploughman (from December 1921+ mesh watermark reprint)

1.63 6m Allegory of Charity + label with 4m surcharge (pair 11 December 1923)

1.64 25m harvesters overprinted Rhein=Ruhr Hilfe and 500m surcharge (from set 19 February 1923)

1.65 5,000m Wartburg Castle and 10,000m Cologne Cathedral (pair May 1923+)

humiliated, with memories of it bitter for many families, and with left and right extremism fighting for supremacy, the designs eschewed the past and highlighted ordinary workers' lives while promoting a peaceful path of recovery. Seven low values featured a numeral, two others blacksmiths, two miners, two harvesters, one a ploughman, three a posthorn, and two numerals on a design akin to a rosette. From December 1921 they were reissued, with an additional 75pf value, with a mesh rather than a lozenge watermark.(1.61) In 1922, as inflation bit, the miners and harvesters designs reappeared on a range of mark values.

A few special issues appeared. In 1922 the Deutsche Gewerbe-Schau (German Trade Show) in Munich was marked by a set picturing a monk with outstretched arms taken from the troubled city's historic coat of arms. He is holding a book – which is variously cited as containing the gospels or the municipal laws.(1.62) On 11 December 1923 two identical stamps with an allegory of Charity – a kneeling figure tending a delicate new plant under a (Christmas?) star – were issued to support children and the elderly. A label advertised the premium and the charity.(1.63) In February 1923 the 5m miners, 25m harvesters and 20m ploughman stamps were reissued overprinted *Rhein=Ruhr Hilfe* (Rhine=Ruhr Help) in Gothic script with surcharges of 100m, 500m, and 1,000m respectively.(1.64) The proceeds supported families enduring hardship in these two regions under Allied occupation, and particularly the thousands engaged in the government supported strike protesting against the French reoccupation of the Ruhr.

In May and July 1923 Weimar's first stamps appeared with a celebratory historic theme. By then inflation was well underway. The first featured Wartburg Castle, and the second Cologne Cathedral.(1.65) Vaguely associated with the 850th anniversary of the castle (first mentioned in 1080) and the 600th anniversary of the cathedral (started in 1248), the themes were shrewdly chosen for their wider associations. In the early sixteenth century Martin Luther had translated the New Testament into German at Wartburg Castle, and in 1817 it was the scene of a famous festival celebrating a trio of events - the victory over Napoleon Bonaparte, the 300th anniversary of the Reformation, and the mounting calls for German unity. In 1848, the great year of European revolutions, another part-cultural and part-political festival was held there. Cologne Cathedral on the other hand represented Germany's Roman Catholic heritage. Work had stopped on its construction in 1473, but between 1842 and 1880 Prussia supported its completion as a positive sign of conciliation towards the Roman Catholics who had been incorporated into the state after 1815 but often made to feel unwelcome.

Inflation had begun in the summer of 1921 when Germany started its war reparations payments in gold and foreign currency. Fatally, the government resorted to printing more money to secure foreign currency at almost any price, and later intensified the looming crisis by doing the same to subsidise the Ruhr strikers. As early as August 1921 several *Germania* pfennig stamps were overprinted with mark values, and a year later as panic grew the bland posthorn image was selected for a set of fourteen values from 2 marks to 50 marks, and soon afterwards the larger rosette design reappeared in a dozen values from 50 marks to 100,000 marks.(1.66) And as inflation soared canny industrialists and speculators cashed in on low production costs, people spent rather than saved, and hyperinflation resulted.

Utter misery spread across Germany as the uncontrollable inflation rendered family savings and wages worthless and prices of ordinary household goods soared into hundreds of thousand and ultimately hundreds of millions of marks. Towards the peak of hyperinflation in late 1923 Germany had to resort to an array of simply designed stamps with vast amounts– *Tausend* (Thousand), *Millione* (Million) and finally *Milliarden* (Billion) – printed or even hurriedly overprinted on them.(1.67) Many communities reverted to bartering goods. Finally in December 1923 a new currency, the *Rentenmark* (Mortgage Mark), was introduced which was backed by bonds linked to the market value of gold. In 1924 one trillion old paper marks could be exchanged for just one new gold-backed mark.

The economic recovery of the mid-1920s gave some stability to the Weimar Republic. American loans to German banks under the Dawes Plan, an increase in commerce, falling unemployment, admission to the League of Nations, and arbitration agreements with France, Belgium, Poland and Czechoslovakia whereby future disputes were referred to international panels, suggested that internal and external peace were now

1.66 First signs of inflation. 5pf and 1¼m Germania revalued at 1m 60 and 3m respectively (from set August 1921)

1.67 50,000,000m and 1,000,000,000m inflation definitives (from series 24 August 1923+)

1.68 20pf (+60pf) St Elizabeth inscribed DIE NACKTEN KLEIDEN (The naked dressed) and 60pf DEUTSCHES NOTHILFE (60pf German Emergency Aid) (from set 25 February 1924)

reasonably assured. New stamp issues reflected the striving for greater national pride, not least by reminders of Germany's past achievements. A new political and religious conservatism was in evidence. The Republic was not popular with everyone but a majority supported it as prosperity returned.

From 1 December 1923 stamps appeared in new pfennig values. In February 1924 a new generation of Welfare sets began with a set of four featuring St Elizabeth of Thuringia (1207-31).(1.68) Significantly she was held in honour by both Roman Catholics and Lutheran Protestants, and had lived at Wartburg Castle as the wife of Landgrave Ludwig IV of Thuringia. He had shared her deep concern for the poor and sick, and after his death in 1227 she had followed the Third Rule of St Francis and devoted her remaining short life to establishing and serving a hospital at Marburg. Miracles of healing attributed to her led to her canonization within a decade of her death. The Austrian painter Moritz von Schwind (1804-71) attained fame by adorning Wartburg Castle during its nineteenth century restoration with paintings illustrating her life. The stamps showing St Elizabeth feeding the hungry, giving drink to the thirsty, clothing the naked and caring for the sick are taken from his works.

Signaling Germany's re-emerging unity but also a recognition of each constituent state's identity, the annual Welfare sets in 1925, 1926, 1918 and 1929

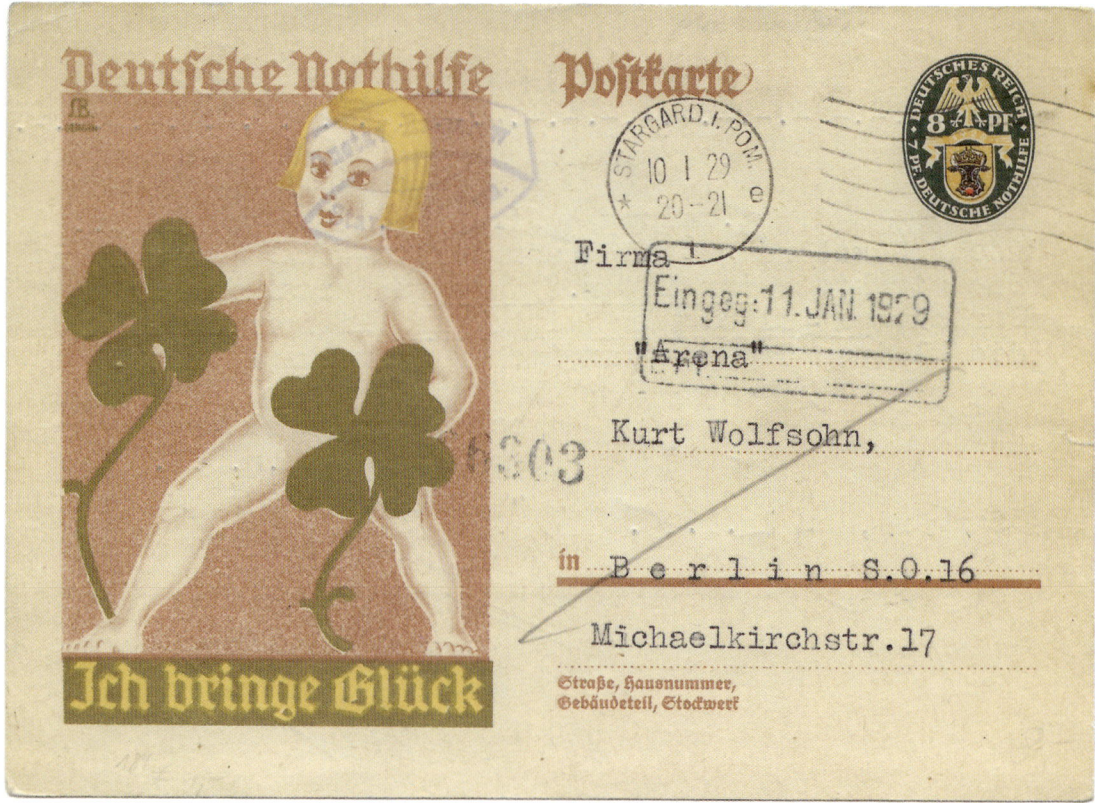

1.69 Children's Welfare Fund postcard with pre-printed 8pf (+7pf surcharge) Arms of Mecklenburg-Schwerin (Bull's Head and Crown) (from set 1 November 1928). The illustration is inscribed Deutsche Nothilfe/Ich bringe gluck (German Emergency Aid/I bring happiness.

progressively featured each one's emblems and Arms.(1.69)

Four stamps issued in 1924 and 1925 centred on famous historic sites, and each one evoked memories of German unity, power and prestige.(1.70) One pictured the medieval Rheinstein Castle (1m) looming above the river valley. Prince Henry of Prussia, Kaiser Wilhelm II's brother, who had been a popular figure and effective commander of the Baltic Fleet during the war, still possessed it. Another featured Speyer Cathedral (5m), long a symbol of Imperial power as the burial place of several medieval Holy Roman Emperors. A third featured the Castle of the Teutonic Knights at Marienburg (3m) whose restoration as a symbol of Prussian nationalism had begun in 1816 and whose architectural style was copied for the German Naval Academy built in Flensburg in 1910. The fourth pictured Cologne (2m) that remained occupied by British troops until 1926 but was formerly one of the great fortresses of the German Confederation and now was leading the recovery of German industry.

In May and July 1925 three stamps were issued featuring a grim looking eagle's head towering above the industrialized River Rhine. The inscription read *Deutsches Reich Deutsches Rheinland* (German Realm German Rhineland) and ostensibly commemorated the region's millenary.(1.71) For much of the time after the collapse of the Emperor Charlemagne's vast empire in the ninth century this rather vaguely defined region had comprised numerous small states, and endured French incursions of varying duration and extent, but nevertheless the set publicly reinforced German convictions that the Rhineland was historically German and remained so. The French had finally left that year.

Other German achievements were highlighted in stamp issues. In 1924 Heinrich von Stephan (1831-97), the prime mover in the federalization of the German postal service and the establishment of the Universal Postal Union, was honoured in a set, and in 1925 the *Reichpost* participated in the *Deutsche Verkehrsausstellung* (German Traffic Exhibition) in Munich and issued two stamps celebrating the four month event.(1.72/1.73) It was the largest post-war trade exhibition to date, and highlighted German and Austrian enterprise in technology for road, railway and marine transport. The stamps featured a steering wheel amidst symbols of power and speed.

In April 1926 new Air stamps appeared around the time the government merged the debt-ridden but pioneering Deutsches Aero Lloyd and Junkers Luftverkehr into the new state airline Deutsche Luft Hansa. Under the Treaty of Versailles the Allies had controlled German air space until 1923 and limited Germany to building small civilian aircraft. Despite

IMPERIAL GERMANY AND THE 'WEIMAR' REPUBLIC

1.70   1m Rheinstein Castle and 3m Marienberg Castle *(from set 11 May 1924+)*

1.73   *10pf German Traffic Exhibition (pair 30 May 1925)*

1.71 (E)   *10pf Rhineland Millenary (from set 30 May 1925+)*

1.74   *40pf Luftverkehr LVG Schneider Biplane (from set October 1919)*

1.75   *1m flying bird (from set July 1922+)*

1.72   *80pf Dr Heinrich von Stephan (from set May 1924+)*

Below: 1.76   *Souvenir card sent by air mail from Erfurt in Saxony to Stuttgart in Wurttemberg with Luftpost label, flight cachet and Drucksache (Printed Matter) handstamp and Erfurt Flugplatz postmarks dated 18.5.28 cancelling 1926 10pf eagle AIR and 1923 3pf Official stamps.*

this, numerous small commercial and passenger airlines had evolved, and encouraged by the Weimar government many Germans perceived travelling by air as a patriotic protest against the Versailles humiliations. Not surprisingly, as early as October 1919 two large Air stamps were issued featuring a winged horn and a Luftverkehr LVG Schneider Biplane.(1.74) This was an offshoot of a successful wartime German fighter plane. In July 1922, during the onset of inflation, these were replaced by a set using a rather bland image of a flying bird that could be pessimistically interpreted as plummeting to earth.(1.75) The 1926 set preferred a powerful eagle with wings poised ready to take off.(1.76)

These images were followed in 1926 and 1927 by a long set of portraits of renowned German painters (Albrecht Durer), poets (Friedrich Schiller), philosophers (Johann von Goethe, Immanuel Kant, Gotthold Lessing and Gottfried Leibniz) and composers (Ludwig van Beethoven and Johann Sebastian Bach). Tucked away amongst them, though, was Frederick the Great, King of Prussia (1740-86), and he was far more celebrated across Germany for his ruthlessly pursued wars against Austria and seizure of Silesia than his friendship with Voltaire and interest in music and philosophy.(1.77)

In 1927 the annual Welfare Fund set featured President Hindenburg in honour of his 80th birthday.(1.78) Alongside General Erich Ludendorff, Field Marshal Paul von Hindenburg had wielded almost total control over Germany's war effort from 1916 onwards, and both were active proponents of the potent post-war accusations that the civil administration and defeatist politicians had 'stabbed the army in the back' by agreeing to the Armistice. On President Ebert's death in1925 Hindenburg's reputation as a war hero remained strong enough to ensure he was elected to replace him. Interestingly he agreed to stand only if the ex-Kaiser, now living in the Netherlands, approved – which Wilhelm did because he thought Hindenburg might restore the monarchy. In the event the new president, although a monarchist at heart, accepted the republican *status quo* and believed that he rather than Wilhelm could restore national unity and stability.

As 1930 approached Germany's rise from the ashes of the war seemed complete with high employment rates, extensive welfare provision, expanding industrial output, international recognition and, at last, peaceful borders. There remained, though, widespread resentment of the Treaty of Versailles and also of the Weimar Republic

1.77 (E) 5pf Friedrich Schiller, 8pf Ludwig van Beethoven, and 10pf Frederick the Great (from set 1 October 1926+)

1.78 (E) 15pf+15pf President Hindenburg (from set 26 September 1927)

whose politicians had accepted it. And the Weimar government itself rested on fragile coalitions of largely Conservative groups, and its weakness became dangerously exposed when the shock waves of the USA's Depression struck Germany. Heavily reliant on USA loans, Germany suffered badly and once again the extremists – the Communists and the Nazis – attracted support from all those disenchanted with republicanism and the Weimar government's inability to stem unemployment and instability. As Federal Chancellors came and went, and no party or coalition secured a majority, and as the growing number of Nazi deputies in the Reichstag deliberately stirred political chaos, so Adolf Hitler rose in the political firmament. Finally in January 1933 President Hindenburg agreed he should become Chancellor in the vain belief he would be amenable to presidential control.

CHAPTER 2
Belgium

After the defeat of Napoleon Bonaparte in 1815 the Congress of Vienna incorporated Belgium into a new United Kingdom of the Netherlands.

Just 15 years later, however, mounting Belgian hostility to the absolutist rule of King William I and the dominance of the Protestant Dutch over the mainly Catholic Belgians led to a short-lived but violent revolution that secured independence and reluctant recognition by the major European powers. In July 1831 Leopold of Saxe-Coburg, perhaps more famous as the *eminence grise* behind the marriage of his nephew, Prince Albert, to his niece, Queen Victoria, became King of the Belgians. Intermittent warfare between Belgium and the Netherlands continued until the Treaty of London in 1839 settled the contested border and, ominously, included Great Britain's guarantee of Belgian neutrality in any future European conflict.

The cross currents of cultural and political differences between the northern Flemings and southern Walloons, and between the influential rural and conservative Roman Catholics and the more secular, liberal and progressive urban middle classes, continually wracked the new kingdom throughout the nineteenth century, but economically it went from strength to strength. A highly efficient railway system was established, and this encouraged industrial growth around the easily accessible coalfields. From the late 1870s onwards Belgian Railways became renowned for its series of *Chemins de Fer* (Railways) stamps for parcels.

The Arts flourished, especially Art Nouveau in the 1890s. In the twenty years prior to 1914 Belgium sought to secure its place in the sun by staging several international exhibitions in imitation of the celebrated Paris Exhibition of 1889. In 1894 a World Fair was held at Antwerp, two more were staged at Brussels in 1897 and 1910, and a fourth at Charleroi in 1911. In deference to regional sensitivities, the Charleroi Exhibition concentrated upon Wallonia's artistic and industrial achievements. And in deference to Roman Catholic opinion most commemorative stamps had religious themes, although they were calculated to appeal to all denominations. Those issued for the 1897 Brussels Exhibition portrayed St Michael as a victorious knight defending Christianity from the machinations of Satan in the guise of a dragon. The strong religious pressures also led to perforated labels stating *Do not deliver on a Sunday* in French and Flemish being attached to all postage stamps between 1893 and 1914.(2.1) If the label remained attached to the stamp on the envelope it would not be included in the deliveries for that day.

2.1 5c and 10c Brussels Exhibition featuring St Michael slaying the dragon (from set 16 October 1896)

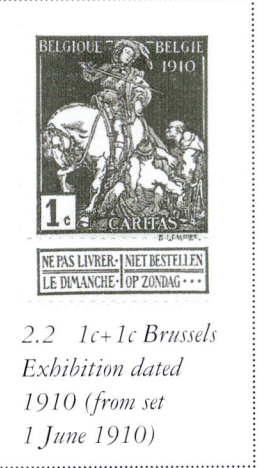

2.2 1c+1c Brussels Exhibition dated 1910 (from set 1 June 1910)

2.3 10c+5c Charleroi Exhibition 1911 overprint (from set June 1911)

The Exhibition stamps issued in 1910 and 1911 take a different stance and show the widely venerated figure of St Martin of Tours in the depths of winter sharing his cloak with a ragged beggar.(2.2/2.3) Each value in each set was produced twice – with a hatched image and with a blocked colour image. Stories vary but most suggest that Martin was a fourth century Roman soldier whose encounter with the beggar led to a conversion to Christianity and eventual enthronement as Bishop of Tours. Great medieval monarchs in France and elsewhere venerated him as a soldier-saint, and in the nineteenth and early twentieth century he became a key symbol in the efforts of Roman Catholics to maintain their influence in Belgian national affairs. Numerous Belgian churches prized their statues of St Martin. These sets and many succeeding ones carried the word 'Caritas' which is best translated as charitable giving in the spirit of Christianity.

Just as King Albert I ascended the throne in December 1909 the heightened international tensions led Belgium to enlarge its army, introduce compulsory military service and set about constructing the National Redoubt – a series of vast fortresses protecting Antwerp, Liege and Namur. Born in 1875, Albert's fervent Catholic faith, extensive cultural interests, simple family-centred life-style, and abiding interest in the welfare of his people made him a far more popular monarch than his predecessor, his disreputable uncle Leopold II, renowned for his autocratic manner, flaunted mistresses, and ruthless exploitation of the Congo. This vast African territory had been his own private property until the never-ending stories of abuse of the Congolese people forced him to cede it to the Belgian state in 1908. Albert's youthful portrait on stamps was in marked, and no doubt welcome, contrast to the elderly, long bearded Leopold.(2.4)

2.4 5f King Albert I (from set 15 April 1912+)

In the summer of 1914 Albert stood firm against German pressure to secure rights of passage through Belgium for its armies to attack France. Speed was of the essence to Germany, and ignoring all protests its armies poured across Belgium's eastern border on 4 August. King Albert had already taken command of the Belgian army, and its recent reinvigoration gave it sufficient strength to slow down the German advance and allow British and French forces to participate in a series of fierce engagements in August and September that generically have become known as the Battle of the Frontiers. It resulted in a German victory inasmuch as German troops retained occupation of most of Belgium and parts of north-eastern France, but in the longer term France was far from conquered and Russian armies were gathering in the east.

The Germans occupied Liege on 7 August, the Belgian government withdrew from Brussels on 18 August, and on 20 August Namur was besieged. By then German troops had crossed into France and were advancing on Nancy. Further battles in the Ardennes and Lorraine resulted in French retreats towards Verdun, Sedan and Stenay in late August. French armies were forced back during the Battle of Charleroi, Belgian troops at Namur had to retreat into France, and the British Expeditionary Force failed to hold the line of the Mons-Conde Canal during the Battle of Mons on 23 August. Within a fortnight German troops had captured Valenciennes, Longwy, Mezieres, Arras, Amiens, Soissons and Reims as they advanced to within 10 miles of Paris. Back in Belgium Louvain had been sacked, and other Belgian forces were blockaded in Antwerp and Liege.

Between 7 and 12 September the key Battle of the Marne was fought which ended the German advance on Paris and any thoughts of a quick victory in the west. The French advancing from the west and the British from the south successfully exploited a large gap between the German 1st and 2nd Armies, and forced the Germans to retreat to the Aisne to avoid the encirclement of the 2nd Army. The swiftly flowing conflict on the Western Front was soon to be transformed into an interminable war of attrition amidst the desolation of hundreds of miles of trenches and the intervening nightmare of 'no man's land'.

The Germans, though, kept hold of Belgium. Belgian troops held out at Antwerp until 9 October, and many men escaped to join King Albert and the remnants of the army in a small strip of territory between the North Sea, French border and the river Yser. Here further German attacks were fought off, and the king and his remaining forces held out for the duration of the war assisted by sea borne supplies and reinforcements. Set against the war as a whole, though, the Yser pocket was of little strategic importance and the Germans had far more important battles to fight.

The Belgian government, although not the King and Queen, fled to Le Havre in October 1914, and German martial rule was imposed on occupied Belgium. Just before the government fled one set of surcharged stamps raising funds for the Red Cross was issued. (2.5/2.6) Three values pictured the embattled king, and three featured the famous Art Nouveau statue erected in 1897

2.5 20c+20c King Albert and 20c+20c Merode Monument (from Red Cross Fund set 2 October 1914)

2.6 Postcard of Le Havre with 1912 Belgian 5c Lion definitive postmarked Le Havre, dated 10.12.1914, sent to Arcachon on the Atlantic coast south of Bordeaux. The exiled Belgian government in Le Havre was permitted to use Belgian as well as French stamps.

in Martyrs Square, Brussels, of Count Louis Frederic de Merode who was killed fighting the Dutch during the 1830 revolution. The statue's inscription *Mort pour l'independence de la patrie* (Death for the independence of the nation) possessed particular poignancy in October 1914. During the Germans frenetic advance through Belgium into France historians estimate that up to 6,500 Belgian and French civilians were executed out-of-hand or because they were suspected of partisan resistance. Tales of torture and abuse abounded.

From 1 October 1914 German stamps overprinted *Belgien* and values in centimes and francs became obligatory in all occupied parts of the country. To ram home German authority, *Germania* stamps were most commonly seen, but the higher values used two designs from 1902 glorifying the Reich – the Germany Union and 25th anniversary of the German Empire.(2.7/2.8)

Once in exile the government produced two sets, printed by Waterlow in London, in support of the wartime Red Cross. They had, of course, limited circulation. One specially designed Red Cross set, in 1915, featured the king, and the other, in 1918 consisted of overprinted surcharges on some of the wartime definitive stamps issued by the Le Havre gov-

2.7 1902 2m German Union overprinted Belgien 1Fr. 50C. (from set 1 October 1914) It was franked on 4 March 1915 in Soignies, 22 miles SW of Brussels. In their first skirmish of the war British and German patrols clashed in woods near Soignies on 22 August 1914 in the prelude to the Battle of Mons that started the following day.

2.8 Four 25pf Germania overprinted Belgien and 20 cents. They are on a celebratory cover postmarked Verviers in Belgium, and, very significantly, dated 11 November 1918.

2.9   20c+20c King Albert (from Red Cross set 1 January 1915)

2.10   2c King Albert (from set issued in exile 1 October 1915+), and 1915 2c overprinted with Red Cross and 2c surcharge (from set 15 January 1918)

ernment.(2.9/2.10)   The thousands of homeless families, destitute refugees and wounded soldiers meant Red Cross aid was sorely needed.

Over a million Belgians fled to France, the Netherlands and Great Britain, and those remaining were subject to a regime enforcing strict rules, high taxation, and the ruthless appropriation of industrial machinery, locomotives and agricultural produce. The general Belgian response was passive resistance; production slowed down and some businesses closed altogether rather than be accused of collaboration. King Albert was deeply distressed by the death and destruction wreaked by the war, but his undercover attempts through diplomatic channels and his widespread family connections (his mother was related to the Kaiser and his wife was a Bavarian princess) to secure a negotiated peace were frustrated by both the Allies and Germany who remained committed, whatever the cost, to total victory.

In October 1915 an elaborately designed set of seven stamps pictured famous Belgian cities and events, all calculated to inspire national pride and patriotism.(2.11) The 35c featured the full glory of the medieval Cloth Hall at Ypres, but now in ruins after artillery fire devastated the city.   Dinant, another ancient city, appeared on the 40c. After the battle for possession, largely against French troops who had fortified the crossing of the River Meuse, the Germans accused the city of encouraging *franc-tireurs* (irregular units) and summarily executed 674 of its citizens.   In yet another reminder of German brutality and aggression, the 50c featured Louvain where German soldiers had gone on the rampage during which the famous library was wantonly set on fire destroying thousands of books and hundreds of irreplaceable manuscripts.   As a result the Germans were condemned as barbarians around the world.

The 1f commemorated the international conference in 1863 that finally revoked the right of the Netherlands under the 1839 Treaty of London to charge hefty tonnage fees on Belgian goods shipped along the River Scheldt to and from Antwerp. As the deeply hostile Dutch knew well, they were strangling Belgian trade.   The 2f showing a group of Congolese in supplication to a newly arrived colonial officer recalled the improvements brought about by eventual annexation and King Albert's personal interest, and perhaps pointedly highlighted relationships between an occupying power and its victims.   The 5f pictured King Albert at a military parade at the city hall in Furnes in the Yser pocket that became his headquarters during the battles in the autumn of 1914.   The 10f contained medallion portraits of the three Belgian kings, Leopold I and II and Albert himself, above the apt wartime inscription 'Unity is Strength' in French and Flemish.   The set remained popular well after the war.

The Germans did considerable damage to internal relations by deliberately favouring the Flemings over the Walloons.   They encouraged Flemish nationalist societies, started a Dutch speaking university at Ghent, and planned to establish a separate Flemish state after the war.   They failed to secure widespread Flemish collaboration but the policy did contribute to post-war difficulties in unifying the nation once again.   And during the Second World War the number of Flemish Nazi sympathisers who joined military units fighting alongside German ones far exceeded those from Wallonia.

One persistent irritation for the Germans was Desire-Joseph Mercier, Cardinal Archbishop of Mechelen and Primate of Belgium.   He published open letters criticizing the German occupying forces, which were read in many Belgian churches and reached Allied and neutral newspapers.   Through this publicity he highlighted and condemned German efforts to incite Flemish nationalism, and was instrumental in persuading the Germans to stop transporting Belgian youths and men to Germany as labourers.   He was briefly arrested in 1915, but his unusually high profile and popularity protected him from further punishment.   He died in 1926, and in 1932 a set of nine surcharged stamps helped raise funds for a memorial statue outside the cathedral in Brussels.(2.12)

In September 1918 King Albert's forces, supplemented with French and British units, joined with the main Allied push of German armies away from the Western Front and out of Belgium.   On 22 November he and his family returned to a hero's welcome in Brussels. The following year new definitive stamps were issued with the dates 1914 and 1918 beside the king

BELGIUM

2.11   35c Ypres, 40c Dinant, 50c Louvain, 1f Freeing of the Scheldt (E), 2f Annexation of the Congo (E), and 10f Kings of Belgium (E) (set 1 October 1915+). The 5f stamp with the value written as 5 FRANKEN (E) was issued on the same day; the identical stamp with the value 5 FRANK was issued in December 1919.

2.12   1f+2f Cardinal Mercier (from set 10 June 1932)

2.14   25c Medieval perron at Liege   (19 July 1919)

2.13.   2c King Albert in wartime military greatcoat and 'Adrian' helmet (from set 19 July 1919+)

wearing his military uniform, greatcoat with upturned lapels and distinctive 'Adrian' helmet.(2.13)

Accompanying these was another psychologically significant stamp featuring the Medieval perron at Liege.(2.14)   A perron was a wide-based stone column topped with an orb and cross that symbolized justice to the citizens of towns possessing them.   All new or amended laws, and important court rulings, had to be

33

read out loud at the site. In 1468 Charles the Bold had seized Liege and signaled his despotic rule by removing the perron. Ten years later, under a more accommodating ruler, the perron, along with the city's rights, was returned and part of the new inscription read, *But these times of bitter servitude have passed: Here I am again against your breast, oh my mother.*

Belgium was only saved from post-war starvation by vast food supplies from abroad, primarily the USA. Burdened by 80% wartime unemployment it embarked upon a determined campaign to reconstruct its devastated railways, factories, farms and houses. The nation also engaged in a frenzy of official and unofficial retribution against all those accused of collaboration and profiteering.

The Paris Peace Conference and the ensuing Treaty of Versailles was a bitter disappointment to Belgium. Its wartime allies - Great Britain, France and the USA – totally opposed its arguments for absorbing the Duchy of Luxembourg, not least because France planned to exert its own influence over this vulnerable duchy. And all the major powers refused to raise yet more international problems by acceding to Belgium's repeated demand that the Dutch hand over territory each side of the vital River Scheldt.

However, the Treaty allotted Belgium a modest share of German reparations, most of which was not forthcoming, and transferred to it several small but keenly contested German territories. Since the 1815 Congress of Vienna Prussia and Germany had controlled Eupen and Malmedy, comprising 730 square miles, on the border with Belgium. Despite their general loyalty to Germany in the war, they were now transferred to Belgium, with a plebiscite in 1920 confirming that an overwhelming majority agreed to the move. However an open ballot was used, and stories abounded of Belgian intimidation and threats that those voting against cession to Belgium would be deported to Germany. In January 1920 several Belgian stamps were overprinted *Eupen & Malmedy* with values in pfennigs, and in March more were added overprinted either *Eupen* or *Malmedy* but retaining Belgian currency.(2.15) In the 1930s Belgium was troubled by considerable agitation and support for the Nazis in the region, especially German speaking Eupen. In 1940 Hitler immediately annexed both areas.

In addition a tiny triangle of contested land around Moresnet that had been administered jointly by Belgium and Prussia since 1830 was finally granted to Belgium in 1919 and renamed Kelmis. No stamps marked the events. However several Belgian definitive and wartime pictorial stamps, including those featuring Ypres, Dinant and Louvain, were overprinted *Allemagne* and *Duitschland* for use by Belgian forces occupying the northern part of the Rhineland from Aachen to Kleve until the general withdrawal of Allied troops from the region in 1930.(2.16) During these years no German forces were allowed west of the Rhine.

2.16 1915 50c Louvain overprinted ALLEMAGNE and DUITSCHLAND (from set 20 September 1919+)

2.17 5c discus thrower, 10c charioteer, and 15c runner (set 2 May 1920)

2.18 10c charioteer overprinted 20c with original value and legend POUR LES MUTILES \ VOOR DE VERMINKTEN (+5c FOR THE DISABLED) obliterated (from set 5 March 1921).

Despite all the devastation the next set issued in 1920 comprised three Classically designed stamps, each selling at 5c above face value, to raise funds for the disabled and for the Olympic Games held that year in Antwerp.(2.17) A promise was being kept as prior to 1914 Belgium had been a candidate for the Games in 1920. Twenty-nine nations took part in 156 events in 29 disciplines. As defeated nations, Germany, Austria, Hungary, Bulgaria and Turkey were not invited, and nor was the internally chaotic Soviet Union. Three new countries took part – Estonia, Czechoslovakia and the Kingdom of the Serbs, Croats and Slovenes, soon to become Yugoslavia. In 1921 the set was reissued overprinted with higher values to help offset the Belgian Olympic Committee's parlous

2.15 1f Freeing of the Scheldt overprinted EUPEN & MALMEDY 1 MK 25 (from set 15 January 1920), and 35c Cloth Hall, Ypres, overprinted Eupen (from set 20 March 1920+)

2.19 1f Leopold I & Albert (from 75th anniversary set 12 June 1925)

2.20 1920 65c Hotel de Ville in Termonde reissued 5 November 1921 paired with 55c overprinted variety

2.21 20c+20c War Invalids Fund (5 July 1923)

2.22 50c+5c Cross of Lorraine and 5f+1f Elisabeth & Albert (from Anti TB Fund set 1 December 1926

even though the Belgians had not dug in to defend Termonde. In 1921 this stamp was chosen for re-issue in pairs – one unaltered and the other overprinted 55c – to make up the 1f 20c express letter rate.(2.20) In 1922 and 1923 single surcharged stamps featuring crippled figures sought funds to support those rendered invalids by the war.(2.21)

Other surcharged sets were issued in most years from 1925 onwards for the national anti-tuberculosis campaign. Some pictured the Cross of Lorraine that had been adopted by the 1902 International Conference on Tuberculosis as the symbol of the global fight against the disease. In 1882 Robert Koch had confirmed it was an infectious disease, and in 1906 the Bacille Calmette-Guerin (BCG) vaccine was created, but its use was painfully slow to spread across Europe. The immediate post-war need was for sanitoriums and isolation wards where victims could receive the best treatment along with the best food in hygienic conditions. Some stamps carried the emotive word *Caritas*. The 1926 set included stamps portraying Queen Elisabeth as well as King Albert.(2.22) The Queen, although German by birth, had made herself extremely popular by visiting troops, staying with her husband in the Yser pocket, and sponsoring nursing units. The 1931 set was devoted exclusively to the Queen.

The 1928 anti-TB set featured the cathedrals at Mons (5c+5c), Tournai (25c+15c), Malines (35c+10c), Ghent (60c+15c) and Brussels, St Gudule (1f75+25c), and also Louvain Library (5f+5f) in their full medieval – and post-war - glory.(2.23) Louvain Library had been rebuilt, and the cathedrals had survived as symbols of hope and faith amidst the wartime death and destruction, and any damage had been carefully repaired.

Under incessant rain in January 1926, rivers right

financial position after the Games.(2.18) It was, in fact, bankrupt.

King Albert had achieved heroic status during the war and in 1925 he was portrayed once again in uniform alongside Leopold I in a lengthy set marking (in 1924) the 75th anniversary of the first Belgian stamps.(2.19) Albert was widely mourned after his death in a mountaineering accident in 1934.

There were also a number of commemorative and surcharged charity stamps connected with the lingering effects of the war. On 5 August 1920 a single 65c stamp pictured the ruined Hotel de Ville (City Hall) at Termonde in Flanders. During the invasion in 1914 German artillery, probably angered and frustrated by the slowness of the advance, had destroyed half the houses in the city along with several churches and the city hall

2.23 60c+15c Ghent Cathedral, 1f 75+25c St Gudule's Cathedral, and 5f+5f Louvain Library (from set 1 December 1928)

2.24 New 30c overprinted King Albert and reprinted 1910 1fr St George with flood relief inscriptions and surcharges (set 10 February 1926)

2.25 1f25+25c Duchess Mathilda retrieving her ring and 2f+40c Cistercian stone mason (from set 15 September 1928)

across north-east France, the Netherlands, Belgium and north-west Germany burst their banks. Fields, factories and mines were flooded, thousands found themselves out of work and/or rendered homeless by the devastation that ravaged cities as far apart as Liege, Mons and Malines as they were recovering from the war. To aid relief funds a recent King Albert definitive stamp was reissued surcharged, and the 1910 1f St Martin of Tours stamp reprinted with a 1f surcharge label.(2.24)

Another issue, in 1928, highlighted the strength of Roman Catholicism in the country and the desire to rebuild celebrated institutions. A striking set of nine surcharged stamps sought funds for the restoration of Orval Abbey; it was the first of several sets over the next two decades until the new church was consecrated in 1948. The Abbey had had a turbulent history, suffering destruction by fire in the 1250s, pillaging in 1637 during the Thirty Years War, and total destruction by French forces in 1793. The site lay fallow until the secular owners donated it to the Cistercian order in 1926 so that a new monastery could be built. In 1929 the set was reissued overprinted '19-8-29' when the first new stone was laid. Three stamps pictured the legend of the trout rising to the surface of the spring with the wedding ring that the widowed Duchess Mathilda of Tuscany (c1046-1115) had lost there.(2.25) In great distress she had prayed for its return, and exclaimed "Truly this place is a Golden Valley' (Val d'Or).

In 1929, and afterwards, the anti-TB sets shifted towards the celebration of Belgium's other attractions and achievements, but the war was far from forgotten. The 1929 set included the pastoral setting of Coo Waterfall, the striking cleft Bayard Rock at Dinant, the Canal at Bruges, and the popular Duchess of Orleans walk (Promenade d'Orleans) at Spa. It also included a stamp featuring the British liner RMS *Aquitania* and the Holland-Amerika Line cargo ship *Dinteldyk* in Antwerp harbor. The former had had a dangerous wartime career as a hospital and troop ship; the latter had been completed in 1922 and was fated to be reduced to a wreck in the German attack in 1940. A sixth stamp featured the Menin Gate Memorial dedicated on 24 July 1927 to 54,395 British and Empire soldiers killed in the Ypres salient who have no known grave.(2.26)

2.26 (E) 5c+5c Co Waterfall, 25c+15c Bayard Rock at Dinant, 35c+15c Menin Gate and 1f 75+25c Aquitania and Dinteldyk, 60c+15c Duchess of Orleans walk at Spa (from set issued 2 December 1929)

2.27 (E) 2fr monoplane flying over Namur (from set 30 April 1930+)

2.29 (E) 1f 75 + 4f 25 Infantry Memorial (pair 4 August 1932)

2.28 60c Leopold I (reigned 1831-65), 1f Leopold II (1865-1909), and 1f 75 Albert I (1909-34) (set 1 July 1930). The dates 1830-1930 on the stamps reflect the year independence and the Provisional Government were proclaimed, and not 1831 when Leopold of Saxe-Coburg was installed as king.

The end of the decade witnessed two other key issues. Belgium's first Air set was issued between April and December 1930, and as in most countries it reflected national pride in the expansion of routes and possession of a national airline – *Sabena* in Belgium's case.(2.27)

The second set, issued in July 1930, marked the centenary of Belgian independence.(2.28) Three stamps portraying Leopold I, Leopold II and Albert marked the passage of a turbulent hundred years.

Two years later, on 4 August 1932, a pair of stamps featuring a battle weary soldier raised funds for a national infantry memorial.(2.29)   Made out of the famous Belgian Merbes-Sprimont granite, the thick towering column surmounted by a crown and featuring soldiers carved in stone and cast in bronze was installed in central Brussels, after considerable argument about its site, in May 1935. It is not far from an Anglo-Belgium memorial unveiled by the Prince of Wales in 1923 to all the Belgians who aided wounded British soldiers and prisoners-of-war.

In August 1932 Adolf Hitler was just a few months away from being appointed German Chancellor.

CHAPTER 3
Luxembourg

The small independent Grand Duchy had been fortunate to survive the tumultuous European upheavals of past centuries. Its formidable castle and location abutting France and the Low Countries had given it great strategic value. Ruled by the powerful House of Luxembourg for several centuries, it had passed to the Hapsburgs in 1477. In 1795 it was conquered by France, but regained a precarious independence in 1815. However until 1890, when it passed to the House of Nassau under a succession agreement, the Grand Duke was also King of the Netherlands.

Its territory periodically shrank. In 1815 Prussia held onto a north-eastern slice it had occupied in 1813, and under the 1839 Treaty of London Belgium acquired over half its remaining territory, which became its French-speaking province of Luxembourg. This left just the city of Luxembourg and its immediate vicinity (today's Grand Duchy) independent. Even so it remained an object of desire by France, Germany and Belgium. Culturally mainly French, economically it was reliant on Germany.

In 1912 Marie Adelaide, aged just seventeen, became Grand Duchess. Luxembourg's constitution allowed its rulers considerable political power, and the scene was set for controversies that long outlasted the impending war.(3.1)

3.1 5f Grand Duchess Marie Adelaide (from set issued 4 May 1914+)

On the night of 1-2 August 1914 German forces ignored all treaties and trade agreements, and crossed into Luxembourg, primarily seeing it as a vital passageway into France and southern Belgium. Marie Adelaide ordered her army of 400 men not to resist, and after a formal protest she accepted German military rule as inevitable, although her greatest fear was formal absorption into the Reich. It was this that led the duchess and her able prime minister, Paul Eyschen, to ensure the duchy and its citizens did nothing to incite the Germans to end the duchy's self-government. In tacit agreement, the Germans acquiesced and Luxembourg stamps, without any overprints signifying German authority, continued in use throughout the occupation.

In October 1915 Eyschen died, and without his guiding hand Marie Adelaide's obdurate Roman Catholicism and innate conservatism began to incite opposition to her personal rule that lead in turn to disturbing political instability. Her unsettling dismissal of several ministries was compounded by increasing shortages of food due to disrupted imports and poor harvests, and then the growth of a rampant black market after rationing was introduced. Civil unrest mounted, and in May 1917 the Germans intervened to repress a strike in the iron and steel works upon which they relied for supplies.

Marie Adelaide's friendly relationship with the German royal family, including the Kaiser who visited her during the war, had not gone unnoticed. It did not help that in August 1918 Antonia, one of her sisters, became engaged to Crown Prince Rupprecht of Bavaria, a German Field Marshal commanding forces on the Western Front.

On the withdrawal of German troops in November local Communists made an bid for power in Luxembourg following the lead of Karl Liebkneckt and Rosa Luxemburg in Germany. This was suppressed, but the Liberals and Socialists, and also the French, were united in their conviction that Marie Adelaide should abdicate, and when part of the army declared in favour of a republic it needed French and American forces to restore order. With the duchy in complete disarray, in January 1919 Marie Adelaide agreed to go. Exiled in Germany, she died of influenza in 1924 aged just 29.

Marie Adelaide's sister, Charlotte, succeeded her. However, her position remained perilously uncertain until the end of the year when the Paris Peace Conference dashed Belgium's hopes of annexation and a referendum declared in favour of a grand duchy, not a republic.

For several years Luxembourg made do with Marie Adelaide stamps, supplemented with a few Duchy Coat of Arms stamps from Grand Duke William IV's reign (1905-12). Some in due course were overprinted with new values.(3.2) Charlotte's first stamp, a portrait of herself, was not issued until 6 January 1921. It had no

3.2 1907 4c Coat of Arms stamp overprinted 5c, and 1914 87½c Marie Adelaide stamp overprinted 80c (from set 1921+)

3.3 15c Birth of Crown Prince Jean (6 January 1921)

3.5 Imperforate 25c Grand Duchess Charlotte (pair 27 August 1922)

3.4 80c Grand Duchess Charlotte, 1f (E) Vianden Castle, 2f (E) Esch Steelworks and 5f (E) Bridge across the Alzette Gorge (from set 25 March 1921+)

inscription and was a low key commemoration of the birth of her son and heir, Crown Prince Jean, the previous day.(3.3)

It was, though, the forerunner of the new definitive set issued from March 1921 with Charlotte's portrait on the lower values, and three scenic views on the higher ones.(3.4) The 1f featured Vianden Castle whose history aptly reflected the sensitive relationship between Charlotte's predessors and the local people. In 1820 the Grand Duke of Luxembourg and Count of Vianden (who was also King William I of the Netherlands) sold the castle to a local alderman who started to strip its roof and paneling for sale. This caused such outrage that William repurchased it to calm things down. Restoration work was still going in 1914. In contrast the 2f pictured the mighty steel works at Esch-sur-Alzette that had contributed much to the duchy's prosperity, and also to the rise of Socialism and militant trade unionism that had contributed to Marie Adelaide's humiliation. The 5f featured the city of Luxembourg itself and the famous bridge over the River Alzette.

Stamp issues fast became important as a source of revenue and a boost to post-war tourism. In 1922 a Philatelic Exhibition was held in Luxembourg, with imperforate 25c and 30c Grand Duchess Charlotte stamps marking the occasion.(3.5)

Single pictorial stamps celebrating the historic and scenic beauties of the duchy were issued every few years. A 1923 stamp featured the fortress town of Echternach on the German border that was recovering its nineteenth century reputation as a tourist centre. It was reissued in 1934. A second 1923 stamp pictured Clervaux in the Ardennes with its Benedictine Monastery completed in 1910; in 1928 a stamp featured Clervaux from a new perspective, and it reappeared in 1934. Different views of the historic city of Luxembourg featured on stamps in 1923, 1828, 1931 and 1934. They all served to reinforce national pride in the duchy, its growing prosperity and its continuing independence.(3.6) And a set of Air stamps in April 1931 featuring a biplane over the Alzette Bridge highlighted the growth of flights in and out of Luxembourg's fledgling airport.(3.7)

In 1921 surcharged pictorial stamps of Clervaux monastery, the city of Luxembourg and its historic

3.6 *3f Echternach (23 Sept 1923), 2f Clervaux (16 October 1928), 10f distant prospect of Luxembourg (March 1923), 20f Ville Base (Lower Town), Luxembourg (20 June 1931)*

3.7 *Cover with four values of the 1931 Air set and special Echternach cancellations dated 17 August 1932 commemorating the first flight to Brussels.*

3.8 *10c+5(c) Clervaux Monastery (from set 2 August 1921) and 15c+10(c) Pfaffenthal additionally overprinted 25(c), and 27 mai 1923 (from set 27 May 1923)*

3.9 *2½fr Grand Duchess Marie overprinted CARITAS and + 1Fr (from set 17 April 1924)*

3.10 *1f Grand Duchess Charlotte (from set 10 November 1926+)*

Pfaffenthal quarter raised funds for a national war memorial. They were reissued two years later overprinted *27 mai 1923* with further surcharges to mark the unveiling.(3.8) The memorial was to the 3,700 Luxembourg citizens, mainly from abroad, who served in the French army and especially the high number, approaching 2,000, who were killed. It took the form of a soaring 21 metre high granite obelisk surmounted by a gilded statue of Nike, the goddess of victory and freedom, holding a laurel wreath. Its striking classical and secular format upset many Roman Catholics, and Grand Duchess Charlotte did not attend the unveiling.

Charlotte shrewdly adopted a far more politically sensitive and less interventionist role than her sister, and indeed the new post-war constitution considerably reduced the ruler's powers. Under mainly popular right-wing governments, fully supported by the Roman Catholic Church, the duchy regained both stability and prosperity, especially with the development of greater industrial capacity. It entered into an economic and monetary union with Belgium, and gradually re-established sound trading connections with Germany. The ruling dynasty recovered security and popularity, and special stamps marked the birth of Princess Elisabeth in 1923. The following year several definitive stamps of Grand Duchess Marie Adelaide were re-issued overprinted with CARITAS and surcharges to mark her death. The hint of Christian forgiveness accompanied the plea for charitable giving.(3.9) Two years later, in November 1926 a profile of Charlotte appeared on a new definitive set.(3.10)

As elsewhere across Europe surcharged sets raised funds for the anti-TB campaign and child welfare charities.(3.11) In Luxembourg child welfare charities were important, and stamps often incorporated members of the expanding grand ducal family in the designs. Shrewdly timed, each year they caught the Christmas mood and surge in post. In 1927, for example, the set featured the young Princess Elizabeth, in 1928 a new Princess Marie Adelaide, in 1929 Princess Marie Gabrielle, in 1930 Prince Charles, and in 1931 Princess Alix.(3.12)

Luxembourg hosted another International Philatelic

3.11 (E)   1fr Anti-Tuberculosis Fund (from set 21 December 1925)

3.12   75c+15c Princess Marie Adelaide (from set 2 December 1926) and 1¾fr Prince Charles (from set 10 December 1930)

3.13 (E)   25c International Philatelic Exhibition (from set 4 September 1927)

Exhibition in 1927, and its Grand Duchess, now the symbol of the increasingly prosperous state, graced the stamps marking the event along with her husband, Prince Felix. In an understated commemoration of the 75th anniversary of the duchy's first postage stamp the set included the dates 1852 and 1927. (3.13)

The 1926 definitive set lasted until the 1940 German invasion when, unlike 1914, they were overprinted with German values. Soon afterwards the grand duchy was incorporated into the Gau of Trier-Koblenz, later renamed Moselleland.

CHAPTER 4
France

After being a nation famed for its military prowess and territorial aggression under Napoleon Bonaparte, France's confidence and reputation suffered a devastating setback with Prussia's shattering defeat of its armies in 1870-71. The national trauma underscored French politics until 1914.

In 1848 Bonaparte's nephew, Louis Napoleon had been elected President of France, and in a *coup d'etat* in 1852 he proclaimed himself Emperor Napoleon III. All went reasonably well until 1870 when Bismark manipulated a war with France that served several important purposes for Prussia. It secured support from the German states still outside the North German Confederation, severely set back France's ambitions to dominate European affairs, and expedited the annexation of Alsace and Lorraine. Besieged at Metz and crushed at Sedan, France's over-confident but ill-equipped forces were no match for Prussia's well-honed modern army, and humiliation was complete when King William I of Prussia was proclaimed Emperor of Germany in the Hall of Mirrors of the Palace of Versailles in January 1871. By then Napoleon III had been deposed in another French revolution.

Napoleon III's head and pointed beard had adorned French stamps during his reign, but a dramatic change occurred under the ensuing Third Republic. Classically-styled allegories of peace, prosperity and human rights dominated all issues until the middle of the Great War. In 1871 Ceres, the ancient goddess of agriculture and motherly love appeared, followed several years later by a series featuring the figures of Peace and Commerce designed by Jules-Auguste Sage and engraved by Louis-Eugene Mouchon.(4.1/4.2)

From 1900 a set by Paul Joseph Blanc portrayed France as the Goddess of Freedom in a Phrygian cap so beloved of revolutionary artists. She is holding the scales of justice and smiling on two cherubs exchanging fraternal kisses.(4.3) Alongside these from 1900 were further Mouchon stamps featuring a seated female figure representing France holding a sceptre of justice and *The Declaration of the Rights of Man and of the Citizen* whose principles had been acclaimed by the National Assembly at the dawn of the French Revolution in 1789.(4.4) The head of what appears to be a lion appears just above the figure's breast, perhaps to suggest that the state would

4.1 2c Ceres stamp (from series 1871+)

4.2 2c Louis-Eugene Mouchon Peace & Commerce (from series 1877+)

4.3 1c Paul Blanc Goddess of Freedom (from set 4 December 1900+)

4.4 20c Mouchon engraved allegorical figure holding sceptre and Rights of Man from the redrawn plate (from set April 1902+)

4.5 40c Olivier Merson Liberty & Peace (from set 4 December 1900+)

4.6 10c Sower with sun and horizon (from set 2 April 1903+) and 10c Sower with ground but no sun (from redrawn set 13 April 1906+)

react aggressively if unduly provoked.

In 1900 a set by Nicholas Luc-Olivier Merson entitled Liberty and Peace pictured a reclining female figure resting in what could be interpreted as a vineyard with her hand on a pitcher.(4.5) In 1903 perhaps the most famous allegorical stamp was issued featuring a female sower set against the sun. With minor design changes all of these stamps had unusually long lives stretching well past 1918 into the inter-war years.(4.6)

Their later popularity belied the initial criticisms of the designs, especially the Sower, as too effete. Critics said they made France appear too inward looking and obsessed with maintaining peace when what was needed were images that conveyed a nation proud of its achievements, optimistic about the future, and ready to defend its interests. The stamps survived the onslaught but the controversy highlighted the deep pre-war divisions in French society.

Several crises prior to 1914 emanated from, and accentuated, these divisions. In the late 1880s Georges Boulanger, an army general of rabidly nationalist anti-German views, achieved sufficient popularity to have attempted a revolutionary coup if his nerve had not failed him at the critical moment. Even more revealing in the 1890s was the widespread anti-Semitism and repeated miscarriages of justice when Captain Dreyfus, a Jewish officer, sought to prove he had been falsely convicted of passing military secrets to the Germans. The nation erupted into violently partisan camps with liberals, republicans and anti-clericals generally supporting Dreyfus and most royalists, conservatives, anti-Semites and many Roman Catholics steadfastly condemning him.

In 1900 republican France did, though, have one unlikely ally in Imperial Russia. The alliance had been forged between 1891 and 1893 after Kaiser Wilhelm II had failed to renew Bismark's carefully contrived treaty with Russia. The Franco-Russian treaty was purely defensive, but it had ominous repercussions. Germany fully appreciated that it now had potentially hostile powers on its western and eastern borders. Inevitably Germany strengthened its own alliance with Austria-Hungary, thereby setting the pattern for future conflict, and started to court Italy.

France's relations with Great Britain were, as in every century, consistently brittle with additional moments of acute crisis. However despite several diplomatic clashes over colonial rights in Egypt, the Sudan and Morocco, French fears of a rampant Germany coincided with those of Britain in this respect and both countries welcomed a formal rapprochement. King Edward VII's state visit to France in 1903 was celebrated amidst effusive signs of mutual admiration and provided the incentive to settle numerous nagging colonial differences – notably in true high-handed colonial fashion allowing Britain to control Egypt and giving France a free hand in Morocco – and seal the 'entente'. There was no obligation on Great Britain to support France militarily, but France was emboldened by the Russian alliance and British 'entente' while Germany, for all its might, felt frustrated and besieged.

When war broke out the rapid defeat of France was Germany's immediate aim. However the massive swing through Belgium, Luxembourg and north-eastern France towards Paris was slower than planned and the British Expeditionary Force arrived quicker than expected. Huge and bloody battles – around Guise and then south of the River Marne – denied Paris to the Germans. In early September, with France bruised but far from defeated, Field Marshal Moltke ordered the German armies to withdraw to the north and regroup. The Allies pursued them and the Battle of the River Aisne began.

The battle was costly and indecisive, and the nature of the war was changing. Along the Aisne miles of entrenchments and machine guns began to dominate the battlefield enabling advancing troops to be slaughtered in their thousands. Henceforth each side was reduced to massive attempts to push back enemy salients along hundreds of miles of well-defended trenches running from the Channel coast to Switzerland. The Germans had some success in an Ypres offensive – they certainly reduced much of Ypres to rubble - and greater success in their Artois offensive in 1915, while the French offensive in Champagne was a disaster and its Somme offensive around Arras and Albert between July and November resulted in a few kilometres advance at the cost of 200,000 casualties.

It was the never-ending carnage at the huge French fortresses circling Verdun-sur-Meuse during repeated German attacks between February and December 1916 that haunted the nation most. Under General Petain 'Verdun' became the symbol of French defiance of the invaders. Defended by no less that 259 regiments, the city of Verdun remained inviolate, and at the end of the year the Germans withdrew. The French, though, had suffered 377,000 casualties; the Germans 337,000.

Meanwhile further slaughter had taken place in a series of battles on French soil at Albert, Fromelles, Delville Wood, Pozieres, Guillemont, Ginchy, Flers-Courcelette, Morval, Thiepal Ridge and the Ancre River during the Allies new Somme offensive between July and November 1916. The Allies advanced around 10 kilometres but failed to take Bapaume, a key objective, let alone break through and outflank enemy lines. Another 200,000 French soldiers became casualties, alongside 400,000 British and Empire combatants, and 500,000 Germans.

In 1917 General Nivelle planned a vast Allied assault involving a million French soldiers along a front stretching from Royle to Reims. He asserted a 'creeping barrage' whereby an advancing succession of artillery bombardments followed up by infantry consolidating each advance, would win the day and, he hoped, the war. In the event confusion reigned. Initial Allied advances in several sectors were checked by German counter-attacks, and for the next three weeks as April turned into May 1917 a host of local engagements ended in stalemate and 350,000 Allied casualties, 187,000 of them French.

The almost incomprehensible slaughter eventually incited a series of French mutinies in late 1917. Although news of the Russian revolution was seeping through, the mutiny did not seek to overthrow the republic but was fundamentally a protest stemming from perceptions that commanders thought nothing of the ordinary soldiers' feelings, conditions and sacrifices. Forty nine of the 113 French divisions were involved to a greater of lesser extent, but a combination of concessions by General Petain involving longer leave and rest breaks behind the lines and the court-martial of around 3,000 men (resulting in 49 executions and 2,878 imprisonments) quickly ended the mutinies. Nevertheless, they represented the air of despondency and exhaustion pervading the nation, and the horror at the devastation and distress across north-eastern France. They represented, too, the enervating air of national pessimism that many commentators perceived in French life after the war – and not least General Petain himself who believed that his dictatorial Vichy regime created in 1940 under Nazi authority was the only way France could be purged and French morale and self-respect regenerated.

After the mutinies French generals used their troops more circumspectively, and in 1918 they were successful in defending the Allies' lines against German attacks in Champagne and across the River Marne. And in what proved to be the last great Allied offensive French armies were instrumental in liberating most of north-eastern France and advancing into Belgium. Other French divisions that year gave much needed support to Italian forces fighting the Austrians on the northern Italian front.

The first French stamp of the war, as early as 11 August 1914, was the 1907 10c Sower stamp overprinted with a red cross and 5c surcharge. This was followed on 10 September with a special printing of the 10c stamp with the red cross and surcharge within the design itself.(4.7) The fury of the sudden German onslaught rendered relief funds vital.

From 1 October 1914 French families and businesses within the German Western Military Command Zone straddling Belgium and France found themselves using German stamps. As the front line stabilized the affected Departments were Pas de Calais, Nord, Somme, Aisne, Marne, Ardennes, Meuse, and Meurthe et Moselle. Until December 1916 the stamps were those overprinted *Belgien* and franc and centime values, but afterwards the overprints for German stamps in French territory merely identified the French value.(4.8)

As shortages grew acute across France in 1916 a range

4.7 1907 10c Sower overprinted with red cross and 5c (11 August 1914), and redrawn 10c Sower inscribed CROIX-ROUGE (RED CROSS) and with red cross and 5c in white tablet (10 September 1914)

4.8 1906 80pf Germania overprinted 1F for use in the French areas of the German Western Military Command Zone (from set 1 December 1916)

4.9 2c+3c war widow, 25c+15c woman ploughing, and 35c+25c flag over trenches (from set August 1917)

of Mouchon definitive stamps began to appear on cheaper grey paper. Charity sets, though, remained important. In a timely issue in August 1917, soon after the mutinies, a pictorial set raised funds for war orphans.(4.9) The images on the lower values highlighted the impact of war on family life. The 2c+3c featured a war widow and the 15c+10c and 25c+15c pictured a woman replacing a man on a farm. The higher values took a different stance. They acknowledged the suffering, while attempting to stiffen patriotic resolve. The 35c+25c featured the French flag flying over a trench, although no soldiers are included.

The 50c+50c pictured the 'Lion of Belfort'. The fortified citadel at Belfort in Alsace had successfully resisted a Prussian siege for 103 days in 1870-71, and a huge sandstone image of a defiant lion at bay 22 metres long and 11 metres high created by Frederic Bartholdi, the sculptor of the Statue of Liberty in New York, was erected there in 1880. In recognition of the resistance Belfort was a tiny part of Alsace that was excluded from annexation by Prussia. However in deference to Prussian protests, the lion ended up facing away from Germany, not towards it. The 1f+1f and 5f+5f featured an allegorical Spirit of War in the form of a female figure

4.11 15c+10c woman ploughing, 50c+50c Lion of Belfort, and 1f+1f Spirit of War (from the August 1917 set overprinted with lower surcharges 1 September 1922)

4.10 5c+5c orphans (March 1919)

4.13 (E) Red Cross Fund (8 Aug 1918)

4.12 New 2c+1c war widow and 50c+10c Lion of Belfort printed with lower surcharges (from set 27 December 1926+)

armed with a sword flying beneath an ominous dark cloak or cloud. All are inscribed ORPHELINS de la GUERRE (Orphans of the War)

These emotive stamps appeared again after the war. In March 1919, a 5c+5c value was added to the War Orphans' set portraying two children looking sadly into the distance.(4.10) In 1922 the complete set was reissued overprinted with black bars obliterating the original charity surcharges and replacing them with considerably lower ones.(4.11) Perhaps numerous charity appeals, however sorely needed, were exhausting people's goodwill, and perhaps by then many people were in a state of denial about the trauma. Nevertheless, the war widow, Lion of Belfort and Spirit of War designs were used again, with the lower surcharges, in 1926-27.(4.12)

In August 1918 as the summer offensives were underway, a single surcharged stamp was issued on behalf of the Red Cross.(4.13) To the left it showed a hospital ship, the converted liner *Charles Roux*, and to the right a nurse in a ruined hospital. The *Charles Roux* survived its duties as a troopship and hospital ship to be refitted as a Mediterranean cruise ship after the war.

By 11 November 1918 all France was long familiar with grieving families – a total of 1,340,000 men had died – and with the constant sight of limbless, blind, burned and psychologically damaged ex-soldiers. Vengeance was to the fore. The Germans, in retreat and with starvation and mutinies back home, signed a humiliating Armistice in Marshal Foch's private train in the Forest of Compiegne, and the Paris Peace Conference led to further German humiliations in the Treaty of Versailles. (4.14 overleaf) Amongst them was the return of Alsace and Lorraine to France, but the exhausted nation issued no celebratory stamps, only a few privately inscribed covers. Significantly there was no Victory issue.

After the war France saw no need to replace the allegorical definitive stamps designed well before 1914. They were regularly reissued with new colours and some new values throughout the 1920s, and the Sower design survived until the Second World War. Significantly by 1923 Merson's Liberty and Peace stamp had become celebrated enough for a 1f variety to be overprinted 'Congress Philatelique de Bordeaux 1923' and used as the symbol of this international event.(4.15 overleaf) Mouchon's Peace and Commerce stamp was reprinted in carmine with a 5f value for sale at the 1925 Paris International Philatelic Exhibition, primarily in a miniature sheet block of four. In 1927 Mouchon's Sower design was given 5f and 10f values and incorporated into a miniature sheet for the Strasbourg Philatelic Exhibition, and two years later the 2f Merson Liberty and Peace stamp was reprinted and overprinted 'Exposition Philatelique Le Havre 1929'. The national allegories remained firmly in favour.

The 1920s witnessed several colourful sets devoted to achievements in science, poetry, and applied arts and crafts. Between May 1923 and November 1926 the work of Louis Pasteur, the celebrated French chemist and microbiologist, was marked with an ever-increasing number of stamps bearing his portrait that became virtually an alternative definitive set.(4.16) His discoveries helped reduce mothers' deaths from puerperal fever, provided the first vaccines against rabies and

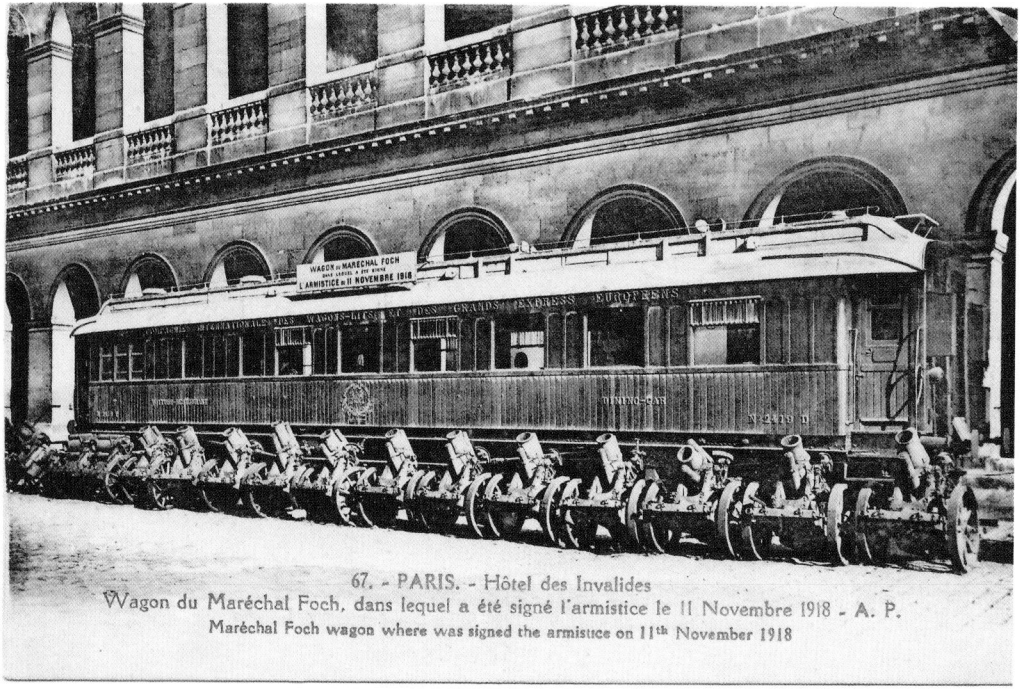

4.14 *French commemorative postcards featuring Marshal Foch's railway carriage in which the Armistice was signed on 11 November 1918? and the Trianon Palace, Versailles, with the special Congres De La Paix (Peace Conference) postmark, dated 11 May 1919.*

anthrax, and prevented the contamination of milk through the process of pasteurization named after him.

In April and May 1924 four stamps publicized the Olympic Games held in Paris between May and July that year.(4.17) The set celebrated Paris as much as it did the Games. The 10c featured a champion athlete wearing the ancient award of a laurel wreath rather than a modern medal with his arm outstretched in salute over a distant view of the stadium and France's famous symbol of military glory, the Arc de Triomphe. Significantly,

since 1920 the Arc de Triomphe had housed France's Tomb of the Unknown Warrior and an 'eternal flame' of remembrance. Significantly, too, the Olympic Committee did not extend an invitation to Germany.

The 25c was even more ambiguous and featured an allegorical figure of France holding a statuette of a winged figure of victory over Paris's medieval Pont Neuf and Notre Dame cathedral. The 30c featured the moment when Milo of Croton, a renowned Classical Greek athlete, sought to prove his strength in old age by

4.15 Souvenir Bordeaux Exposition Philatelique cover with overprinted 1fr Merson Liberty & Peace and special Exposition handstamp dated 21.6.1923.

4.16 45c Louis Pasteur (from set 25 May 1923+)

4.17 1924 Paris Olympic Games (set 1 April 1924+)

splitting a tree trunk along a cleft already in it. The stamp, however, ignores the story's outcome that highlighted the folly of vanity and the fleeting nature of glory. Milo's hand caught fast in the cleft and he was attacked and eaten by wolves. The stamp's design was based on the Louvre's statue of Milo's death throes, although the sculptor, Pierre Puget, chose a lion as the killer, not wolves. The 50c was straightforward, and highlighted the antecedents and continuity of the Olympic Games by picturing a modern athlete wearing a laurel wreath. Unfortunately for France's parlous post-war finances the games made a loss of five and a half million francs.

In October 1924 the anniversary of the birth of the Renaissance poet Pierre de Ronsard (1524-85) was commemorated.(4.18) Living mainly in Paris Ronsard had witnessed the religious wars and political instability that wracked sixteenth century France, and he owed his wealth, and indeed his liberty, to the favour of King Charles IX and his brother Henry III. Famous in his lifetime for his mastery of the styles favoured by the poets of ancient Alexandria, after his death he was largely forgotten until the end of the nineteenth century. Possibly his life story matched France's sombre post-war mood as did his works celebrating the countryside, re-imagining Classical and mythical characters, and praising the virtue of patriotism.

4.18 Pierre de Ronsard (6 October 1924)

Issued over several months in 1924 and 1925 a set of six stamps

4.19 10f abstract RF design, 15f vase, 25f terrace garden and steps, and 75f potter (from International Exhibition of Modern Decorative Arts set 8 December 1924+)

publicised the International Exhibition of Modern Decorative Arts in central Paris.(4.19) From this event evolved the name Art Deco with its characteristic bold lines, bright colours, stark contrasts and use of new materials such as ivory and ebony. The set's four designs featured a typical clean lined Art Deco abstract design, a stylized vase, a potter, and an Art Deco terraced garden and steps. The style had made its appearance prior to 1914, and originally the Exhibition had been planned for 1915. Nevertheless with 15,000 exhibits from 20 countries, the 1925 event not only set the seal on Art Deco's world-wide influence in architecture, interior décor, furniture, glass, jewelry and advertisements, but also ensured France reigned supreme in the glamorous world of modern art and design. Germany was not invited.

In 1927 a stamp commemorated the centenary of the birth of Pierre Marcellin Berthelot (1827-1907).(4.20) A distinguished French chemist, Berthelot showed that organic chemistry was a constructive science, not merely an analytical one. His research expedited the creation of a range of synthetic sugars, fats and hydo-carbons, and successive governments particularly valued his development of new explosives. Indeed, at the time of the 1870-71 war with Prussia he was president of the government's scientific defence committee.

In 1920 the Pope had finally canonized the French heroine, Joan of Arc, but more than a century earlier, in 1803, Napoleon Bonaparte had declared her a national symbol. A stamp picturing her on horseback with a standard held aloft commemorated the 500th anniversary of her relief of the siege of Orleans in May 1429.(4.21) Widely believed to have been divinely inspired, her charisma and advice had restored a demoralised and defeated country's battle-winning pride and self-confidence. The aptness of her achievements had not gone unnoticed.

Starting in 1927 a series of annual surcharged stamps were issued in support of the government's Sinking Fund. The country was deep in debt, and inflation was high – the ordinary internal postage rate had risen from 10 cents in 1917 to 50c in 1926. France has borrowed heavily to finance the war and then undertake massive restoration projects. It owed the USA four billion dollars. Much of occupied France had been devastated and the retreating Germans had destroyed most industrial plants they had not already transported back to Germany.

France demanded 70% of the reparations Germany was obliged to pay the Allies, and asserted that war damages should take priority over Great Britain's claims to the actual costs of fighting the war. In the end Germany was saddled with a bill of 132 billion gold marks, of which 52% would go to France, 28% to Britain and the rest to Belgium, Italy and Serbia. In the event Germany paid only about 22 billion gold marks and then only after long delays while its economy recovered. In addition repeated German protests led to reductions in the amount, and by 1930 the Allies had lost the will to impose further sanctions.

In desperation, in 1926 France's Sinking Fund attempted to accumulate funds to set aside to repay debts. To assist this a series of surcharged stamps was issued between 1927 and 1931. In common with all special stamps they were carefully designed to attract collectors in addition to well-wishers of the fund. In 1927 the Pasteur portrait and two different Sower designs were selected for stamps printed (not overprinted

4.20 Pierre Marcellin Berthelot (7 September 1927)

4.21 (E) St Joan of Arc (3 March 1929)

later) with the inscriptions 'C A' or 'Caisse d'Amortissent' (Sinking Fund) and modest surcharges.(4.22) In 1928 the three stamps were reissued in different colours - and in yet more colours in 1929, 1930 and 1931.

In 1928, too, a striking 1f 50c Sinking Fund stamp featuring sturdy male and female workers was issued with a massive 8f 50c surcharge. And possibly with serious collectors in mind, the lines above 'f' in the surcharge tablet come in three different broken and unbroken forms. In 1931 a Sinking Fund stamp with similar close-up portraits of women in provincial bonnets appeared. The year before, though, witnessed a particularly appealing stamp featuring the famous smiling angel of Reims Cathedral.(4.23) Carved in the thirteenth century, a German shell shattered its head in September 1914, and the damaged statue became a wartime icon symbolizing French culture and German barbarity. The pieces were collected and preserved, and the angel was carefully restored in 1926. Despite all the attention to detail, probably the multiplicity of issues, the high surcharges, and the lack of appeal of the Sinking Fund itself accounted for the poor sales overall. There were no more issues after 1931 although the Sinking Fund itself continued throughout the decade.

In 1927 memories of the war were once again revived when 20,000 men and women of the USA's veteran association, the American Legion and Auxiliary, visited France in September for their Ninth Convention. They paraded through Paris and visited cemeteries and battlefields, and notably the bridge over the Marne where several US divisions had fought in 1918. Two identical stamps packed with details of the kindred spirit between the two republics marked the Convention.(4.24) The images highlighted the American Revolution and the present day but significantly omitted any reference to the recent war. Possibly the disappointment and embarrassment associated with the US Senate's refusal to ratify the Treaty of Versailles and to join the League of Nations established after the war had much to do with the omission.

The left of each stamp featured the dashing Marquis de Lafayette (1757-1834). A French aristocrat and soldier, he became an enthusiastic supporter of the American Revolution and a successful field commander under George Washington. Back in revolutionary France he helped frame the *Declaration of the Rights of Man and of the Citizen* and became commander of the National Guard. However he spoke out against extremism, narrowly escaping arrest and execution, and he refused any government post under Napoleon. His reputation remained high after 1815 as an opponent of the absolutism of the restored Bourbon kings. On the right the stamps featured George Washington (1731-99), the revered commander-in-chief of the American army that defeated the British who became the first president of the United States (1789-97). In the centre of the stamps was a tiny image of the *Spirit of St Louis*, the monoplane in which Charles Lindbergh attained fame by being the first person to fly non-stop across the Atlantic from New York to Paris (3,600 miles in 33½ hours) in 1927. It is shown flying over the French liner *Paris*. At 34,569 tons *Paris* was the largest liner under the French flag and renowned for its luxurious décor, much of it in the striking Art Deco style. It was, though, an unlucky ship. In 1929 it ran aground twice, first in New York Harbour and then off the Eddystone Rocks in Cornwall, and later that year caught fire at Le Havre and sank but was refloated and refitted. In April 1939 it caught fire again at Le Havre and capsized, and remained there until cut up in 1947.

By the dawn of the 1930s French stamps were undergoing a sea change. Between 1929 and 1933 a set became the precursor of numerous issues celebrating France's culture, countryside and historic sites.(4.25) It included Reims Cathedral (3f) that was still undergoing

4.22   Sinking Fund (set 26 September 1927)

4.23   Sinking Fund issues: 1f 50+8f 50 workers (15 May 1928) and 1f 50+ 3f 50 smiling angel (15 March 1930)

4.24 (E) 1f 50 American Legion's visit (pair 15 September 1927)

  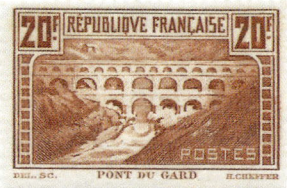

4.25 *90c Le Puy-en-Velay, 2f Arc de Triomphe, 3f Reims Cathedral, 5f Mont St Michel, 10f La Rochelle and 20f Pont du Gard (set 1929+)*

restoration after extensive damage by German artillery in 1914, Mont St Michel (5f), the fortified island off Normandy that defied English attacks in the Hundred Years War, the port of La Rochelle (10f) in the south-west that saw the English evicted in 1372 and withstood English attacks in 1627-28, the mighty Roman aqueduct in southern France (20f) known as the Pont du Gard, the celebrated Arc de Triomphe in Paris (2f), and a panoramic view of the peaks of Le Puy-en-Velay (90c) in south-central France. On the peak in the centre stood a huge statue of the Virgin Mary cast from 213 Russian guns captured in the Crimean War.

In addition France remained proud of its extensive African, Caribbean and Far Eastern Empire. It had been secured largely in rivalry with the British over the past few centuries, and more often than not gained and held by force of arms. Despite the revolts and controversies tens of thousands of colonial soldiers had fought alongside French troops in the war. The first post-war stamp drawing attention to French colonies appeared on 1 January 1930 to mark the centenary of the conquest of Algeria. It featured an enticing Bay of Algiers viewed through Moorish arches.(4.26)

Unsurprisingly, culture and crafts rather than conquest and control characterized the International Colonial Exhibition in Paris in 1931. Indigenous people from across the globe were imported to display domestic tasks and crafts in recreated buildings and villages, and French aid and support rather than exploitation were highlighted. Belgium, the Netherlands, Portugal and Great Britain were among the other participants. The Exhibition lasted six months and attracted nine million visitors. Three stamps portraying a Fachi tribeswoman from French Niger and a 1f 50 stamp featuring colonial people from across the Empire promoted the event.(4.27)

The sombre post-war mood of national pride tempered by horror at thought of renewed military

4.26 *Centenary of conquest of Algiers (1 January 1930)*

4.27 *International Colonial Exhibition (from set 17 November 1930+)*

4.28 *2c Sower and 1f Peace (from set 1932-39)*

combat was, perhaps, best summarized by the introduction of a definitive series in 1932 that harked back to the pre-war allegorical designs of Mouchon, Merson and Blanc. Designed by the artist Paul Albert Laurens, the new stamps pictured a female figure in a Classical tunic but also wearing the Revolutionary Phrygian or Liberty cap holding out an olive branch of peace.(4.28) It was called Peace, and significantly the Sower was reintroduced for some values.

In 1933 Adolf Hitler became Chancellor of Germany, while in France the Sower and Peace set was extended with new values and colours until 1939.

CHAPTER 5
Poland

Over the centuries Poland had expanded and shrank in size depending upon the military prowess, internal cohesion, and enterprise of its rulers and enemies. When the vast Polish-Lithuanian Commonwealth was created in 1569 stretching from the Baltic Sea nearly to the Black Sea and from Smolensk to Posen it was the largest country in Europe. During this 'Golden Age' King John III Sobieski (1674-96) achieved cult status by defeating Ottoman Turk armies at Khotyn in 1673 and outside Vienna in 1683, but he was the last Polish king to be a major player in European affairs. A century later, through a series of invasions and partitions in 1772, 1793 and 1795 the fatally weakened country was erased from the map by its powerful neighbours, the Russian Empire, the Hapsburg Empire and the Kingdom of Prussia.

During the Congress of Vienna in 1815 the victorious allies created a new Kingdom of Poland (commonly known as 'Congress Poland') but although it possessed its own army and constitution its ruler was also the Russian Tsar. Centred on Warsaw it stretched from Lublin in the east to Kalisz in the west and just short of Kracow in the south with a narrow northern corridor reaching into southwestern Lithuania. (see map overleaf). To the chagrin of Polish patriots vast stretches of ex-Polish-Lithuanian lands east of Congress Poland remained absorbed within the Russian Empire itself, and Prussia and Austria retained most of the territory they had purloined in the 1790s. The bitter memories of past glory, humiliating partition and the disappointment of the Congress of Vienna lasted well into the twentieth century.

The nineteenth century saw Poles engaging in bloody but unsuccessful revolts against Russian and Austrian overlordship. After the 1830-31 revolt Czar Nicolas I abolished the Kingdom's army and constitution, and after the 1863-64 revolt the Kingdom was downgraded to 'Vistula Land' and treated little better than a mere province.

Polish political parties evolved in all three Empires, but overall their voices were fragmented and weak. Political frustrations, nationalist feelings, and the sense of second-class citizenship never went away though, and Congress Poland joined in the prolonged but unsuccessful revolution across Russia in 1905. Two key figures in this were Roman Dmowski and Jozef Pilsudski who were to dominate Polish affairs until the 1930s. They loathed each other and not only took opposing sides in the 1914-18 war but possessed very different views on the size and constitution of any restored Polish state

The outbreak of war saw the beginning of the convoluted resurrection of an independent Poland. Poles found themselves conscripted into the armies of Russia, Germany and Austria-Hungary, and often fighting each other on the Eastern Front. As the war descended into the nightmare of relentless attrition all three empires attempted to secure Polish loyalty by offering pledges of political concessions and even autonomy once they had won the war, but their wartime actions towards the Poles rarely matched their conciliatory utterances. Russia secured some support by allowing the creation of a Polish National Committee and promising to create a large autonomous Poland embracing east Poznan, south Silesia and western Galicia. Roman Dmowski made great efforts to secure the western Allies support for Russian promises. Jozef Pilsudski on the other hand saw liberation emerging from a Russian defeat and created a Polish Legion in support of Austria-Hungary, even though he abhorred Germany for its relentless suppression of Polish culture

Much of the fighting on the Eastern Front occurred across Congress Poland. In 1914 Russian armies neared Krakow before being halted, and in early 1915 Galicia to the east endured the scorched earth policy of the retreating Russians and hundreds of thousands of Poles were evicted and deported. By the end of the year the Germans occupied all Russian Poland, and an abortive Russian campaign in 1916 only exacerbated the people's suffering.

After Germany's failure at Verdun and Austrian setbacks in Italy there were renewed attempts to encourage Polish support. Initially the Germans and Austrians had turned Congress Poland into an administrative unit blandly known as the General Government with the north-west half ruled by Germany

5.1 20pf Germania overprinted Russisch Polen (from set 12 May 1915) and 60pf Germania overprinted Gen.-Gouv. Warschau (from set 1 August 1916+)

in Warsaw and the south-east controlled by Austria in Lublin. On 12 May 1915 five *Germania* values had been issued overprinted *Russisch Polen* (Russian Poland) for use in the German sector. On 1 August 1916 these began to be replaced by eleven *Germania* stamps from 2½pf to 60pf overprinted *Gen.-Gouv. Warschau* (General Government Warsaw).(5.1)

In the Austrian sector Austrian stamps along with some Austro-Hungarian Military Post and Bosnia-Herzegovina issues were used. No overprints were applied, but postmarks were usually inscribed *K. u. K. Etappenpostamt* (Austrian Empire and Kingdom of Hungary official district post office) with the name of the town in Polish.(5.2) (see also Chapter 8 Austria-Hungary)

The German and Austrian stamps paid for mail to be delivered to district post offices, but not individual

5.2 Souvenir cancelled to order card with preprinted 8 heller conjoined Austrian Empire and Kingdom of Hungary Arms and 2 h Emperor Charles K.u.K. Feldpost postmarked K. u. K. Etappenpostamt Dabrowa in Polen, dated 9.X.18, and 3g local delivery stamp inscribed Poczta miejska wZarkach (Municipal post office at Zarkach). Zarckach was a town north of Katowice.

5.3 Cover with 5pf shaded Germania overprinted Russisch Polen with two 1915 local delivery stamps from Warsaw featuring the Polish eagle (10 Groszy), one of them overprinted 2gr, and another local delivery stamp featuring the sword bearing mermaid Arms of Warsaw overprinted 6gr. The Germania stamp and local delivery stamps have Warsaw cancellations a day apart as this collector's item was addressed and posted within the city.

addresses. Many local councils set up local delivery services; some printed special stamps for this service, others used handstamped cachets to signify payment, and a few used both.(5.3)

In November 1916 the Germans and Austrians turned the General Government into a new puppet Kingdom of Poland. It was ruled by German and Austro-Hungarian governors, and in due course possessed an advisory and administrative Regency Council, but never a king. However few Poles saw the Germans as liberators, and despite all the eulogistic propaganda the new Kingdom was perceived as little more than a dumping ground for Poles moved from western districts areas abutting Germany so that they could be settled by German families and in due course formally annexed. Poles were subject to forced labour, and industrial output and agriculture centred on German, not Polish, needs. Germany overrode the more liberal ideas of Austria-Hungary for the kingdom, including suggestions for a Hapsburg archduke to become king.

For a time, however, Pilsudski cooperated with the new puppet Kingdom of Poland, and became co-leader of its Council's Military Commission. He saw it as a pragmatic stepping stone to independence, but frustration quickly mounted at the lack of progress and the dominance of German rather than Austrian control. During this period of fragile collaboration many Poles in the Russian army left to join an autonomous Polish Legion under Pilsudski's command. However in the summer of 1917 Pilsudski and other Polish Legion officers were imprisoned for refusing an oath of loyalty to an unknown future king and commitment to an alliance with Germany. Even at this late stage, however, Pilsudski had been prepared to negotiate an agreement with Austria.

Nevertheless the growing Polish Legion remained intact, if largely unused as yet. By arrangement with the German Field Post authorities its mail was accepted using Imperial Russian stamps overprinted with the Polish eagle and *Pol. Korp*, and sometimes new values.(5.4) Pilsudski remained acutely aware of the value of the Legion as a vehicle of propaganda as well as a potent military force.

After the conquest of Russian Poland German forces had seized Russia's southern Baltic provinces. Vilnius was occupied on 18 September 1915, and Courland and the old Polish-Lithuanian province of Livonia straddling modern southern Estonia and northern Latvia by the end of the year. From January 1916 a dozen *Germania* stamps up to one mark appeared in these regions overprinted *Postgebiet Ob. Ost.* (Postal territory of the Commander-in-Chief East).(5.5)

Although Bolshevik Russia's exit from the war was confirmed in the Treaty of Brest-Litovsk with Germany in March 1918, Congress Poland was not mentioned as it was already firmly in Germany hands. In the treaty Russia renounced all claims to the Ukraine and the Baltic areas of Estonia, Latvia and Lithuania, all of which now came under the command of the German Commander-in-Chief East.

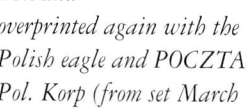
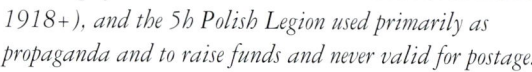

5.4 *Russian Romanov eagle overprinted 10k and overprinted again with the Polish eagle and POCZTA Pol. Korp (from set March 1918+), and the 5h Polish Legion used primarily as propaganda and to raise funds and never valid for postage.*

5.5 *2½pf and 10pf Germania overprinted Postgebiet Ob. Ost. (from set 15 January 1916+). The 10pf has a Riga postmark*

When Germany faced total defeat a few months later its High Command hurriedly grasped thoughts of a negotiated peace that accepted President Woodrow Wilson's view that a fully independent Poland, far larger than Congress Poland, should be established On 3 October Germany's new Chancellor, Prince Max of Baden, concurred and ordered the immediate termination of military control in all occupied countries. Not surprisingly, on 6 October the Regency Council in Warsaw adopted Wilson's proposals as the basis for negotiations. On the same day the command over Polish forces serving Germany and Austro-Hungary were transferred to the Regency Council.

On 10 November Jozef Pilsudski arrived back in Warsaw from a German prison, and his political reputation and command of the Polish Legion ensured he slipped easily into a leadership role. Meanwhile his rival Roman Dmowski was in Paris seemingly secure in French approbation. Whereas Pilsudski sought a Poland comprising mainly Poles Dmowski wanted the largest possible Poland and cared little that significant minorities of Germans, Austrians, Czechs, Russians, Ukrainians, Lithuanians and Estonians might be under Polish authority. Both, though, argued that a Baltic port was essential.

The Allies urged Pilsudski and Dmowski to work together, and successfully encouraged the charismatic and internationally renowned Polish pianist and patriot Ignacy Paderewski to cement a working relationship, and this he achieved. Pilsudski would remain head of state and the armed forces, Paderewski would become prime minister of a coalition government and speak for the government alongside Dmowski at the Peace Conference.

The Poles had a battle-hardened army, territory they called their homeland, significant international support and a central European power vacuum they could exploit. On the other hand they were surrounded by enemies, and there were no agreed borders. The Austro-Hungarians vacated their territory on 29 October 1918. The Germans started to evacuate the General Government soon after 11 November, but ominously hung onto the heavily Germanised western province of Poznan until 27 December and to Pomerania and Danzig until February 1919.

Soon after the Armistice the Warsaw government instructed post offices to continue using existing stocks of German and Austrian stamps but ensure all cancellations had Polish place names. Many offices, however, went further and overprinted the stamps with variations of *Poczta Polska* (Polish Post).(5.6/5.7) Some of these were postally used, but many were produced speculatively with collectors uppermost in mind.

However on 17 November the government introduced as far around Warsaw as possible four highly patriotic but hitherto unissued stamps printed originally for the city's

POLAND

5.6 40pf Germania with Deutsches Reich obliterated and overprinted Poczta Polska with new value (November 1918)

5.7 10pf Germania overprinted Gen.-Gouv. Warschau with the further overprint Polska Poczta and Ostrow applied in the city of Ostrow Wielkopolski. The two bars of the Ostrow overprinting failed to obliterate the German overprint. Ostrow Wielkopolski attained fame on 10 November 1918 for declaring itself an independent Polish republic, and preparing to rise in revolt against the Germans. It was soon overtaken by wider events

5.8 Warsaw local post issues overprinted Poczta Polska and 5, 10, 25 and 50 Fen values (set 17 November 1918)

5.9 2½pf and 3pf Germania overprinted Gen.-Gouv. Warschau and further overprinted with varying degrees of accuracy Poczta Polska, 5 g values and obliterating bars (from set 5 December 1918+)

local post.(5.8) They had been overprinted with the value in fenigs at the top and *Poczta Polska* at the bottom. The new Polish currency of fenigs and markas was equivalent to German phennigs and marks. The 5 fen featured the huge column in Warsaw commemorating Sigismund III Vasa, King of Poland and Duke of Lithuania from 1587 to 1632, who seized Smolensk and briefly held Moscow, and for a time was also King of Sweden. The 10 fen pictured the armed mermaid Arms of Warsaw, the 25 fen the outstretched Polish eagle, and the 50 fen Warsaw's impressive statue of King John III Sobieski.

Meanwhile large residual stocks of *Germania* stamps and postcards already overprinted *Gen.-Gouv Warschau* were further overprinted with black obliterating bars and *Poczta Polska*, and issued in the evacuated German parts of Congress Poland from 5 December.(5.9) The hasty emergency printing resulted in many shifts of bars and double printing. Not surprisingly, stamps and postcards without *Poczta Polska* were banned from 16 December.

In the ex-Austrian part of Congress Poland, the Polish administration in Lublin told post offices to use up existing stocks of Austrian stamps. Several post offices decided to apply their own *Polska Poczta* overprints, but during December Lublin supplied post offices with all the remaining Austro-Hungarian stamps complete with the *Polska Poczta* overprint and heavy obliterations of the Hapsburg portraits.(5.10) In this region the Austrian haller and krone currency continued in use. One of the many problems facing the emerging new country was the variety of currencies in use.

After the Austro-Hungarian army left the old Hapsburg subordinate Kingdom of Galicia and Lodomeria (straddling the present day border of Poland and Ukraine) in late October 1918 the territory was administered by a coalition of Polish political parties termed the Polish Liquidation Commission. The ancient kingdom had been part of the Polish-Lithuanian Commonwealth until annexed during the eighteenth century partitions. Here unaltered wartime Austrian stamps picturing the Imperial Austrian Crown, Coat of Arms and the Emperors Franz Joseph or Charles continued in use for a time, although once again some post offices added *Polska Poczta* or *Poczta Polska* handstamps. On 10 January 1919 a range of superannuated Austrian definitive, Postage Due and

5.10 1918 45h Emperor Charles Imperial & Royal Welfare Fund with portrait obliterated by a circular Polish eagle and overprinted POLSKA POCZTA (from set 5 December 1918)

5.11 1916 80h Arms of Austria overprinted POLSKA POCZTA and 25h value (from set 10 January 1919)

5.12   70h Western Galicia (from set 25 February 1919)

Newspaper stamps appeared with official *Poczta Polska* or *Polska Poczta* overprints. (5.11) Unoverprinted Austrian stamps were banned ten days later.

Despite all the turmoil, on 25 February 1919 the Polish Liquidation Commission was able to issue its own set of eleven specially designed stamps for Western Galicia featuring the Polish Eagle.(5.12) They were imperforate and sold without gum.

On 27 January 1919 the Austrian currency, although termed halerzy and korony in Polish, appeared on a specially designed set of twelve stamps primarily for south Poland's ex-Austrian provinces.(5.13) Two images featured the Polish eagle, one of them set between two ancient Roman fasces – the axe contained within a bundle of rods that represented the state's authority and was carried in front of all Roman magistrates. Two others pictured peaceful farming scenes, representing national recovery, while the fifth design represented national defence in its picture of a Polish Uhlan, the renowned cavalryman, with his sword drawn and horse rearing up ready to charge. The set was available from the same date in ex-German provinces with the values printed in fenigow or marki.

It is perhaps significant that May 1919 saw the first Polish Philatelic Exhibition. There were few specially designed Polish stamps but a plethora of overprinted German and Austrian ones to highlight the enormity of recent events and stimulate Polish pride. The Exhibition was supported by a set of five stamps using two current Polish eagle designs overprinted with 5f surcharges, a white outlined cross, and the inscription *T POLSKA WYSTAWA MAREK* (literally The Polish Exhibition of Brands/Types).(5.14) The set also supported the Polish White Cross whose founder was Helena Paderewska, wife of the Prime Minister, Ignacy Paderewski (January to November 1919). During the war Helena had been instrumental in attracting many Polish American women to work as White Cross nurses in Polish military hospitals.

Soon afterwards, on 15 June 1919, the Prime Minister himself appeared on a stamp (15f) in a set commemorating the opening of the first session of the independent Polish National Assembly, known as the Sejm from an ancient Slavic word for 'gathering'.(5.15) Other values featured Jozef Pilsudski (25f) and Adalbert Trampczynski (20f), the new governor of Poland's Poznan province and a key member of Poland's Upper House, the Senate. Three

5.13   Ex-Austrian Poland 50h Polish eagle, 1k farming, 2k 50 'ploughing in peace', and 5k Polish Uhlan (from set 27 January 1919)

5.14   1919 5f and 25f Polish eagle varieties with Polish Philatelic Exhibition overprint (from set 3 May 1919)

5.15   The first session of the Sejm (set 15 June 1919) (A smaller version of the 20f was issued in 1920).

further values featured an outstretched eagle above a Sejm commemorative tablet (10f), an eagle over a galleon (highlighting sea-borne trade) (50f), and a griffin clasping the fasces (1m). The symbol of the fasces was not confined to Italy, although Mussolini's Fascists were soon to make it their own.

However the Polish claims to huge swathes of land were aggressively challenged. Many Germans, smarting at the Armistice, still harboured hopes of retaining Poznan and East Prussia, and the Lithuanians to the north, Czechs to the south, and Ukrainians and Bolsheviks to the east all coveted territory claimed by Poland.

While Pilsudski attempted to bring cohesion and overall control to the Warsaw administration, and Dmowski sought the Peace Conference's support for a Poland nearing the old Polish-Lithuanian Commonwealth in size, the Peace Conference's Commission on Polish Affairs set to work guided by Woodrow Wilson's conviction that ethnic factors should determine international borders and somehow or the other Poland must be able to access Danzig. Its task was daunting. First, although some areas were dominated by ethnic Poles others possessed a bewildering array of racial majorities and minorities. And second, the Poles were busy determining their future for themselves, and were not shy of using force. In January 1919 Pilsudski stationed Polish troops in Poznan, and ordered forces north into Lithuania and south into Galicia where fighting soon erupted with the Ukrainians.

In the event the Treaty of Versailles did secure Poland the province of Poznan and a large 'corridor' of territory through East Prussia that included eastern Pomerania and Soldau leading towards Danzig. In August 1919 five *Germania* stamps were issued across Poznan overprinted *Poczta Polska* with 5pf or 10pf values.(5.16) Possibly they eased a shortage of stamps, but possibly the new Polish issues of 27 January could have been used. Overprinted *Germania* stamps, however, thrust the change of territorial ownership firmly down German throats.

However Poland did not get Danzig or its hinterland. Justified fears of enmity between Poland and Danzig's predominantly German population meant it became a Free City under League of Nation's guardianship. Poland did, though, receive significant commercial rights in Danzig and established its own Post Office in an old German military hospital. Polish stamps overprinted PORT GDANSK were used.(5.17) It was a sign of the deep and lasting German enmity that the Poles captured after defending the Post Office in September 1939 were executed as illegal combatants.

Other East Prussian territory also evaded Poland's clutches. The Treaty of Versailles ordered plebiscites in the provinces of Marienwerder and Allenstein and both voted overwhelmingly to stay in Germany.

In German Upper Silesia the Allies overrode the

5.16 *20pf Germania overprinted Poczta Polska and 5h (from Poznan set 5 August 1919)*

5.17 *1928 25g Polish eagle overprinted PORT GDANSK with a Gdansk cancellation dated 31.7.35*

5.18 *60pf optimistically featuring a dove of peace flying over rural and industrial Haute Silesie (Upper Silesia) from the Inter Allied Commission set (26 March 1921). 'Upper Silesia' appears in French, German and Polish.*

5.19 *10f and 50f Polish eagle and 4m Silesian miner (from Polish regional set 19 June 1922+)*

recommendation of the Peace Conference's Commission that all 4,200 square miles of this ethnically mixed industrialised region should be awarded to Poland. Despite Silesia's angry Poles rising in rebellion, the Allies ordered a plebiscite for 20 March 1921. This was organized by a hard pressed French led Inter-Allied Commission that publicized and funded the event with a lengthy set of stamps.(5.18) In the end the south chose Poland, the north and west Germany, but the valuable industrialised central region was evenly divided. Deadlock, and further violence, ensued until an international commission of four disinterested nations – Belgium, China, Spain and Brazil – awarded 70% of the territory to Germany but as the remainder had most of the mines and factories Poland ended up the winner.

In June 1922 Polish Silesia enjoyed a special set of stamps. Some featured the Polish eagle and others a Silesian miner shouldering a pick-axe.(5.19) To great

German acclaim Hitler reoccupied the region in 1939.

Poland completely disregarded the Commission of Polish Affairs' recommended eastern border. This approximated to the 1919 Curzon line that had divided the vaguely defined region of Lithuania roughly in half and ran directly south passing west of Brest Litovsk (Brzesc in Polish). Polish forces, however, staked out claims 150 miles to the east. Poland deeply desired Vilnius, but the Lithuanians wanted it as their capital. When German forces withdrew, prolonged fighting between Polish, Lithuanian and Soviet Russian forces saw the city and region change hands several times.

Both Lithuania and Poland fought the Soviet Union but not as allies. The Poles captured Vilnius in April 1919, and tried unsuccessfully to overthrow the Lithuanian government. Some months later the Russians briefly pushed back the Poles and handed the city to the Lithuanians. In late October 1920 Poland's Pilsudski acted deviously to negate an armistice he had made with Lithuania earlier in the month that implied Vilnius was on the Lithuanian side of the border. The Polish General Zeligowski pretended his troops had mutinied and that he had been unable to prevent them occupying Vilnius – where they stayed. The Republic of Central Lithuania was set up, and when all the League of Nations attempts at resolving the situation failed, Poland annexed it on 24 March 1922. In 1923 the League of Nations Conference of Ambassadors agreed that the region was Polish, and Lithuania, utterly incensed, broke off all relations with Poland until 1938. Among many complications, this meant a letter from Poland to Lithuania had to go to a neutral country where it was repackaged to remove any signs it was Polish and then posted on to Lithuania.

The short-lived Polish controlled Republic of Central Lithuania produced numerous stamps inscribed *SRODKOWA LITWA* (CENTRAL LITHUANIA) to continuously reinforce its presence and claim. In October 1920, and again in February 1921, sets of three stamps

5.20 2m conjoined Arms (from set 20 October 1920), and 10s 1919 Lithuanian Arms overprinted with the conjoined Arms of Poland and Lithuania and 4m (from set 23 November 1920)

5.21 2m Ostrabrama Gate, Vilnius and 4m St Stanislaus Cathedral, Vilnius (from set December 1920).

5.22 50f government offices, and 2m medieval Polish-Lithuanian castle on Trakai Island (from Postage Due set February 1921)

5.23 (E) 4m Queen Jadwiga/King Wladislaw, 6m Stefan Bathory University, 10m Union of Poland and Lithuania, and 20m Kosciuszko/Mickiewicz (from set April 1921+)

showed conjoined Polish and Lithuanian Arms. More insultingly in November several Lithuanian Arms stamps appeared overprinted SRODKOWA LITWA with the conjoined arms and new values.(5.20)

From December 1920 onwards several pictorial sets were issued.(5.21) Even a Postage Due set helped stamp a Polish identity on the region with views of government offices, cathedrals and castles.(5.22)

Other issues rekindled memories of the medieval Polish-Lithuanian Commonwealth and its rulers.(5.23) Those from the summer of 1921 included a scene of the union of Poland and Lithuania in 1569 (10m), and portraits of Queen Jadwiga and King Wladislaw II Jagiello (4m). Jadwiga was Queen of Poland (1384-99) in her own right and despite her Christian faith she married Wladislaw, the pagan Grand Duke of Lithuania in 1386, thereby creating a far larger kingdom. The frontiers were extended, plots thwarted, and in 1410 Wladislaw broke the power of the Teutonic Knights at the celebrated Battle of Grunwald. The 20m featured two Polish-Lithuanian heroes. One was Tadeusz Kosciuszko (1746-1817) who fought the British in the American War of Independence and was prominent in the unsuccessful 1794 uprising against Russia. The other was Adam Mickiewicz (1798-1855), the national poet of Poland, but also celebrated in Lithuania, whose works encouraged nationalist movements and led to his long exile. The 6m was equally pointed in its portrayal of Vilnius University. Long closed by the Russian Tsar, Pilsudski had been instrumental in reopening it recently as Stefan Bathory University, named after a renowned late sixteenth century King of Poland and Grand Duke of Lithuania

In early 1921 a surcharged set of Central Lithuanian joint Arms stamps even raised funds for Poles to travel to participate in the Upper Silesian plebiscite.(5.24) And later that year all pretence that a mutiny caused the seizure of Vilnius was swept aside by two stamps celebrating its first anniversary with scenes much like a hero's victory parade.(5.25)

In the south Poland faced further conflict over ex-Austrian Galicia. The western half was mainly Polish as was the historic city of Krakow, and their annexation proved uncontroversial. In the east there were far more Ruthenians (Catholic Ukrainians), and fierce fighting occurred as the Ruthenians much preferred an independent Ukraine. Indeed they were attempting to create one with other Ukrainians, although against stiff Bolshevik opposition (see Russia). Effectively helpless, the Allies procrastinated, and in the end Ruthenian protests were ignored and Poland's hard won occupation was formally recognised in 1923.

The Poles wanted to push their border far into Byelorussia (Belarus). Pilsudski's forces got as far as Kiev in April 1920 only to be relentlessly pushed back dangerously close to Warsaw by the Red Army. However

5.24 25f joint Arms overprinted NA SLASK (For Silesia) and 2m to support the Upper Silesian plebiscite (from set February 1921+)

5.25 100m Polish forces entering Vilnius and 150m General Zeligowski (from set November 1921)

5.26 10m Russian Peace Treaty (from set May 1921+)

5.27 1919 5k Uhlan overprinted S.O. 1920 (from set 1920)

in August a brilliant counter attack saved Warsaw, forced a hasty Soviet retreat and overtures for peace that resulted in the Treaty of Riga in March 1921. Poland's eastern borders now stretched well beyond the Curzon Line and far to the east of Lwow (Russian Lvov). Four million Ukrainians and one million Belarusians were added to Poland's population. Between May and August 1921 Poland marked the treaty with three stamps (10m, 15m, 20m) featuring a rainbow of hope with a figure sowing seeds but, significantly, with his sword ready at hand.(5.26) The 10m and 20m values were reissued in different shades and slightly different sizes in 1922.

To German, Lithuanian and Soviet Russian antagonism was added Czechoslovak resentment over the fate of the small ex-Austrian Duchy of Teschen and its coalfield on the Silesian borders of the two new nations. All attempts by the Allies to stop Czech and Polish troops and workers fighting, and to secure agreement for a plebiscite failed, and in desperation in July 1920 they awarded the coalmines to Czechoslovakia and divided the border city of Teschen on the Olza river between the two. Until then both countries had been permitted to sell stamps in the region overprinted *S.O. 1920*.(5.27) The French had had the uneviable task of attempting to keep the peace, and S.O. stood for *Silesie Orientale* (Eastern Silesia).

5.28 6m Uhlan (from set February 1920, 40f eagle and fasces with redrawn value tablet (May 1920) and 8m eagle (from set 1920+)

5.29 Twin coloured 100m Polish eagle (from set June 1921) and single coloured 2,000m stamp (from set February 1923+)

5.30 5m Uhlan overprinted with Red Cross and 30m surcharge (from set 5 March 1921)

Between 1921 and 1923 growing inflation led to a new large Polish eagle series of stamps with steadily increasing values from 25 to 2,000 marki.(5.29) Chronic inflation had arisen from the huge cost of the Poland's wars, the instability of the marki, and the impossibility of further economies in a war ravaged country.

In a sign of the dire welfare problems, on 5 March 1921 four of the Polish Uhlan stamps (5m, 6m, 10m and 20m) appeared with large premiums of 30 marki each in aid of the new Polish Red Cross that had been established recently by Helena Paderewska.(5.30)

In 1923 the Treaty of Riga and some eagle stamps were hurriedly overprinted with tens of thousands of marki, and in 1924 the bottom of the large eagle stamp had to be redesigned to accommodate values up to 2,000,000 marki.(5.31)

On 2 May 1921 seven stamps with three allegorical designs celebrated Poland's new constitution voted through, as each stamp notes, on 17 March. Based on the French model, it established a republic, asserted Sejm and Senate supremacy, abolished all royal and aristocratic titles, and banned all racial and religious discrimination. The stamps featured allegories of the nation's new dawn (2m, 3m, 4m), new prosperity (6m, 10m), and new peace (25m, 50m).(5.32)

As inflation continued to soar the stamps issued between June and November 1923 to mark the 450th anniversary of the birth of Nicolaus Copernicus (1473-1543) and the 150th anniversary of the death of Father Stanilaus Konarski (1700-73) had values in thousands of marki.(5.33) Poland was eager to claim Copernicus, the mathematician and astronomer who showed the planets circled the sun, was Polish (just as the Nazis claimed he was German) as he had been born in Thorn (modern Torun) in Royal Prussia which then was a domain firmly within the independent Kingdom of Poland. Stanislaus Konarski probably was selected because his educational

As a practical sign of emerging central government authority, from 1 February 1920 stamps had been issued for the whole of Poland rather than merely its emerging regions. At first the spread eagle, agricultural and Uhlan images from the 1919 southern and northern Poland issues were reintroduced with fenigow and marki values up to 200m. (5.28) In 1920 and 1921 the two spread eagle stamps were redesigned, and new values placed on them.

5.31 25m+2m Polish eagle and 10m Peace Treaty inflation overprints (from series 1923+) and 500,000m redrawn Polish eagle (from set January 1924+)

5.32 2m, 6m and 50m new constitution (from set 2 May 1921). The 6m has the additional date 3/VI 1794 that almost certainly refers to the time Tadeusz Kosciuszko announced the granting of civil liberties to all during his ill-fated uprising against Imperial Russia.

5.33 5,000m Nicolaus Copernicus and 3,000m Stanislaus Konarski (from set June 1923+)

5.34 50g Polish eagle, wreath and fasces (from new currency set 1 May 1924) and smaller reprint with NA SKARB and 50 GR in the design (from set 1 January 1925)

5.35 1g Holy Gate, Vilnius, 3g King Sigismund III Vasa's Column, 20g Galleon, and 30g King John III Sobieski's statue (from set 1925+)

5.36 President Ignacy Moscicki (May 1928)   *5.37 Jozef Pilsudski (May 1928)*

arguments propounded the importance of citizenship training and character building, including notions of duty and service, and his political writings advocated government by constitution and the supremacy of a majority vote. The set was issued at the time the new Commission on Public Education was instituted.

In 1924 a drastic reform of the currency took place and from 1 May 1924 all stamps used the groschen and zloty. A hundred groschen equaled 1 zloty, and at the changeover 1 zloty equalled 1,800,000 markis. In an unusual step on 1 January 1925 a set of eleven Polish eagle postage stamps were offered for sale overprinted with 50 groschen premiums and the blatant inscription *NA SKARB* (FOR THE TREASURY).(5.34) Across the largely rural country income from taxation was relatively low, and any income from collectors was welcome. Not surprisingly, perhaps, throughout the rest of the 1920s a flurry of commemorative stamps appeared with income as much as the encouragement of national pride in mind.

A lengthy set gradually issued between 1925 and 1927 epitomized the twin aims. Two images highlighted the Holy Gate in recently acquired Vilna (1g) and the town hall in the ex-German city of Poznan (5g). Three others paid tribute to Poland's major cities and illustrious past. They featured Warsaw's King Sigismund III Vasa's Column (3g, 10g), Krakow's Wawel Castle, the seat of many Kings of Poland and a popular symbol of Polish statehood (15g, 40g), and Lwow's King John III Sobieski's statue (2g, 30g). The final stamp pictured a galleon in full sail, symbolizing the revitalized state and its renewed access to the sea.(5.35)

In October 1924 Stanilaus Wojciechowski, President from December 1922 to May 1926, featured on a stamp, and so did his successor Ignacy Moscicki in May 1927 and May 1928 who held the presidency until the German occupation in September 1939.(5.36)

Ignacy Moscicki combined a high profile career as a research chemist with active support for Jozef Pilsudski's opposition to foreign occupation. Pilsudski had retired from active politics after the adoption of the new constitution, largely because it reduced the power of the executive and his political opponents were temporarily in the ascendancy. By 1926, however, the situation had changed and widespread dissatisfaction with the National Assembly's chronic divisions and weak government led to Pilsudski staging a successful coup. His nomination of Moscicki for President was readily accepted, but for the next decade Pilsudski held almost dictatorial powers. He rarely, and only briefly, held any political post again, but through his personal prestige and command of the armed forces his decisions were rarely, if ever, challenged. His renowned grizzled features appeared on several stamps, and as a mourning issue in 1935.(5.37)

Poland continued to be troubled by its ethnic minorities, and its neighbours continued to view it with frustration and hostility – until they took their revenge in 1939.

CHAPTER 6
Imperial Russia and the Soviet Union

THE LAST DAYS OF IMPERIAL RUSSIA

In February 1913 royalty, aristocrats and other dignitaries from across Europe and much of Asia crowded into St Petersburg, Russia's capital city, for the three hundredth anniversary of the Romanov dynasty. Enveloped in all the ceremonial trappings of power, Tsar Nicholas II, Tsarina Alexandra, their son Alexei and daughters Anastasia, Maria, Olga and Tatiana attended a service of thanksgiving and then several days of dazzling receptions before a tour following the route taken by the first Romanov, Michael, after his election as tsar.

Everything about the tercentenary sought to reinforce loyalty to Nicholas as the embodiment of the God-given autocrat dedicated to the well-being of his people. Portraits of all the Romanov rulers lined the streets, images of the Romanov double-headed eagle were everywhere, and the Eastern Orthodox Church's elaborate ceremonies repeatedly hallowed the role of the Tsar. A series of stamps marked the anniversary with images of the Kremlin, the great Winter Palace, and the Moscow birthplace of Michael, together with portraits of past Romanov tsars thought worthy of attention.(6.1) Peter the Great (reigned 1682-1725) appeared on two values, as did Nicholas II. The unpopular Peter III, who was quickly murdered in 1762 to make way for his wife, Catherine the Great, was one of those omitted. These stamps were the first to portray the Romanovs, and it was said that some postal officials were too awestruck to sully their images with postmarks.

The tercentenary was in fact the exotic swansong of the dynasty. There was plentiful evidence that Romanov rule was unpopular and unfit for the effective understanding, governance and development of a vast empire, many of whose regions – and notably Russian Poland, the Ukraine and Baltic provinces – deeply resented Russian overlordship. And various sections of society across the Empire, including the Russian heartlands, believed with considerable justification that Nicholas was a diehard conservative autocrat who was convinced that political concessions were akin to denying his Divine birthright. If ever he was inclined to waver, his wife Alexandra, to whom he was devoted, restored his faith in absolutism. A Hesse princess by birth, Russians disliked her cold manner, were convinced she despised Russian culture, and believed she encouraged pro-German policies.

One earlier set of stamps in 1904 was inadvertently associated with a major Russian disaster that had humiliated the nation and weakened Nicholas's prestige. It was the first Russian pictorial issue; prior to this Russia had contented itself with designs centred on the Romanov eagle. When Japan and Russia clashed over territorial and commercial rights in China, Nicholas was pleased to go to war, sensing an easy triumph. However under widespread international scrutiny Russian forces were pushed back into Port Arthur where they were obliged to surrender in January 1905 and after sailing halfway round the world the Russian Baltic Fleet was all but annihilated in the Strait of Tsushima between Korea and south Japan in May. In December 1904, just before these disasters occurred, a set of stamps was issued and sold at 3k above face value in support of war orphans.(6.2) They evoked

6.2 3k Admiral Kornilov Monument, 5k Pozharsky and Minin Monument, and 10k Kremlin (from set December 1904)

6.1 1k Peter the Great, 7k Nicholas II, 14k Catherine the Great, and 3r Michael's birthplace, Moscow (from set 2 January 1913)

6.3 35k Romanov Arms from 1883 design reprinted 1909

6.4 50k Romanov Arms from 1889 design reprinted 1909

6.5 (E) 5k and 10k Romanov Arms with new designs c1912

memories of past Russian heroes, and no doubt sought to raise hopes of new ones, while in reality they were to exacerbate the sense of national decline. One featured the monument to Vice Admiral Vladimir Kornilov (3k) who achieved fame for capturing a large Turkish warship in the Crimean War and died defending Sevastopol. The 5k featured the huge memorial in Moscow to two seventeenth century heroes to whom Michael, the first Romanov tsar, owed his throne in 1613. During a period of chaos Dmitry Pozharsky led a volunteer force from Nizhny Novgorod to force the Polish army occupying Moscow to surrender. Winning several more battles, Michael called him 'the Saviour of the Motherland'. Alongside him was Kuzma Minin, a merchant who was instrumental in creating the volunteer force and became an equally celebrated commander. A third stamp pictured Tsar Peter the Great whose demonic energy, and ruthlessness, saw St Petersburg created out of marshland, and Russia modernized, equipped with a navy, and expanded into an Empire after the defeat of Sweden and Persia. The contrast with Nicholas II could not have been greater. The 10k featured the Kremlin, the scene of Pozharsky's triumph.

From 1902 a variety of stamps featured the Romanov Arms – a double-headed Romanov eagle clutching a scepter and orb. Various values had different decorative surrounds, some new and some dating back to the 1880s, and several different size perforation machines were used.(6.3/6.4/6.5) As we shall see, the Romanov Arms stamps would long outlast the Imperial family

During the early twentieth century two seemingly opposing trends occurred. Russian industrial output expanded dramatically, primarily through French investment and loans, and not far from the gilded palaces of the very wealthy the ghettoes of an ever-expanding urban working class spread inexorably in extent. The economy grew but so did expectations and mounting dissatisfaction with the disparities in wealth, the absence of popular representation in government, and press censorship. Strikes, riots and assassinations were perceived as the only means of protest in a nation whose autocracy and wafer thin glittering aristocratic veneer barely concealed the grinding poverty and desperation beneath. In 1905 thousands of workers seeking to present a petition to the tsar whom they believed would listen sympathetically were fired upon as they approached the Winter Palace in St Petersburg and then charged by Cossacks with drawn swords. A hundred died.

Shocked by the workers' actions rather than the repression, Nicholas allowed a State Duma, an advisory council composed of regional representatives, to meet. Its optimistic expectations of reform were totally dashed by the tsar's fundamental dislike of any democratic processes. He ensured the Duma remained virtually powerless and bitterly frustrated in its efforts to promote political and social reform. In the end Nicholas only succeeded in accentuating extremism.

WAR AND REVOLUTION

In July 1914 Nicholas faced a dilemma. He did not desire a general war but did not wish to desert Serbia. Despite advice to the contrary, he ordered mobilization, perhaps thinking this would kick start talks. Instead Germany interpreted the order as provocative and declared war when Russia refused to demobilize. With vast numbers of men but few reserves of equipment and munitions two Russian armies advanced into East Prussia. Although initially surprised, the Germans counter-attacked and in quick succession halted and threw back the Russians in the Battles of Tannenberg in August 1914 and the Masurian Lakes in September. Russian losses totaled 300,000 men killed, wounded or captured.

On 26 November the sole wartime charity set was issued. It incorporated an eclectic mix of images, but all of them purveyed messages of hope in perilous times.(6.6 overleaf) One was Ilya Muromets, a legendary knight-errant who saved Kiev for Prince Vladimir, defended Chernihiv from invaders and killed a dangerous forest monster. Another was St George whose exploit slaying a dragon was recorded on an eleventh century icon from Georgia. A third stamp was an allegory of Mother Russia gathering up her children. The fourth showed a smiling Don Cossack shaking a girl's hand in welcome or

6.6 1k Ilya Muromets, 3k Cossack and girl and 7k Mother Russia (from set 26 November 1914) and 10k St George (from 1915 reprint). The 1914 set had coloured paper, the 1915 set white.

6.7 10k Nicholas II and Cyrillic inscription on reverse 'Having circulation on a par   *with silver money' (from set October 1916)*

6.8 2k Alexander II overprinted '2' and reverse of 3k Alexander III stamp   *with inscription 'Having circulation on a par with copper money' (from set March 1917+)*

farewell. The Cossacks had traditionally supported the dynasty against its internal and external enemies in return for generous grants of land and acceptance of their tribal organization, and they continued to so – at least in the early stages of the war. Each stamp had a 1k premium, and the set was reissued in different colours in 1915. Around the same time the German sounding St Petersburg became the Russian sounding Petrograd.

The Russians had greater success against the Austro-Hungarian armies in Galicia, but in attempting to stop the combined enemy armies advancing through Russian Poland and into Belorussia and Lithuania in the spring and summer of 1915 another two million men were killed, wounded or captured. Many officers and troops loyal to the Romanovs had been lost, and the country was incapable of replacing the vast quantities of equipment captured, destroyed or abandoned. In September 1915 Nicholas made a fatal mistake when he took personal command of the armed forces and left Alexandra as regent. He was blamed for the war, and she for all domestic chaos.

During 1916 Russia edged ever closer to collapse with mounting riots and desertions, food prices soaring and the railways in chaos. Currency was in short supply and three 1913 stamps portraying Tsars Alexander I, Nicholas I and Nicholas II were reissued in slightly different shades on thin card to be used as currency as much as postage stamps. The message on the reverse, below the Romanov eagle, stated 'Having circulation on a par with silver money'.(6.7) In 1916 and 1917 those picturing Peter the Great, Alexander II and Alexander III were also reissued on card with the inscription 'Having circulation on a par with copper money'.(6.8) Few could have failed to notice the difference in Imperial affairs since 1913.

Calls for Nicholas to abdicate came from all classes including aristocrats, the Duma and senior generals. On 15 March 1917 the Duma unilaterally created a Provisional Government in the face of a widespread soldiers' revolt in St Petersburg. Fearing for his family, with civil war and a German onslaught threatening, and isolated and powerless at Psov, Nicholas abdicated. A power struggle quickly evolved in which the Soviets – the soldiers' and workers' councils that had sprung up – vied with the far more moderate Provisional Government under, first, Prince Georgy Lvov, and then the lawyer, Alexander Kerensky. For a time an uneasy partnership evolved with the influential Petrograd Soviet pressurizing Lvov and Kerensky for greater political and welfare reforms rather than attempting, as yet, to seize power.

Kerensky was a committed Socialist but chose to continue the interminable war, and the misery this brought along with the growing shortages of food, and indeed the expectations of better times now the Romanovs had gone, led many soldiers and civilians to rally to extremist groups. It probably did not help Kerensky that the plethora of stamps issued from 1912 displaying the Romanov Arms continued to be used. These were reissued imperforate throughout 1917 and 1918 and without the crucial publicity value of any overprint signifying the change of regime and ideals.(6.9)

6.9 Imperforate 20k and 5r Romanov Arms (from new series 1917+)

6.10 5k Romanov eagle overprinted PY.b (1920)

6.12 35k cutting the fetters (pair November 1918)

6.11 15k fiscal and 1k and 5k postal savings bank stamps used for ordinary postage dated 21.8.1918

There were a plethora of stamp issues across Russia during the long civil war, but most of them came from White Russian sources. The hard-pressed Bolshevik government continued to use Romanov Arms stamps, and as inflation mounted in 1920 the kopek value stamps were authorized for sale, without official overprints, up to one hundred times the face value. Some post offices, however, hand stamped them 'PY.b' or 'P' as abbreviations for roubles.(6.10) Alongside these, from January 1918 1k, 5k and 10k Postal Savings Bank stamps were hurried into use as postage stamps.(6.11) In November 1918 the regime at last managed to issue limited stocks of newly designed 35k and 70k stamps with the revolutionary image of a sword cutting through chains.(6.12)

The first long Russian SFSR set of stamps had to wait until August 1921. With inflation rapidly growing, values from 1r to 40r appeared on 10 August and those from 100r to 1,000r just two weeks later. A new modernist style had been adopted with designs aimed to promote the dynamism and determination of the new regime. In common with many early Soviet stamps they were sold imperforate. One pictured a bare-chested worker slaying a dragon from a typically triumphalist work by an early Soviet artist, Mikhail Antonov. Others centred on the new hammer and sickle emblems of the regime, or featured symbols of agriculture, industry, science and the arts.(6.13) The clear message was the state embraced everything, and everything served the state. Perhaps, though, not all the symbols and messages were equal. Five values highlighted

As 1917 wore on Bolshevik influences in the Petrograd and Moscow Soviets grew as casualties and mutinies mounted. In July Lenin and the Bolsheviks failed to take advantage of a major protest against Kerensky's government, but amidst the continuing chaos they staged a successful coup in October. Civil war immediately broke out with a variety of liberal, moderate socialist and monarchist forces challenging the Bolsheviks' new Socialist Federal Soviet Republic (SFSR) and their hurriedly recruited 'Red Army'. The war would last four years, and in places much longer, and cost tens of millions of lives in battles and massacres, and from famine and disease. Although the Red Army's opponents were collectively known as 'White Russians' they comprised diverse and sometimes mutually hostile entities – a major factor in their eventual defeat. And adding to the chaos, the war against Germany continued alongside the civil war until Lenin brought peace through the Treaty of Brest Litovsk in March 1918.

6.13 2r agriculture, 20r hammer and sickle, and 40r Triumph of Revolution (from set 10 August 1921) and 250r science and arts and 1,000r industry (from series 25 August 1921)

6.14 100r Fourth Anniversary of the October Revolution (from set 5 November 1921)

6.17 250r Science and Art overprinted 7,500r (from set March 1922)

6.15 2,250r Volga relief work (from set 31 December 1921)

6.16 35k cutting the fetters overprinted 250r and also a further 250r famine relief surcharge (from set February 1922). The Cyrillic inscription reads 'famine relief.'

6.18 2T (2,000r) Obligatory Payment Famine Relief (from set 19 April 1922)

6.19 3k Romanov eagle stamp overprinted Philately for the Children 19-8-22 (from set 19 August 1922) (E), and Famine Relief Fund goods train and freighter 'Lenin' (from set 18 November 1922)

agriculture, three industry, but art and science only one.

On 5 November 1921, with the Red Army finally in sight of winning the civil war, a set of three stamps featuring a star, the dates 1917 and 1921, and the regime's initials PCCP within a decorated oval frame marked the fourth anniversary of the October 1917 revolution.(6.14) In a sign of the devastation caused by the war and drought, the following month two striking designs were used for a set of four high value 2,250 rouble stamps in aid of Volga famine relief. Two hundred roubles from each stamp were earmarked for the relief. One featured life along the River Volga, the other aid reaching a victim.(6.15) In February 1922 the 'cutting the fetters' stamps from 1918 were reissued overprinted with 100 and 250 roubles postage values and 100 and 250 roubles famine relief surcharges.(6.16)

Hyperinflation as well as social, political and economic chaos was blighting the country. In March 1922 the 250 rouble science and art stamp was hurriedly reissued on a variety of papers overprinted 7,500 and 100,000 roubles.(6.17) In April four large stamps featuring simple drawings of rural workers were introduced for obligatory extra payments in support of famine relief on the postage of registered letters, money orders and parcels.(6.18)

In August stocks of the 1k to 10k 1906 Romanov Arms stamps were recalled into use. Overprinted *Philately for the Children 19-8-22*, they were offered only in Moscow and only for one day at five million times their face values with 80% of the money earmarked for children's charities. With millions of people starving, that November a specially printed set of four stamps featuring a train, aeroplane, freighter and lorry – optimistically transporting food – were issued. They were printed without values as inflation was rising and prices constantly changing(6.19)

However all new Bolshevik issues remained in short supply, and initially new sets targeted Petrograd, Moscow and Kharkov. And the desperate shortages of materials meant that dies and stocks of Romanov Arms stamps continued in use despite their despised images

THE WHITE RUSSIANS

As civil war erupted across Russia various White Russian leaders, usually ex- Imperial Russian senior officers, sprang into prominence. A large force led by Pavel Bermondt-Avolov, an avowed monarchist, joined with German Freikorps units to keep the Red Army at bay in the newly independent areas of Lithuania and Latvia. Very much the stooge of the Germans who sought control of these emerging Baltic states, Bermondt-Avalov's 'Western Russian Army' captured most of Courland, Zemgale, Samogitia and Riga. In Autumn 1919 he issued sets of Latvian stamps overprinted with an encircled Russian Orthodox cross with the traditional slanted foot crosspiece pointing up to heaven and down to hell.(6.20) In November a variety of Imperial Russian Arms stamps were overprinted to the point of obliteration by a framed design with rays pointing to the cross and the letters L P for *Latwija Pashparwalac* (Independent Latvia).(6.21) Bermondt-Avalov's adventure ended soon afterwards. Lithuanian and Latvian forces mounted counter-attacks, and under pressure from the Allies and Weimar Republic he and his remaining forces withdrew into Germany in December 1919.

Also in the Baltic area, White Russian forces under General Alexander Rodzianko occupied Pskov and the region around Lake Peipus in February 1919. His campaign survives in five crudely printed imperforate floral stamps inscribed *OKCA*, the initials of *Osobiy Korpus, Severnoy Armiy* (Special Corps, Northern Army).(6.22) His force later joined General Nikolai Yudenich who by August 1919 had gathered together a substantial if polygot anti-Bolshevik army ranging from avid monarchists to moderate socialists. Significantly he was in receipt of military aid from both Great Britain and the White Russian government that Admiral Alexander Kolchak had already established in Omsk.

In early October Yudenich's North-Western Army advanced towards Petrograd, taking several towns, but Bolshevik reinforcements were rushed in by rail to enable the attack to be defeated on the city's outskirts. Shrewdly the Bolsheviks acknowledged Estonian independence, something Yudenich refused to do, and Estonian forces duly disarmed and interned the army as it retreated back to the Baltic States. Philatelic evidence

6.20 Early 1919 5k Latvian Arms overprinted with Western Russian Army's encircled cross with slanted foot crosspiece (from set 13 October 1919)

6.21 1908 Romanov Arms overprinted with black border and network enclosing cross with slanted foot crosspiece and letters LP and 50k (from set 9 November 1919)

6.22 20k Northern Army inscribed OKCA (from set 20 August 1919)

6.23 1889 1r Romanov Arms overprinted Sev. Zap. Armia in Cyrillic script (from set 1 August 1919)

of his brief tenure of power survives in several varieties of Imperial Russian Arms stamps overprinted *Sev. Zap. Armia*, an abbreviation of *Severo-Zapadnaya Armia* (North-Western Army).(6.23)

In 1917 Admiral Kolchak was the distinguished commander of the Baltic Fleet, and vehemently opposed to the Bolsheviks. With British support, in November 1918 he was elected Supreme Ruler of the White Siberian Regional Government after a Cossack coup against its largely Socialist Revolutionary leadership. From Omsk Kolchack subjected vast swathes of central Russia to his virtually absolutist rule. He returned factories and estates to their previous owners, issued and upheld draconian laws, and savagely repressed all Bolshevik inspired revolts. In 1919 his White armies seemed poised to strike towards Archangel, Ufa, Kazan and Samara, but after initial successes his supply lines were overstretched, Red Army reinforcements were rushed in, and in a fatal error the increasingly dictatorial Kolchack alienated his Czechoslovak Legion, Polish and Japanese allies. The revitalised Red Army broke through the Urals and on 14 November 1919 Omsk had to be evacuated. Kolchack lost authority, resigned and was captured by the Czechs who handed him over to the Socialist Revolutionary committee running Irkutsk. Soon afterwards the Bolsheviks seized power there and executed him on 7 February 1920. His brief attempt at autocratic capitalist rule was accompanied by the use of Imperial Russian Arms stamps without any overprints except higher values as inflation took hold.(6.24)

In late 1917 the former Imperial Russian general, Lavr Kornilov became commander of the Don region's anti-Bolshevik Volunteer Army, and at his behest undertook a campaign of terror against all communities suspected of Bolshevik sympathies. However in February 1918 the Red Army seized Rostov and advanced on the Don capital of Novocherkassk. Kornilov's army then undertook a famed and perilous 'Ice March' across the steppe towards the Kuban River region abutting the Black Sea. Here he was killed during the attack on Ekaterinodar (modern Krasnodar).

General Anton Denikin, Kornilov's colleague, took over the South Russian forces and instituted a government that also preserved whatever order it could through terror tactics, especially against the Jews. Denikin's army advanced optimistically on Moscow in the summer of 1919, but the Red Army stood its ground and forced a steady retreat back to the Crimea. After a bitter dispute with General Wrangel over strategy and tactics Denikin resigned the following year. However,

6.24 1909 4k and 1917/18 1k Romanov Arms overprinted 1r and 70k by the government of Admiral Kolchak (from set 1919+)

6.25 70k and 1r St George with inscription One Russia (from Denikin set May 1919)

6.26 3k Romanov Arms overprinted 25r (from series issued 1918+) and 20k Yermak Timofeyevich (1919)

6.27 5k Romanov Arms overprinted 5r (from set 1920)

6.28 3k and 25k Romanov Arms overprinted 10,000r and 5,500r for use in the refugee camps (from series 1920)

his government had managed to design and issue its own stamps across the Don and Kuban regions. All included the central figure of St George surrounded by the inscription *Edinaya Rossiya* (One Russia).(6.25) Basically most White commanders detested all thoughts of separatism and ethnic autonomy.

Despite this conviction, political expediency had led Denikin to recognise the internal autonomy of a Kuban Cossack Republic and a Don Cossack Republic that had been set up in October 1917 and January 1918 respectively. Both used Romanov Arms stamps with inflationary overprints. However in 1919 the Don region also used a 20k currency stamp for postage featuring Yermak Timofeyevich, a celebrated leader of the Cossacks in their campaigns against the Tartars of Siberia until his death, in an ambush, in 1585.(6.26) Ironically his campaigns were at the behest of Russia's Tsar Ivan the Terrible. Inscriptions on the reverse of the stamps proclaimed the Rostov-on-Don branch of the State Bank had issued them.

General Pyotr Wrangel had been an aggressive commander of the anti-Bolshevik Volunteer Army based at Ekaterinodar. He enjoyed a series of successful engagements, and in April 1920 he became commander-in-chief of the White forces in and around the Crimea where he established the Government of South Russia and secured agreements with the short lived independent republics of Ukraine and Georgia. Wrangel authorized Romanov Arms stamps to be used overprinted *South Russia* and much higher inflationary values. However by the summer of 1920 the Red Army was overwhelmingly strong and in November he had to evacuate the Crimea. Large numbers of civilian evacuees were placed in Turkish, Serbian and Greek refugee camps where Romanov Arms stamps and some of General Denikin's issue were available for use overprinted with heavy surcharges from 1,000 to 20,000 roubles in tune with inflation.(6.27/6.28) Many were subsequently printed

6.29 15k Romanov Arms overprinted DBP and 7k (from set September 1920+)

6.30 7k and 20k Far Eastern Republic (from Chita set December 1921)

6.31 2k Romanov Arms overprinted 35, and 1k overprinted 70 by the Far Eastern Republic and further overprinted Priamur Rural Area (from series 10 October 1922+)

in Paris to sell direct to collectors.

In April 1920 extensive parts of eastern Siberia fell under the control of the Far Eastern Republic based in Chitra. This was a coalition of Social Democrats, Social Revolutionaries and Communists tolerated by Lenin, who had more pressing problems to deal with, as a temporary buffer state against the opportunist Japanese who had occupied parts of the Siberian coast earlier in the civil war. Its first stamps were ordinary Romanov Arms ones together with some inherited from the Kolchak regime overprinted with higher values. To avoid the fraudulent use of imported Imperial Russian stamps, some months later the regime ordered all stocks to be overprinted in a flowing script with *DBP*, the initials of *Dalne-Vostochnaya Respublika* (Far Eastern Republic).(6.29) Only these could be franked. A currency based on 1 gold rouble being equal to 1 Japanese yen was used. In December 1921 the Far Eastern Republic printed numerous crudely designed values centred on an anchor crossed with a scythe encircled by ears of corn and a star.(6.30)

The unstable Far Eastern coalition split asunder in March 1921 when White Russians led by Spiridon and Nikolai Merkulov backed by the Japanese took control of the Priamur and Maritime Provinces. Decidedly anti-Bolshevist, they established the Provisional Government of the Priamur and lasted long enough to reissue the four recent Arms stamps overprinted with an oval and the celebratory legend *26.V.1921-1922* marking the regime's first anniversary. However in June 1922 the Japanese caused panic by announcing their imminent withdrawal from Russian soil. The regional assembly (zemsky sobor) gratefully confirmed the White Russian General Mikhail Diterikhs as both military commander and civil governor of a newly created Priamur Rural Area Government. Clearly distancing himself from the Far Eastern Republic he ordered all stamps to be overprinted *Priamurskii Zemskii Krai* (Priamur Rural Area).(6.31)

A former colleague of Admiral Kolchak, Diterikhs had regularly liaised between the White forces in Siberia, and now began to court support throughout the region for the restoration of a Romanov monarchy. The zemsky sobor formally agreed on 8 August 1922, but when the Japanese left in October Priamur quickly fell to the Bolshevik backed rump of the Far Eastern Republic, and in November Diterikhs and his remaining forces fled from Vladivostock in Japanese ships. The chaotic Far Eastern Republic was soon absorbed into the Russian Socialist Federal Soviet Republic (RSFSR).

THE UKRAINE

The Ukraine suffered particularly badly during the fighting on the Eastern Front during the 1914-18 war, and several attempts to create an independent republic afterwards were blighted not only by the constant conflict between White and Red armies that ravaged the region until late 1921 but also by the territorial ambitions and aggression of Poland and Czechoslovakia.

A Socialist *Tsentraina Rada* (National Council) established in Kiev proclaimed independence on 22 January 1918 and signed a separate peace with Germany and Austria on 9 February, but was challenged from its outset by a rival Bolshevik Soviet Republic in Kharkov. In April Pavlo Skoropadsky, an ex-Imperial Russian General, ousted the *Rada* with German support and established a conservative Ukrainian State that lasted until the Germans left in November. In July 1918 the fragile state managed to issue one eclectic set of stamps mixing the Ukranian heritage with hopes for its future through images of the ancient trident from the Arms of the national hero Vladimir the Great, Ceres the goddess of agriculture, a peasant, and a victory wreath.(6.32) In

6.32 10sh trident, 20sh peasant and 30sh Ceres (from set July 1918)

EUROPEAN STAMP ISSUES AND THE FIRST WORLD WAR

6.33 Trident overprints from Odessa on the Wrangel Russian refugees inflation overprints on 1909-17 Romanov eagle stamps (from series October 1918+)

6.35 20hr Petliura Directorate (January 1919)

6.34 40h Austrian Feldpost overprinted Poshta Ukr. N. Rep and 40 (Western Ukraine National Republic Post 40 shahiv) (from set March 1919) and 15h Emperor Charles overprinted with trident and letters З Y H P (Western Ukraine People's Republic) (from set May 1919)

6.36 10k+10k Spectre of famine, 20k+20k Taras Shevchenko, 90k+30k Death and peasant, and 150k+50k Ukraine giving bread (set June 1923)

April the set was printed on card with a note on the reverse proclaiming it could be used as paper money.

Various places such as Odessa, Kiev, Kharkov, Kherson, Poltava and Yekaterinoslav supplemented these with huge numbers of Romanov Arms stamps locally overprinted with various forms of the Ukrainian trident to avoid the fraudulent use of unofficially imported stocks.(6.33) Surplus stocks had flooded in from printers in Constantinople and Paris commissioned originally by General Wrangel for use in the refugee camps.

The German withdrawal opened the way to further warfare between rival factions. General Skoropadsky left with Germans, and the Ukrainian nationalist Symon Petliura became leader of the Directorate of Ukraine that for most of 1919 fought both White Russians and Bolsheviks in a desperate attempt to maintain its independency. The ambitious and aggressive Poles seized Eastern Galicia, and ended its short period of internal autonomy as the Western Ukraine National Republic. Its brief existence centred upon Lviv, Przemysi and Stanislaviv had lasted from early November 1918 to July 1919, but its aspirations remain recorded in the numerous overprinted Austrian stamps it introduced.(6.34) In the event, very few were actually used for postage.

However as the Bolsheviks gained ground Symon Petliura accepted the lost of Galicia, and made peace with the Poles. They joined forces against the Red Army which was not only threatening the Ukraine but also Warsaw. Poland defeated the USSR, but the Ukraine did not and in November 1920 Petliura and many of his men sought refuge in Poland. His philatelic legacies are a single ornate stamp issued in January 1919 together with the 1918 Skoropadsky pictorial set overprinted with Polish values for army use.(6.35)

The Bolshevik Soviet Republics across the Ukraine won the day. They had united in March 1919, allied with the Russian SFSR in December 1920, and became part of the USSR two years later. A brief period of internal autonomy remained, and in 1923 the Ukrainian Soviet Republic issued a set of surcharged stamps to help relieve the widespread famine.(6.36) Strikingly designed, one pictured skeletal Death visiting a peasant, another the cloaked spectre of Famine, the third the State distributing bread, and the fourth the renowned liberal and anti-Romanov Ukrainian artist and poet Taras Shevchenko (1814-61) who had celebrated the region's countryside, its people and their cultural and political aspirations.

THE USSR

As the civil war faded in intensity in 1922, the victorious Russian Federal Soviet Government remained beset by daunting problems. Chief among them were the consolidation of its authority, the promotion of Marxism, the crushing of dissent, the restoration of shattered industries and, most crucial of all, the reinvigoration of agricultural production. Savage warfare, extensive destruction, and social dislocation along with natural disasters had led to widespread famine. The Bolsheviks had broken up the great landed estates of the aristocracy and although peasant holdings had soared in number the Bolsheviks had resorted to seizing any surpluses to feed the Red Army and supply the industrial towns. In 1921 the New Economic Policy (NEP) evolved to replace the unpopularity of the war emergency restrictions, and peasants were allowed to operate on a freer market. The state, though, kept strict control of all industry and banking, and in both agriculture and manufacturing it sought to repress what it considered undue profiteering. Prices were controlled and any trusts or syndicates broken up. Many people preferred bartering, especially during soaring inflation.

In these desperate times Romanov Arms stamps, some designed in the 1880s, continued in use, and by April 1922 the kopek values were sold at one million times face value and the rouble values at ten thousand times. Finally in December 1922 they were issued heavily overprinted with the proletarian symbols of a star enclosing a hammer and sickle.(6.37) In addition Postal Savings Bank stamps sold at well above their stated values continued to serve as postage stamps.

In 1922 inflation was at its worse and four stamps issued in March and April promoting economic growth had values of 5,000, 7,500, 10,000 and 22,500 roubles. They shared two designs in the grand heroic style soon to be a feature of most Soviet issues. One was a revalued reprint of the 1921 Agriculture and Industry stamp and

6.37   50k Romanov Arms overprinted with Soviet symbols and 30r value (from series December 1922+)

6.38   7,500r Agriculture & Industry, and 22,500r Industry (from set March 1922+)

6.39   5r Fifth Anniversary of the October Revolution (from set 7 November 1922)

6.40   10r worker and 100r soldier (from imperforate and perforated sets December 1922+)

the other featured a fist clutching a hammer against a background of smoking factory chimneys. (6.38) The ribbon contained the early Communist cry *Workers of the World Unite* – an outcome Lenin and Trotsky optimistically thought might occur across depressed post war Europe.

In the same month, March 1922, the People's Commissariat of Finance ordered a new rouble redeemable in gold. By March 1924 this had saved the situation but only after a period of utter chaos and widespread suffering while the old so-called 'goods rouble' was still paid as wages. Each gold rouble was never equated with less than 10,000 'goods roubles', and often several thousands more.

The first stamps with gold rouble values were a set of five on 7 November 1922 marking the fifth anniversary of the October revolution. Russia had changed from the Julian to the Gregorian Calendar on 1/14 February 1918. As a result the Revolution of 7 November 1917 (Gregorian Calendar) remains known as the October Revolution as it began on 25 October in the Julian Calendar. In a strange semblance of an ancient Egyptian stone mason, each value featured a loin-clothed worker finishing chiseling *PCCP 1917=1922* on a stone tablet.(6.39)

In late December 1922 the Russian SFSR, the Transcaucasian SFSR, the Ukrainian SSR and the Byelorussian SSR agreed to form the Union of Soviet Socialist Republics (USSR). In October 1924 the Uzbek SSR and Turkmen SSR, and in 1929 the Tajik SSR, were admitted.

1922 witnessed the introduction of long lasting philatelic images concentrating upon those sections of society through whose efforts the Communist regime would prosper – the workers and soldiers. The 50r, 70r and 100r stamps pictured a floral frame enclosing a soldier in the familiar Russian peaked cap looking reverentially upwards, while a single value, the 10r, featured a young male worker staring directly at the viewer.(6.40) It was said the sculptor Ivan Shadr (real name Ivan Ivanov) used working people from his home town of Shadrinsk as models.

6.41   3r worker, 4r soldier, and 5r peasant (from set May 1923)

6.42   2r worker (from set December 1923+)

6.43   1921 100r agriculture overprinted 'USSR For the victims of the flood in Leningrad 3k+10k', and 1,000r industry overprinted 'USSR For the Leningrad proletariat 23 IX 1924 20k+50k' (from set November 1924)

perforated and imperforate between 1923 and 1925. The rouble values were given more elaborate twin coloured designs that accentuated the feeling that the figures were intoxicated with Marxist ideology.(6.42)

Setbacks such as the disastrous floods in and around Leningrad in late 1924 were turned into opportunities to unite ordinary people across the still fragile nation. Early Soviet stamps promoting agriculture and industry were reissued with new values and surcharges, and the inscriptions *For the victims of the flood in Leningrad* and *For the Leningrad proletariat 23 IX 1924*.(6.43) The 'K' values refer to the gold currency stabilizing Soviet finances.

The USSR's first specially designed publicity set complementing the workers' definitive series was issued on 19 August 1923, the opening day of the All-Russian Agricultural and Handicraft Exhibition in Moscow.(6.44) The title was inscribed on each of the elaborately designed stamps, and the set featured a sower (2r) and a reaper (1r), a view of the exhibition (7r) and a Ford tractor (5r). Although the USA did not recognize the USSR until 1933, Ford managed to sell 20,000 tractors and the accompanying technical expertise to Amtorg, the USSR's intermediary purchasing company.

Lenin was the first notable figure to appear on a stamp, and did so on 28 January 1924, exactly a week after his death in office as President of the Council of People's Commissars.(6.45) There were three printings within three months, all in slightly different sizes. In 1925 Lenin's mausoleum in Moscow featured on a set, and in 1925, 1926, and 1927 slightly different pairs of stamps perpetuated his memory. No opportunity was lost to elevate the already legendary leader to cult status. In 1927 and 1929 his portrait was included amongst those of soldiers and workers in the restyled definitive sets.(6.46)

By the mid 1920s the USSR had got into its philatelic stride and the long definitive sets portraying the working classes as revolutionary heroes were accompanied by visually dramatic sets celebrating their role in past revolts. Everything, the sets implied, led to today's proletarian victory. On 20 December 1925 three stamps using works from the new generation of Socialist Realism artists marked the twentieth anniversary of the 1905 revolt with detailed images of workers marching (3r), an orator clutching a lamp post to address a crowd (7r), and a

Communist leaders continued to eschew portraits of themselves in favour of persuading the working classes they were the beneficiaries, even 'owners', of the revolution as well as its instigators and defenders. In May 1923 the same worker and soldier appeared on simplified versions of the stamp. They had no floral framework and just the date 1923 and PCCP. The pair were now were joined by a rural peasant from the third key group meriting commemoration.(6.41)

These three figures were used again in 1923 and 1924 for a set of ten definitive stamps, this time inscribed *zolotom* (in gold) and *CCCP* (USSR). They were the precursor of a lengthy set ranging from 1k to 5r printed in a variety of perforation gauges and available both

6.44   The Agricultural Exhibition set (19 August 1923)

6.45 20k mourning Lenin (from perforated set February 1924+)

6.46 14k Lenin and 50k farm girl (from set August 1929+) Female factory and farm workers were only included in 1929

Moscow barricade (14r).(6.47)

On 28 December another equally dramatic set marked the centenary of the 'Decembrist Revolt' in St Petersburg when a group of aristocrats and officers led an army revolt against Tsar Nicholas I assuming the throne after his older brother Constantine renounced his succession rights.(6.48) The rebels, some 3,000 strong, were easily crushed by artillery fire, five were executed and many others exiled to Siberia. The Decembrists had been motivated by thoughts of a more liberal regime promoting elected assemblies, peasant rights and welfare reform, and in Siberia the Decembrists became renowned for striving to practice and promote these ideals. The sets shows Decembrists at work in exile (3r), the revolt under way in Senate Square, St Petersburg (7r), and the profile of the five rebels who were executed (14r). In 1925 Senate Square was renamed Decembrist Square and the plaque shown on the 14k stamp adorned the monument erected at the execution site.

October 1927 provided the opportunity to celebrate the tenth anniversary of the final revolution with another detailed set eulogising the roles played by ordinary citizens.(6.49) One stamp acknowledged the ethnic diversity, and by implication the Bolshevik comradeship, within the USSR, and another showed the USSR stretching from the Black Sea to the straits opposite Alaska. However once again Lenin was far from forgotten. A stamp featured the Smolny Institute in Petrograd where he established his headquarters before moving to Moscow

6.47 (E) 20th anniversary of the 1905 revolt (set 20 December 1925)

6.48 Centenary of the 1825 Decembrist Revolt (set 28 December 1925)

and where, in 1927, a statue was erected to him.

By 1927, however, Joseph Stalin had firmly established his authority over the Communist Party and the USSR. The revolution had been won under Lenin but its consolidation would take place under his successor, a man Lenin deeply distrusted and thought unfit for the highest office.

6.49 7k Smolny Institute, 8k comrades in arms, 14k map, and 28r USSR ethnic groups (from set October 1927)

CHAPTER 7
The Baltic States

ESTONIA

Estonia fell under Russian control after the Treaty of Nystad in 1721 when Tsar Peter the Great defeated his great rival, King Charles XII of Sweden, for Baltic supremacy. There was little agitation among the mainly German nobility or the mainly Estonian lower orders against Russian overlordship until the mid nineteenth century when the tsars imposed repressive policies of Russification after revolts elsewhere, notably in Russian Poland. And in 1905 the abortive revolution in Russia incited vigorous calls for greater political representation and freedom of the press.

In late 1917 Russia's Provisional Government granted internal autonomy to a newly created state of Estonia. It comprised the ancient northern province of 'Danish Estonia' and also the northern half of 'Livonia', another ancient province straddling modern Estonia and Latvia. Elections to a provisional assembly, the *Maapaev*, took place, but the minority Bolshevik faction violently usurped power just two days before the October Revolution in Russia.

Although marginalized, on 24 February 1918 an anti-Bolshevik 'Salvation Committee' of the *Maapaev* in Parnu declared Estonia an independent republic. The following day German forces invaded and drove the Bolsheviks back into Russia, primarily in an attempt to force Lenin to agree peace terms. At the Treaty of Brest-Litovsk on 3 March 1918 Lenin accepted the loss of both parts of Estonia, and it fell under the authority of the German Eastern Command Army.

During the occupation influential Baltic Germans avidly petitioned the Kaiser to create a United Baltic Duchy embracing modern Estonia and Latvia that would be ruled, much like other Imperial states, by a German prince – the Duke of Mecklenburg-Schwerin was suggested - under the Kaiser. In the event, in October 1918 the last Imperial German Chancellor, Prince Max of Baden, proclaimed that Germany would abide by the wishes of Estonia and Latvia, and the following month both formally declared independence. Four rather innocuous stamps inscribed *EESTI POST* (ESTONIAN POST) marked the event. Two appeared in Russian kopeks in November 1918, and two in new Estonian pennis in January 1919.(7.1)

German troops withdrew, and the Estonian

7.1 15k (from set November 1918) and 70p (from set January 1919) marking independence

7.2 2k Romanov Arms handstamped Eesti Post(from set 7 May 1919)

7.3 5p EESTI VABARIIK (13 May 1919)

Provisional Government took up office again only to face an immediate Bolshevik invasion. However the hard-pressed Estonian army rose to the challenge and forced the Red Army to retreat during early 1919. With numerous other enemies to combat, the Russian SFSR signed the Treaty of Tartu on 2 February 1920 renouncing all territorial rights in Estonia.

From early May 1919 war torn Estonia's Provisional Government resorted to stocks of Russian Romanov Arms stamps handstamped, often crudely, *Eesti Post*.(7.2) Between 5 and 7 April the Constituent Assembly was elected, and in May the currency was formally changed from Rusian kopeks and roubles to Estonian penni and marks. On 13 May a single 5p stamp was issued featuring a soaring seagull and inscribed *EESTI VABARIIK* (THE REPUBLIC OF ESTONIA).(7.3)

A couple of days later the first stamps in a new set of nine values appeared. The penni values had either abstract designs or the soaring seagull, while the mark values featured a Viking longboat at sea.(7.4) The Viking image represented a significant throwback to the region's past as a major Viking settlement, much like the Danelaw in eastern and northern Britain. Most likely the soaring seagull and the warlike longboat were

7.4 *70p soaring seagull and 1m Viking longship (from set 15 May 1920+)*

7.5 *25p Tallinn skyline and wave (from set March 1920+)*

7.6 *35p+10p War Victims' Fund (from set June 1920), and 3½m (inc 1m premium) Red Cross Fund (pair 26 April 1922)*

7.7 *1m weaver and 5m blacksmith (from definitive set issued 1922+), and 100m map of Estonia (14 March 1923)*

7.8 *70m National Theatre (9 December 1924)*

philatelic symbols of the new state's positive intent.

The great aristocratic estates were divided up among veterans and peasants, the country became a member of the League of Nations in 1921, and sound trade relations established across western Europe and with North America. Between 1920 and 1924 a set of eight stamps was issued featuring the skyline of Tallinn, Estonia's capital and a major seaport, set significantly within a rolling wave.(7.5)

Other issues in the early 1920s, however, recalled Estonia's recent troubles. In June 1920 two surcharged stamps picturing wounded soldiers raised funds for war victims. A pair of Red Cross stamps featuring a nurse sought further funds in August 1921 and were reissued in April 1922, October 1923, and June 1926.(7.6) They were overprinted *Aita hadalist* (Help the unfortunate) in 1923, and with higher mark values in 1926.

No opportunity was lost to highlight the enterprise and vibrancy of the new country. Between 1922 and 1925 eleven definitive stamps were issued up to 20m displaying either a blacksmith or a woman weaver at work, and in 1923 and 1924 two particularly high value stamps displayed a map of Estonia (no doubt for the international market).(7.7) In 1924 a stamp featured the National Theatre and in 1927 a matching stamp featured Tartu's Vanemuine Theatre.(7.8)

Estonia was proud to publicise its developing air links. As early as March 1920 a triangular 5m stamp for prepaying the air premium featured the LVG Schneider biplane that also adorned contemporary German and Polish stamps.(7.9) The largely wooden machine had evolved from a successful German design for a wartime reconnaissance plane. The Estonian stamp was issued for a route between Tallinn and Helsinki that failed to survive.

However in 1924 and 1925 a striking set of five triangular Air stamps featured the German Sablatnig PIII and Junkers F-13 aircraft with wheels, skis and floats as used by Estonia's fledgling Aeronaut.(7.10) The PIII was a wooden aircraft carrying six passengers, and when the Treaty of Versailles severely limited German aircraft production several were built in Estonia. In contrast the advanced F-13 was the first all metal monoplane, and used by Aeronaut in the mid 1920s for carrying passengers – just four at a time – as well as transporting goods.

7.9 *5m LVG Schneider (13 March 1920)*

7.10 *10m Sablatnig PIII with skis, and 15m Junkers F-13 with floats (from set 15 July 1925)*

7.11 (E) 5m+5m Kuressaare Castle, 10m+10m Tartu Cathedral and Fortress, 12m+12m Parliament House, 20m+20m Narva Castle and 40m+40m old Tallinn (set 19 November 1927)

7.12 10m blacksmith overprinted 1918 24/II 1928 (from set 24 February 1928)

On 19 November 1927 a set of five surcharged stamps featuring key historic sights raised funds for the War of Liberation Commemoration.(7.11) The 5m+5m pictured the fourteenth century Kuressaare Castle built on Saaremaa Island by the Teutonic Knights during their crusade against the pagan post-Viking Estonians. The 10m+10m featured the ruins of Tartu Cathedral and Fortress. In the thirteenth century the region's Christian conquerors had built a bishop's castle and cathedral on the site of a pagan stronghold, but after the Protestant Reformation the buildings were abandoned. In common with Kuressaare Castle, in the nineteenth century the site had become a public park. The 20m+20m featured Narva Castle in the far north east. Built in the thirteenth century by the Danes it had opposed the Russian Ivangorod Castle on the opposite bank of the Narva River – as it did again in the 1920s. Of the remaining two stamps, the 40m+40m featured the historic skyline of Tallinn and the 12m+12m the new Parliament House opened in 1922. Perhaps with Estonia's wartime experiences and future tasks in mind, the new parliament building looked comfortingly traditional on the outside but was starkly Expressionist in the inside.

In 1928 the tenth anniversary of independence was commemorated with several blacksmith and weaver stamps issued overprinted *1918 24/II 1928* and values in the new senti and kroon currency.(7.12)

By then Estonia had just a dozen years of independence left. In the 1930s its stamps continued to highlight its culture, charities and achievements, and a new definitive set in 1936 portrayed Konstantin Pats, the elected Head of State, who had assumed dictatorial powers two years earlier. In the summer of 1940, however, the Russians returned with a vengeance.

LATVIA

Latvia travelled a more tortuous and bloodstained road to independence. Under Russian occupation since 1721, a nineteenth century national revival led to conflict with the Baltic German aristocracy as well as resentment at the policy of Russification ordered by Tsar Alexander III. In 1905 Latvians were prominent in the abortive Russian revolution although their hostility targeted the Baltic Germans as much as the Russians. In the ensuing campaign of brutal retaliation the Baltic Germans and Cossacks executed several thousand Latvians, and many more were exiled or fled.

In summer 1915 Russia implemented a scorched earth programme as the German army advanced. Thousands of Latvians trudged to Russia, leaving burning houses and farms, and empty and wrecked factories behind them. The Germans captured Jelgava, the capital of Courland, but failed to secure the key cities of Riga or Daugavpils. Thousands joined the Volunteer Latvian Rifle units and served alongside the Russian army. The Germans were held along the Daugava River until the Russian army finally disintegrated in mid 1917 and opened the way for the Germans to occupy Riga.

Under the relatively liberal rule of Kerensky's Government various centrist Latvian politicians meeting in Valka in Latvia's relatively safe far north established a Provisional National Council which the following month proclaimed itself the sole authority for all ethnic Latvian lands. At the same time, though, the Bolshevik inspired *Iskolat* government, also in Valka, denied the National Council possessed any authority. However when Lenin's fragile rule seemed to buckle under German onslaught's, on 30 January 1918 the National Council declared that Latvia comprised the four regions of Courland, Semigallia, Livonia and Latgale, and would become an independent democratic republic.

In March 1918 the Treaty of Brest-Litovsk ceded Latvian Courland and southern Livonia to Germany, and here, as in Estonia, many Baltic Germans sought the creation of the United Baltic Duchy under the German Emperor. By then, though, the region had been devastated, and even greater suffering was on the way. After the Armistice the numerous Latvian political parties outside the Bolsheviks reached agreement and on 17 November the new People's Council formally proclaimed independence and created the Latvian Provisional Government.

In violent opposition the Latvian Bolsheviks proclaimed Latvia was part of the Russian SFSR, and on 1 December a Soviet army, strengthened by numerous Latvian Volunteer Riflemen, advanced from Pskov and Daugavpils. The Red Army entered Riga on 3 January 1919, and a Latvian SFSR was proclaimed under Peteris Stucka who immediately ordered land confiscations and the execution of all those considered class enemies – notably German nobles, capitalists and priests. Thousands died in the chaos and terror.

The Provisional Government's control was reduced to a region around Liepaja. It had issued its first stamps on 18 December. Printed on the back of surplus German military maps the first was a 5 kapeikas value featuring the sun enclosing ears of corn.(7.13) While enduring the Red Army's onslaught and gathering strength for a counter-offensive the same design was extended to many more values printed on a variety of papers with different perforation sizes.

In cooperation with the German Freikorps, the Provisional Government's army belatedly but successfully fought back. The Freikorps recaptured Riga in May 1919 and the event was marked by a set of three stamps featuring two women clutching each other by a skull lying amidst briars with Riga's profile in the background.(7.14) The earlier Red terror was duly matched by the Freikorps own White terror against all Bolshevik sympathisers.

The post-war ambition of Germany to reclaim Baltic territory led to disagreements and eventual military conflict between the Freikorps and the Provisional Government. After defeat by Latvia and under international pressure, on 23 June 1919 the Germans agreed to leave but many were assimilated into Colonel Avalov-Bermondt's White West Russian Army that was also striving to conquer the region, but primarily to keep

7.13 5k sun and wheat (18 December 1918) and reverse

7.14 15k Liberation of Riga (from set 9 June 1919)

7.15 10k rising sun issued in northern Latvia (3 July 1919)

7.16 1r first anniversary of independence (from set 22 January 1920+) and reverse

it Russian. The disruption this caused to communications led to the Estonian commander in Livonia hastily printing new 10k stamps for northern Latvia when supplies of normal issues failed to get through.(7.15) They incorporated a new design of a rising sun that was later reflected in the Latvian coat of arms definitive issue introduced in October 1921 and often reprinted.

On 5 October 1919 the West Russian Army seized the west bank of the Daugava River and part of Riga itself but by the end of November Latvian and Polish forces had driven it from the city (with the help of British warships) and then from the country. Despite the Red and White armies lingering presence, on various dates from 18 November 1919 a striking set commemorated the first anniversary of independence. Each stamp featured a young woman in national costume (symbolizing the state) clutching a sword and holding a large wreath encircling the legend '*1918 18 nov. 1919*. Shortages of paper, and probably wry propaganda, led the 1 rublis value being printed on banknotes being prepared, but never finished, by the embryonic Riga Soviet.(7.16)

EUROPEAN STAMP ISSUES AND THE FIRST WORLD WAR

7.17 *10k liberation of Courland (from set 16 December 1919+)*

7.18 *50k liberation of Latgale 50k (from set 24 March 1920) and reverse*

7.19 *1r inscribed SATVERSMES SAPULCES PEEMINAI (Commemorating the Constituent Assembly) (from set 30 April 1920+)*

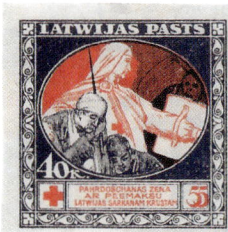 

7.20 *40k+15k Red Cross Fund (from set 18 March 1920+), and reverse showing its Riga Soviet banknote origins. Stamp inscription reads 'Price includes a charge for the Latvian Red Cross 55k'*

7.21 *5r Latvian Coat of Arms definitive (from set 6 October 1921+)*

7.22 *10l Great Seal of Latvia (from second printing 5 December 1923+)*

Below: 7.23 *Illustrated Red Cross air mail cover (flown from Riga to Vienna) with set of Latvian Arms overprinted with the War Invalids Fund logo and inscription.*

Other equally striking issues marked the final campaign to secure independence. In December 1919 a colourful set featuring a dragon slayer commemorated the liberation of Courland.(7.17)

Bolshevik rule was driven back to Latgale in the east where it survived for several months before final dissolution after the Battle of Daugavpils in January 1920. Polish forces had joined with Latvian ones by this stage. The Poles were engaged in a life or death war with the Russian SFSR and they saw the Latvian front as part of their own struggle for survival. On 24 March 1920 the liberation of Latgale merited a pair of stamps featuring a mother welcoming a child home. It was printed on the back of banknotes over-optimistically prepared by the White West Russian Army.(7.18)

A few days later another celebratory set, this time with a young woman in national costume at the helm of a boat looking steadfastly ahead, marked the first meeting of the Constituent Assembly.(7.19)

The future might look more hopeful, but the casualties of war were ever-present   Starting in March 1920 four surcharged stamps picturing a woman symbolizing Latvia protecting a wounded soldier with a shield were issued in support of the Red Cross. Three printings were undertaken, in March on Bolshevik blue banknotes, in May on green White Western Army ones, and in August on brown, green and red Riga Soviet ones.(7.20) They were issued again through the Red Cross in May 1921.

On 11 August 1920 Soviet Russia signed a peace treaty with Latvia and relinquished all claims to its four provinces. Latvia became a member of the League of Nations in September 1922. At home the great estates were broken up and granted to peasant farmers who in due course were to exert considerable political power. Briefly the country's future looked assured.

In 1921 the Latvian coat of arms with the rising sun of freedom above the red lion of Courland and silver griffin of Livonia adorned a new definitive set, and was repeated in a set in 1923 in the new currency of santinu and lats.(7.21) The elaborate Great Seal of Latvia with its oak leaves and extra lion and griffin supporters made a rare public appearance on a set in 1923.(7.22) In that year, too, the lingering legacy of the brutal war of independence was remembered when the 1s, 2s and 4s Arms stamps were offered overprinted with a Maltese Cross, a 10s surcharge and the legend *KARA INVALIDIEM* (FOR THE WAR INVALIDS). (7.23)

Stamp issues in the later 1920s avidly promoted Latvia's history, culture, recent achievements, and unity. Sets embraced Liepeja's tercentenary in 1925, and in 1928 marked the tenth anniversary of independence and supported the fund for a Liberty Memorial.(7.24/7.25)

In 1932 two surcharged pictorial sets raised funds for the Army Reserve, a reminder of the re-emerging tensions across Europe. The first set pictured medieval Latvian warfare and heroes, but the second featured modern soldiers in action (6s-25s and 7s-35s), receiving first aid (10s-45s), and around a field kitchen (12s-55s), and finally the determined features of General Janis Balodis (15s-75s), a distinguished officer in the wars of independence, and Minister of War from 1931 to 1940.(7.26). However, Latvia had just eight more years of independence before the Red Army returned in overwhelming force.

7.24 *Liepeja Tercentenary 6s-12s Liepeja Harbour and lighthouse (from set 29 May 1925)*

7.25 *Liberty Memorial Fund 6s-16s Venta, 10s-20s Allegory of Latvia' and 1l-1l 10 soldiers in trenches at Riga Bridge (from set 18 November 1928)*

7.26 *Militia Maintenance Fund (second set 12 May 1932)*

EUROPEAN STAMP ISSUES AND THE FIRST WORLD WAR

LITHUANIA

With Poland as well as Bolshevik Russia and Germany making claims on Lithuanian territory from 1918 onwards, its struggle for independence was the most perilous of the Baltic States. The claims went back to the vast Polish-Lithuanian Commonwealth and to the creation of Congress Poland in 1815. During the nineteenth century the Poles and Lithuanians cooperated in abortive revolts against Russia, and paid the penalty of Russian repression.

However two ultimately opposing movements emerged as separate Lithuanian and Polish campaigns for independence gathered momentum. In 1915 Germany occupied Lithuania, with the key city of Vilnius falling on 19 September. The German Eastern Command took control, and Lithuania's Germans joined the agitation for an internally autonomous state within the German Empire.

7.27 20s from the second printing in Kaunus (from set 18 February 1919)

7.28 30s, 50s and 1a Vytis (from fourth issue May 1919+)

Late in 1917 a widely representative Lithuanian Conference met in Vilnius with the agreement of the German occupation administration that assumed it would vote for annexation. Instead it declared autonomy, although as a German protectorate. On 16 February 1918, though, it went further and proclaimed complete independence as a democratic republic. For the rest of the war it played a delaying game with Germany by endlessly discussing the recreation of a Kingdom of Lithuania under the German Duke of Urach who was a scion of the House of Wurttemberg rather than a Prussian Hohenzollern.

These convoluted debates ended at the November Armistice. The Germans withdrew, Lithuania formed its first government, and then, in December, Soviet forces arrived and the Lithuanian-Russian War began. The government in Vilnius just had time to issue its first stamps on 27 and 31 December – merely a rectangle of circles enclosing the statik values and the logo *LIETEVOS PASTA* (LITHUANIAN POST).

However when German troops evacuated Vilnius on 1 January 1919 they handed it over to local Polish units, forcing the beleaguered Lithuanian government to retreat west to Kaunas. Between 28 January and 3 March further primitive stamps, although slightly differently designed, were issued from Kaunas to maintain some continuity and a semblance of authority.(7.27)

By mid-January, though, the Red Army had occupied most of Lithuania, and Vilnius became the capital of the Lithuanian Soviet Republic. Both Lithuania and Poland were now fighting the Soviet Union but not as allies. The Poles recaptured Vilnius in April 1919, and tried unsuccessfully to overthrow the beleaguered republican Lithuanian government. It survived, though, and then rallied sufficiently to drive Soviet forces from the country by August 1919, and by December to force back the

7.29 15s Lithuania receiving independence, 60s Lithuania arises, 1a Lithuania breaking the chains, and 5a Vytis over Vilnius (from set 15 February 1920) The stamps are dated 1918-II-16.

7.30 15s Vytis, 20s Vytautus, 80s Gediminas and 1a oak and altar (from set 25 August 1920)

White West Russian Army that had invaded from the north.

During this perilous period there were four Lithuanian stamp issues using a variety of available papers and perforators and three carefully composed and highly symbolic designs. They were inscribed *LIETUVOS PASTO ZENKLAS* (LITHUANIAN POSTAL CODE). Each design centred on a portrait of the *Vytis*, the legendary Lithuanian armoured knight with a flowing saddle blanket and raised sword riding a white charger.(7.28) It had been the motif of the medieval Grand Dukes of Lithuania, and the shield displayed the double armed cross of the first Christian rulers of the Jagiellonian dynasty. The *Vytis* had become the Lithuanian national image during the nineteenth century revival, especially after the Russians banned its display. It came to represent the repulsion of occupiers and invaders, and never more crucially than in the post 1918 crisis.

On 15 February 1920, during a brief respite from war, a striking set of eleven stamps with four designs celebrated the second anniversary of the bold wartime declaration of independence.(7.29) The images were symbolic. The first showed Lithuania being granted the blessing of independence, the second Lithuania allegorically portrayed as a mother and child arising from the winter of oppression, the third the figure of Lithuania breaking free from chains, and the fourth the *Vytis* flying over the Tower of Gediminas, the symbol of the contested city of Vilnius.

In April 1920 Lithuania's Constituent Assembly was elected, and on 12 July a peace treaty was signed whereby the Russian SFSR recognized a fully independent Lithuania together with its claims to Vilnius. On 25 August a set of eleven stamps with four striking designs marked the Assembly.(7.30) Two stamps were inscribed *STEIGIAMASIS SEIMAS 1920* (CONSTITUENT ASSEMBLY 1920) with one featuring the *Vytis* and the other the ancient images of the life-bringing sacred oak tree and flaming altar. The other two portrayed greatly revered grand dukes of Lithuania at the height of its medieval power. One was Gediminas (1275-1341) whose military and diplomatic successes, largely against the Teutonic Knights and Livonian Order, led to the Grand Duchy of Lithuania stretching from the Baltic to near the Black Sea. The other was Vytautus the Great (c1350-1430) who won the key Battle of Grunwald in 1410 from which the Teutonic Knights never fully recovered, and was also elected King of Poland.

However the Polish-Soviet War was still going on, and when the Russians briefly pushed back the Poles they handed Vilnius to the Lithuanians. The situation remained dangerous, though, as Russia had not abandoned thoughts of recreating a Lithuanian Soviet Republic, and Poland coveted Vilnius. When all the League of Nations attempts at resolving ownership failed,

7.31 20s sower and 40s Kestutis (from set May 1921)

7.32 5a Junkers F-13 aircraft in flight (from set June 1921+)

7.33 40s Allegory of Flight (from set 6 November 1921)

on 24 March 1922 Poland ordered its troops to occupy the city and its hinterland under the pretext that uncontrollable mutinous units had taken the initiative. In 1923 the League of Nations Conference of Ambassadors agreed that the region was Polish, and Lithuania, utterly incensed, broke off all relations with Poland. The 1922-23 puppet Republic of Central Lithuania produced numerous stamps inscribed *SRODKOWA LITWA* (CENTRAL LITHUANIA) and these are discussed and illustrated in the chapter on Poland.

Throughout the 1920s regular issues highlighted both Lithuania's past glories and its recent re-emergence as an independent state. In May 1921 a long definitive set centred on four designs.(7.31) One featured a sower, another a reaper, the third a dramatic rendering of the *Vytis,* and the fourth Kestutis (c1297-1382), the warrior son of Gediminas. Kestutis was a pagan, like his father, whose life revolved around keeping the Christian Teutonic Knights at bay while foiling the plans of a treacherous nephew to remove him from any power-sharing roles. To modern Lithuanians his trials and tribulations must have made him an apt choice.

Several distinctive Air issues ensured publicity was given to Lithuania's fledgling air connections. Between June and October 1921 a set of seven stamps appeared, some featuring a flying posthorn, and others the highly successful German Junkers F-13 monoplane in flight.(7.32) They commemorated the new Kaunus to Konigsberg air route, which soon became part of the route from Berlin to Moscow. In November that year a set portraying an allegory of flight marked the launch of a regular airmail service.(7.33) In 1922 yet more Air stamps pictured the F-13.

7.34 40s Lieut Juozapavicius, 50s Dr Basanavicius and 8a Antanas Smetona (from set 27 September 1922)

7.35 5c Vytis OFFICIAL overprinted Klaipeda (Memel) and 10 markiu (from set 5 February 1923), and 1,000m Vytis incorporating Klaipeda and Memel in the new design (from set 1923+)

7.36 (E) 80m liner at Memel (from set 12 April 1923)

In 1922 thirteen people who made key contributions to the cultural and political life of Lithuania as it strove for independence and international recognition were featured in a set marking the country's acceptance as a member of the League of Nations the previous year.(7.34) Among them was Lieutenant Antanas Juozapavicius (40s) who was killed defending the town of Alytus on 12 February 1919 as the Red Army advanced towards Kaunus. Another was the scholar and nationalist Dr Jonas Basanavicius (50s) who was the first person to sign the Act of Independence on 16 February 1818 and attained fame for stoically enduring Polish repression when he stayed working in Central Lithuania's Vilnius. A third was Antanas Smetona (8a) whose work as a publicist and politician would lead to his presidency in 1926. By 1929 he exercised almost dictatorial powers, and used them to repress Polish influences, suppress Communism and, in due course, restrain Nazi influences, most noticeably those pervading Memel (Lithuanian Klaipeda).

The port of Memel and its hinterland had been part of the German Empire but despite its urban population being mainly German its predominantly ethnic Lithuanian rural population caused the Allied post-war peace settlement to detach it from Germany while it future was decided. When nothing was finalized, in January 1923 Lithuanian troops disguised as civilians surprised the small French garrison protecting 'Memelland' and seized it.

Stamps were immediately issued to confirm the occupation. Initially these were Lithuanian Official stamps overprinted *Klaipeda (Memel)* and values in markiu, but after March 1923 *KLAIPEDA, MEMEL* and markiu values were incorporated into a new but strikingly similar design.(7.35) From April three pictorial designs appeared showing Memel harbour, its lighthouse and Arms.(7.36)

The League of Nations quickly accepted the situation

7.38 (E) 10c wayside cross (from new currency set 24 February 1923), and 3m wayside cross overprinted KARO NASLAICIAMS (WAR ORPHANS) with 3c surcharge (from set February 1924+)

7.39 10c President Smetona and 1l Lithuania's Resurrection (from 10th anniversary of independence set 20 February 1928)

7.37 (E)　1c Arms of Memel, 25c Ruins of Trakai Castle, and 1l Memel Harbour, 3c Chapel of Birota, 10c Kaunas war memorial (from set 12 July 1923)

but ensured Klaipeda retained considerable internal autonomy so that Polish trade through the port was not suppressed. On 12 July 1923 Lithuania celebrated the union with an exuberant set of thirteen stamps in eye-catching diamond shapes featuring the Arms of Memel and Lithuania, Memel's harbour, Kaunas war memorial, and two famous historic sites.(7.37) These were the chapel of Biruta, a priestess of the Goddess of Fire who married Kestutis – although legends vary in her willingness to do so – and the ruins of Trakai Castle west of Vilnius that was the seat of the Grand Dukes of Lithuania. From this time onwards Klaipeda used ordinary Lithuanian issues. The stamp values were in centu and litu, the new currency introduced in 1922.

The wartime conflicts had devastated many families and dislocated the economy. In 1924 and again in 1929 numerous stamps were overprinted with various designs and surcharges in aid of the War Orphans' Fund.(7.38)

However, Lithuania was at last free from military conflict, and a plethora of stamps throughout the inter-war period continued to imbue pride in the country's illustrious past. President Smetona was successful in providing national stability and repressing the extremism of the inter-war period until overwhelmed by the might of Stalin's Soviet Russia working in brief but shattering partnership with Hitler's Germany. Sets of stamps celebrated Lithuania's tenth, fifteenth and, in 1939, its twentieth years of independence but as in Estonia and Latvia there were no more after that until the 1990s.(7.39)

CHAPTER 8
The Austro-Hungarian Empire, the Austrian Republic and Regency Hungary

In 1919 the Treaty of Versailles turned Austria and Hungary into small and separate republics with little political influence and severely limited military power. In 1914 things were very different; Austria and Hungary were much larger territorially and were the key components of a powerful if rather ramshackle central European entity generally known as the Austro-Hungarian Empire or the Dual Monarchy. At the outbreak of the First World War His Imperial and Royal Apostolic Majesty Franz Joseph was not only Emperor of Austria and King of Hungary, but also King of Bohemia, Dalmatia, Croatia, Galicia, Illyria and Slavonia. Amongst a host of other titles, he was Grand Prince of Transylvania, Princely Count of Tyrol, Kyburg, Gorizia and Gradisca, Prince of Trent and Brixen, Margrave of Moravia, Grand Duke of Tuscany and Cracow, Duke of Upper and Lower Silesia, Lorraine, Salzburg, Styria, Carinthia, Carniola and Bukovina, Lord of Trieste, and Grand Voivode of the Voivodeship of Serbia.

The vast number of titles, although now long forgotten, are important inasmuch as they reflect the disparate array of ethnic groups under Franz Joseph's rule who saw their own particular identities, aspirations and grievances as far more important than any unifying force holding them together. The First World War saw this Empire shatter into racial and cultural fragments.

Franz Joseph lost his authority over the northern Italian states of Lombardy-Venetia (1859) and Piedmont-Sardinia (1860) when they allied with France and their joint forces decisively defeated Austria. This paved the way for the unification of Italy. In 1863 Austria joined Prussia in a war they provoked against Denmark which led the Danish provinces of Schleswig and Holstein to become part of the German Confederation. However three years later when Austria and Prussia disagreed over the administration of the new territories Bismarck seized the opportunity to provoke Austria into a war, comprehensively defeat it, and end its active involvement in German affairs.

Hungary took immediate advantage of the humiliation to intensify its demands for autonomy within the Hapsburg Empire. This it achieved in 1867 when the Dual Monarchy was established. Two separately governed nations were united only in the person of Franz Joseph as Emperor of Austria and King of Hungary. Cisleithania – the Austrian part – incorporated swathes of central Europe including Austria, Bohemia, Moravia, Polish Galicia, Dalmatia, Gorizia and Trieste. Transleithania – the restored Kingdom of Hungary – embraced Hungary, Transylvania, Croatia and Slavonia. There were two capital cities – Vienna and Budapest – and two parliaments, but the emperor/king retained considerable powers, and notably so regarding foreign policy.

From 1868 Austrian Cisleithania and Hungarian Transleithania issued their own stamps, and until 1900 Transleithania preferred to do without Franz Joseph's portrait, much preferring images of a posthorn or a letter. However above both the posthorn and the letter appeared St Stephen's crown, the greatly revered Holy Crown of Hungary that Franz Joseph wore at his coronation in Budapest.(8.1) The gold and enamel crown with its familiar bent cross, or at least parts of it, was said to date back to Stephen I who was crowned in or around 1000AD.

8.1 10k Hungarian Crown and envelope (from set August 1898+)

In 1900 a new Hungarian currency led to two new stamps, with several subsequent reissues and several perforation sizes. One featured a turul, the mythical bird of prey that came to symbolize Hungary after an ancient war lord dreamt a flock of them came to his rescue by attacking enemy horsemen. On the stamp it is flying over the Hungarian plain. St Stephen's Crown is in the

THE AUSTRO-HUNGARIAN EMPIRE, THE AUSTRIAN REPUBLIC AND REGENCY HUNGARY

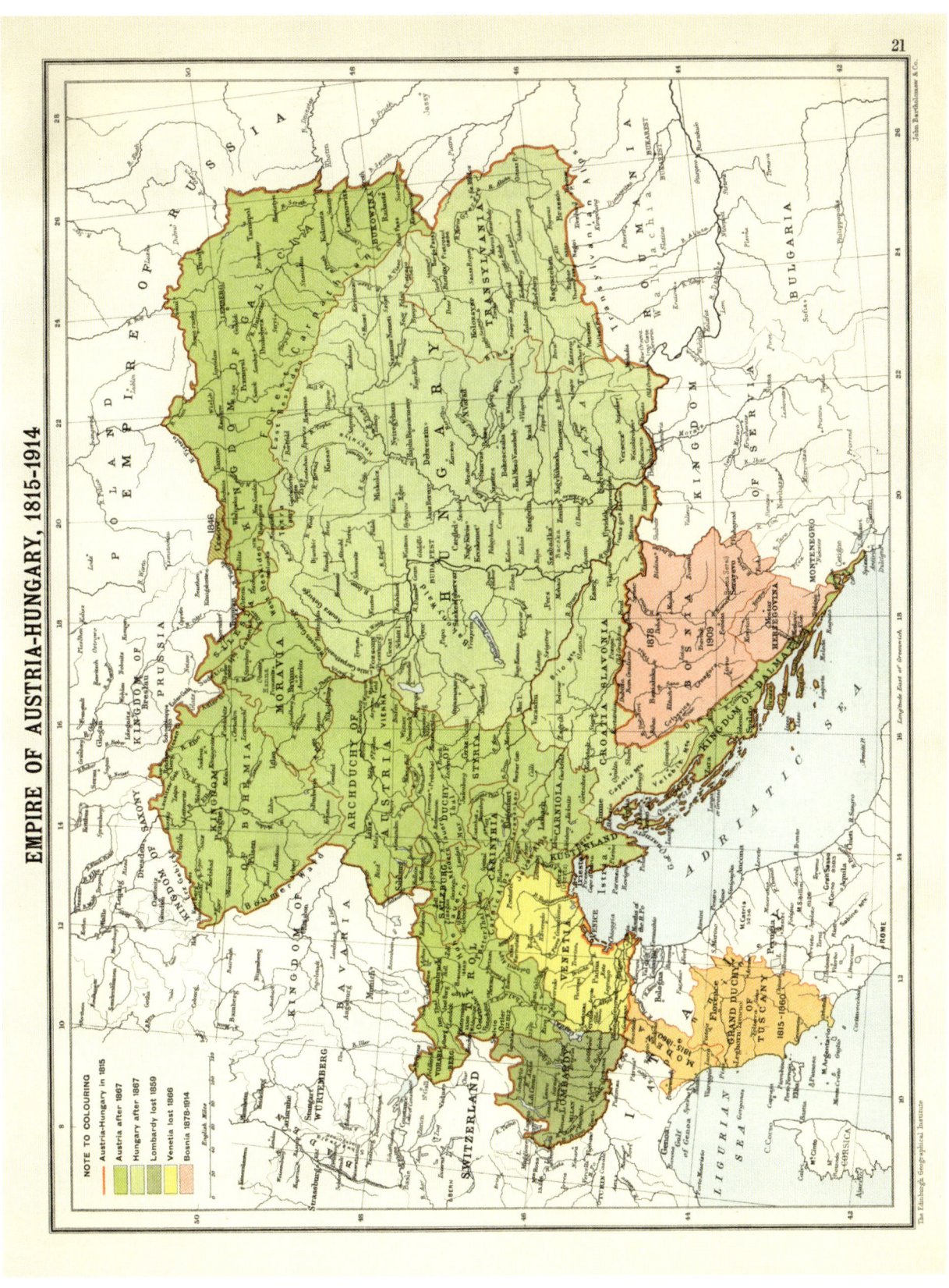

8.2 3f turul and 2k Franz Joseph as King of Hungary (from set 1904+), and 35f and 1k reprinted with Flood Relief labels (from set 20 November 1913)

foreground. The companion stamp features Franz Joseph wearing the crown as King of Hungary. The stamps are inscribed *Magyar Kir.(alyi) Posta* (Royal Hungarian Post).(8.2) A new newspaper stamp featured the ancient Hungarian coat of arms. In November 1913 the turul and Franz Joseph stamps were reissued with a 2f surcharge and additional label seeking support for the victims of the flood when the Danube burst its banks just below Budapest.

For all its nationalism, once Hungary achieved power it showed little sympathy for the strivings of ethnic groups such as the Slovaks, Romanians and Ruthenians within its borders, and as a result the internal fissures in the Dual Monarchy's edifice grew wider.

In 1908 Franz Joseph celebrated the 60th anniversary of his accession. A massive jubilee pageant was organised drawing participants from across the Dual Monarchy but it served mainly to highlight the deepening ethnic divisions. The Hungarians said there was no jubilee to celebrate, as Franz Joseph had only been crowned as their king in 1867, and refused to participate. The Czechs left early feeling snubbed by the Viennese authorities, and the Italians and Croats thought aspects of the pageant merely confirmed their subjugation. The Ruthenians (in from the east) enjoyed their participation, only to be mercilessly mocked by the Viennese for their peasants' look, clothes and gait.

Nevertheless the anniversary produced Austria's first commemorative set. Designed by the renowned Koloman Moser in the fashionable Art Nouveau style several values pictured Franz Joseph in military uniform or wearing the robes of Austria's Roman Catholic Order of the Golden Fleece. Two landscape stamps featured his vast Schonbrunn and Hofburg palaces in Vienna and ensured the essentially Austrian centre of power was emphasized.(8.3) The inscription read *Kaiserliche Konigliche Osterreichisch Post*. This translates as Imperial-Royal Austrian Post, and the omission of the word *und* (and) is highly significant as the inscription does not refer to the Kingdom of Hungary, but only Cisleithania which included not only Imperial Austria but also several ancient subordinate kingdoms, notably that of Bohemia.

Other stamps in the set portrayed Franz Joseph's more recent predecessors.(8.4) It seemed an indestructible dynasty, and the perils its past and present members endured and survived reinforced this view. Among them were Joseph II (1780-90) who alienated the Hungarians by making German the official language, the nobility by making many posts open to talent rather than mere birth, and the Roman Catholic Church by ending tithes, closing monasteries, and requiring senior clergy to swear loyalty to the Crown. The 6h featured his brother, Leopold II (1790-92), who achieved peace with the Turks, and diplomatically pacified Hungary. The 12h showed Francis I (1792-1835) whose turbulent reign throughout the Napoleonic Wars saw numerous defeats but eventual victory as part of the Allied coalition. After 1815 he became more autocratic and conservative as revolutionary ideas and nationalist aspirations swirled around his vast and far from homogenous lands. The 20h featured Ferdinand (1835-

8.3 (E) 50h and 1k (in robes of the Order of the Golden Fleece) Franz Joseph and 2k Schonbrunn Palace (from set 1 January 1908+)

8.4   3h Joseph II, 6h Leopold II, 12h Francis I, 20h Ferdinand, and 30h Franz Joseph in 1848 (from set 1 January 1908+)

48) whose mental deficiency and epilepsy meant his uncle, Archduke Louis, and the able foreign minister, Prince Metternich, were *de facto* rulers. Their innate conservatism, though, had little success in stemming the mounting tide of nationalism, and in 1848 the Hungarians, Italians, Slovenes, Czechs, Slovaks, Croats, Serbs, Romanians and Ruthenians all staged revolts seeking greater autonomy or complete independence. Ferdinand was obliged to abdicate, Metternich to resign and flee, and Archduke Louis to retire. Ferdinand's nephew, the young Franz Joseph, succeeded him, and Austrian and Russian forces eventually crushed the revolts, but the ideas fuelling them lived on.

In 1910 the set was reissued, but this time with the additional dates '1830' and '1910' to mark Franz Joseph's 80th birthday. There was little joy in his life – in 1867 his brother Maximilian, Emperor of Mexico, was executed by victorious republicans, in 1889 Rudolph, his only son and heir, committed suicide with his mistress, and in 1898 Elizabeth, his estranged wife, was stabbed to death in Geneva by an Italian anarchist. Franz Joseph's heirs presumptive were, first, his younger brother Archduke Karl Ludwig, and when he died in 1896 Karl's eldest son, Archduke Franz Ferdinand.

Franz Joseph had little time for Franz Ferdinand. He had married Countess Sophie Chotek, a woman far beneath him in rank, and the emperor denied her any share in his rank, precedence or privileges. Although perceived as an arch-conservative and hostile to the Slavs, a view that probably contributed to his assassination, Franz Ferdinand was, in fact, in favour of increased regional autonomy under a single central government. The emperor disagreed, and the two men rarely met.

In one respect, foreign affairs, Austria-Hungary generally operated as an entity. Pushed out of German affairs, and encouraged by the astute Bismark, Austria-Hungary increasingly concentrated its attention on the Balkans where a dangerous power vacuum was looming.

In 1526 the feared Ottoman armies under Suleiman the Magnificent had occupied Hungary and in 1683 they very nearly seized Vienna. Since then uneasy stalemates interspersed with probing trials of strength had existed between the Hapsburg and Ottoman Empires until the early 1800s when a combination of rising Balkan nationalism and Russian expansion began to triumph over waning Ottoman power. Greece secured its independence in 1829 and Serbia, Wallachia, Moldavia and Montenegro moved towards greater autonomy within the Ottoman Empire under home-grown dynasties only nominally acknowledging Turkish overlordship.

With Russian backing, in 1875 Wallachia and Moldavia (soon to be united as Romania) along with Serbia and Montenegro declared their complete independence. As Turkish forces moved in, the Bulgarians joined the revolt. Russia declared war on Turkey partly to recover territory lost after its Crimean War defeat and partly to enhance its influence across the Balkans. At the Treaty of San Stefano in 1878 the defeated Ottoman Empire granted complete independence to Serbia, Montenegro, Romania and Bulgaria, but at the Congress of Berlin a year later the major European powers, including Austria-Hungary, enforced a revision of their borders partly to prop up the fading Ottoman Empire against further Russian encroachment and partly to stop any new Balkan state gaining too great a degree of power and local dominance. Bulgaria lost vast tracts of Eastern Rumelia and Macedonia to Turkey, and Romania lost part of Bessarabia to Russia. The major achievements were to heighten the underlying jealousies between the new states, and intensify the enmity between Austria-Hungary and Russia. It was a seminal moment in European affairs.

The Congress of Berlin also permitted Austria-Hungary to administer Bosnia-Herzegovina but under Turkish sovereignty and with Turkish forces still present alongside its own. For many Bosnians and Herzegovinians this meant they had two hated occupiers rather than one. In 1908 Austria-Hungary took advantage of an internal upheaval in Turkey itself and suddenly annexed the provinces causing widespread Balkan alarm at its aggression. Famously, several aggrieved Bosnians were directly involved in the assassination of Archduke Franz Ferdinand a few years later in June 1914.

The Hapsburgs dominated the stamps of Bosnia-Herzegovina long before 1908, as well as afterwards. In 1878 troops in these provinces used both Austrian and

8.5 1900 1k Coat of Arms (from Bosnia-Herzegovina set 1 January 1900+)

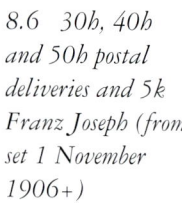

8.6 30h, 40h and 50h postal deliveries and 5k Franz Joseph (from set 1 November 1906+)

pacify the province and wean it away from the hostility of other Balkan states.

No issue marked the controversial annexation in 1908, but in 1910 the whole 1906 set was reissued in a slightly larger size with '1830-1910' added in commemoration of Franz Joseph's 80th birthday.(8.7) On both sets the images were the ancient city of Doboj, Mostar's famous stone bridge, the medieval castle and new Franciscan monastery of St Luke in Jajce, a canyon on the River Neretva, the Rama Valley, the River Vrbas, Jezero village and lake, and the Bey's Mosque, Bazaar and old commercial quarter at Sarajevo. Three values featuring horse drawn deliveries, a mail wagon, and motorized mail delivery highlighted the expanding postal service. Not surprisingly, the highest value pictured Franz Joseph.

Between 1912 and 1914 a lengthy Bosnia-Herzegovina set featuring the aged Franz Joseph appeared with the additional Dual Monarchy inscription *K.u.K. Militarpost*. This was an abbreviation of *Kaiserliche und Konigliche Militarpost* translated as Imperial (Austrian) and Royal (Hungarian) Military Post. In marked contrast the 1913 provincial Newspaper stamps pictured a girl in Bosnian costume.(8.8)

During the first decade of the twentieth century jealousies and resentment across the Balkans exploded into open warfare. Bulgaria, Greece, Montenegro and Serbia came together in the Balkan League to push Turkey out of the Balkans altogether and in doing so acquire more territory themselves and, not least, the land taken from them under the Congress of Berlin. In the First Balkan War of 1912-13 the League decisively defeated Ottoman forces and Turkey was almost driven out of Europe. However the League failed to hold together when the spoils were discussed. Serbia and

Hungarian stamps, but from 1879 when the post was widened to include civilians a design bearing the Hapsburg coat of arms, and possessing a bewildering series of printings and perforations, was introduced.(8.5) Interestingly no country was named on these stamps, but presumably the awesome heraldry was considered adequate provenance.

However in 1906-07 a lengthy set of 19 stamps, with *BOSNIEN HERZEGOWINA* included, appeared featuring picturesque and deceptively peaceful views of towns, villages and countryside.(8.6) The set honoured the province's ancient towns and magnificent scenery and in doing so reflected the Dual Monarchy's considerable but ultimately unsuccessful efforts to develop as well as

8.8 1h Franz Joseph K.u.K Militarpost (from set 4 October 1912+), and 20h Bosnian girl (from set 15 October 1913)

8.7 1h Doboj, 20h Mostar Old Bridge, 25h Bey's Mosque, Sarajevo and 1k St Luke's Campanile, Jajce inscribed 1830-1910 (from set 18 August 1910)

Greece decided to hold on to most of Macedonia despite originally agreeing to the territory going to Bulgaria. Enraged, Bulgaria started the Second Balkan War in June 1913 but reeled under counter-attacks from Serbia and Greece. And sensing an advantage, Romania and Turkey joined them. Forced to cede much of its gains from the First Balkan War Bulgaria was utterly humiliated.

The build up to the First World War was well underway. Austria-Hungary now sought to expand in the Balkans, and secure an Adriatic port at the expense of the crumbling Ottoman Empire and to oppose any other nation, especially Russia, from doing the same. It was particularly at loggerheads with Serbia over its constant agitation against the annexation of Bosnia. As 1914 dawned Serbia was very much in Russia's orbit, and Bulgaria, now isolated, drew closer to Austria-Hungary and Germany.

In 1913 Franz Ferdinand became inspector-general of the armed forces, and in this capacity in late June 1914 he took his wife on a rare tour where she could be equally honoured. In a poorly organized visit to Sarajevo in Bosnia on 28 June they were shot and killed. Few mourned them, but many hawks surrounding Franz Joseph seized the outrage to settle scores with Serbia which, with justification if no hard evidence, they assumed had encouraged and assisted the Bosnian assassins. The Austro-Hungarian High Command and Foreign Office decided on a firm response and a declaration of war if necessary, and Germany's Kaiser and senior ministers committed themselves to support Austria-Hungary – in effect they signed 'a blank cheque'. Perhaps Germany thought the time was ripe to prove to the belligerent Slavic states and their aggressive Russian protector that the Teutonic nations would not stand for any westwards expansion or, indeed, further provocation. Perhaps, too, with France and Russia in alliance Germany had convinced itself that now was the time for a lightening strike to reduce the perils of a war on two fronts.

After dithering for a time, Austria-Hungary sent an ultimatum to Serbia assuming its guilt and demanding its king dismiss all nationalist officers, suppress all nationalist societies, and publicly declare against any territorial expansion. In addition Austria-Hungary demanded the right to involve itself in suppressing subversion within Serbia. It expected, and indeed hoped, that Serbia would reject the insulting demands – and on 25 July it did. Serbia seemed doomed. Only Russia had encouraged its intransigence. Great Britain, France and Italy had urged compromise, and Greece, Romania and Montenegro had sent messages of vague support but no-one promised military aid. On 28 July 1914 Austria-Hungary and Serbia were at war. The only question was who else would join in.

Everyone soon found out. The Serbs rebuffed two Austrian attacks at the battles of Cer and Drina but with huge losses on both sides. In 1915 overwhelming numbers began to tell, and with Bulgaria thirsting for revenge and with German military support forthcoming to stiffen Austrian resolve, Serbia was finally occupied. Its army retreated towards the Adriatic, and after untold hardships the remnant eventually embarked for Corfu. However, by the end of 1914 Austrian losses already amounted to 215,000 men, and the total kept rising as Italy as well as Russia had entered the war on the Allied side.

Not surprisingly in early October 1914 two surcharged stamps using the familiar bewhiskered portrait of Franz Joseph were issued in aid of war charities.(8.9) A set of five specially designed war charity stamps followed in May 1915 featuring the Austrian infantry (3h+1h), cavalry (5h+2h), artillery (10h+2h), the navy (20h+3h) and an early biplane (35h+3h).(8.10)

The army had three components. First, there were regiments recruited from all parts of the Dual Monarchy – the Kaiserliche und Konigliche Armee (Imperial and Royal Army). Second, there was the Kaiserliche-konigliche Landwehr (Imperial-Royal) Landwehr

8.9 5h+2h War Charity (pair 4 October 1914)

8.10 War charity set (1 May 1915) The surcharge is printed as HEL 2 LER

recruited only from Cisleithania, and third there was the Konigliche Ungarisch (Royal Hungarian) Honved recruited only from Transleithania.

With ports at Trieste, Pola, Fiume and Ragusa the *Kaiserliche und Konigliche Kriegsmarine* (Imperial and Royal War Navy), abbreviated as *K.u.K. Kriegsmarine,* had built several all-big gun battleships on Great Britain's Dreadnought model. The navy also included several submarines, one of which was commanded by the famous Captain Ludwig von Trapp. The greatest service provided by the Dual Monarchy's navy during the war was to tie down the rival French and Italian navies in the Mediterranean through sporadic bombardments of the Italian coast and attacks on Allied cargo ships and convoys.

The *Kaiserliche und Konigliche Luftfahrtruppen* (Imperial and Royal Aviation Troops), or *K.u.K. Luftfahrtruppen*, had 10 ballons and around 40 serviceable aircraft at the outbreak of war. On 28 July 1914 an Austrian pilot flew on a reconnaissance mission over Serbia, and met a Serbian aeroplane. The encounter probably represents the first aerial encounter of the war, but as the pilots had no weapons they merely waved at each other.

Austria-Hungary conscripted 7,800,000 men throughout the war. In 1915 its eastern army was defeated at Lemberg and German armies were required to stem Russian advances and then force a lengthy retreat. Despite the slaughter Russia recovered and in 1916 its vast Brusilov Offensive was only repelled after Austro-Hungarian losses of a million men killed, wounded and taken prisoner. There were huge Russian losses, too, and the collapse of the offensive was a significant incentive to the 1917 revolution. During this campaign around 3,500 members of the Czech Legion, mainly ex-prisoners of the Russians, fought for the Russians against Austria-Hungary.

Austro-Hungarian armies fought equally muddled, exhausting and bloody battles on the Italian front. In 1915 an Italian invasion of Austria itself was halted after a dozen battles around the Isonzo River, but at a cost of 200,000 casualties. And in 1916 further Italian incursions ended in lengthy lines of trenches much like the Western Front. In 1917 the Austro-Hungarians attacked at Caporetto and advanced 100 miles towards Venice before being stopped at the Piave River. In June 1918 the Italians returned to the attack and advanced across the Piave causing 90,000 casualties and capturing over 400,000 men. The military disasters and the continuing senseless slaughter fuelled the growing ethnic rebellions within the Dual Monarchy. Its total collapse was nigh.

From September 1916 three new designs appeared specifically for Austrian Cisleithania.(8.11) They featured Franz Joseph, the Imperial Austrian Crown, and the Arms of Austria surrounded by a decorative border and the inscription *Kaiserliche Konigliche Osterreichisch Post*

8.11 3h Imperial Austrian Crown and 80h Arms of Austria (from set 28 September 1916+)

(Imperial Royal Austrian Post). The Arms comprised a black double-headed eagle surmounted by the Imperial Crown and clutching a sword, sceptre and orb, and in the centre the medieval red and white Hapsburg escutcheon.

These Arms came about as in 1915 Franz Joseph succumbed to pressure from Hungary to introduce a new Dual Monarchy coat of arms to replace the existing one highlighting the double-headed eagle that symbolized only the Cisleithanian half of the union. The new common coat of arms featured two side-by-side shields of Cisleithania and Transleithania under the Imperial Crown and Hungarian Crown of St Stephen respectively, linked by the crowned Hapsburg-Lorraine armorials and (with the benefit of hindsight) the hollow motto *indivisibiliter ac inseparabiliter* (indivisible and inseparable).(8.12)

Franz Joseph died in November 1916 and was succeeded by Charles I, Franz Ferdinand's nephew. He had married Princess Zita of Bourbon Parma in 1911, and on 30 December 1916 Hungary celebrated their coronation in Budapest that day with a pair of stamps portraying them wearing the Hungarian crowns.(8.13)

In 1917 Charles began secret talks with the Allies using Zita's brother, an officer in the Belgian army, as intermediary. No progress was made as Charles refused the Allied demands to recognize Italy's claims to further Austrian territory. Around this time, in April 1917, a set of four stamps appeared bearing the portrait of Charles set within a design reminiscent of a glittering breast-star of an Imperial award.(8.14)

Despite the involvement of Bosnian nationalists in Franz Ferdinand's assassination thousands of Bosnians joined Austro-Hungarian regiments during the war, and stayed loyal until the disintegration of the Dual Monarchy in 1918.

However, the mounting casualties led to recent Bosnia-Herzegovinia 5h and 10h stamps being overprinted '1914', then '1915', and then '1916' together with 7h or 12h surcharges for war charities. (8.15/8.16/8.17). In July 1916 two dramatic Bosnia-Herzegovina *K.u.K Militarpost* (Imperial and Royal Military Post) stamps portraying wounded soldiers appeared with 2h premiums in support of the War Invalids' Fund.(8.18)

8.12 *Prepaid postcard with 8h K.u.K. Feldpost conjoined Coats(s) of Arms stamp (and 3h Emperor Charles Feldpost stamp) on censored cover from Krusevac in Serbia to Geneva, postmarked 13 December 1917.*

8.13 *Souvenir first day of issue (30 December 1916) cover from Zagreb with the Hungarian Charles and Zita coronation set.*

8.14 25h Charles I (from set 10 May 1917+)

8.17 1912 10h Franz Joseph overprinted '1916 12 Heller' (pair 19 January 1916)

8.15 1906 5h Mostar Old Bridge overprinted '1914 7 Heller' (pair 1 November 1914)

8.18 War Invalids' Fund (pair 10 July 1916)

8.16 1906 10h Vrbas Valley (pair 10 July 1915) and 1912 10h Franz Joseph overprinted '1915 12 Heller' (pair 9 October 1915)

8.19 1912 3h Bosnia-Hercegovina K.u.K Militarpost overprinted K.U.K FELDPOST (from set 28 April 1915)

8.20 Below: 20h Franz Joseph K.u.K. Feldpost (from set 1 July 1915+), and left: 15h K.u.K. Feldpost on cover with the ETAPPENPOSTAMT cancellation dated 14.1.18 from Noworadomsk (then in Congress Poland, now known as Radomsko), red censor handstamp, and 10f Warsaw local delivery charge handstamp.

Alongside these a series of army field post issues, some overprinted, reflected Austro-Hungarian successes in seizing and at least temporarily holding onto Italian, Montenegran, Romanian and Serbian territory. On 28 April 1915 the 1912-14 Bosnia-Herzegovina set of *K.u.K. Militarpost* stamps featuring Franz Joseph were diagonally overprinted *K.U.K. FELDPOST* for wider use in all occupied areas.(8.19)

From July 1915 these were supplemented with a specially designed issue featuring Franz Joseph with the field post inscription but no other territorial designation.(8.20) In 1917 they were superseded by a set featuring Charles, and a few days before the Armistice a newly designed set portraying Charles, ironically

THE AUSTRO-HUNGARIAN EMPIRE, THE AUSTRIAN REPUBLIC AND REGENCY HUNGARY

8.21 12h Charles K.u.K. Feldpost (from set 1917+), and 10h from redesigned but unissued set 1918

8.22 1912 3h Bosnia-Hercegovina Franz Joseph K.u.K Militarpost overprinted SERBIEN (from set 6 March 1916)

8.23 1915+ 15h K.u.K Feldpost overprinted K.U.K. MILIT. VERWALTUNG MONTENEGRO (pair 1 March 1917)

8.24 6 BANI Charles K.u.K Feldpost (from set 1 March 1918)

8.25 40h Charles K.u.K Feldpost overprinted 43 Centesimi (from set 1 June 1918)

8.26 40h Franz Joseph K.u.K Militarpost (from set 1 October 1916+), and 20h Charles K.u.K. Militarpost (from set 1 July 1917)

within a laurel wreath, was printed but never used by the demoralised and fast collapsing armies.(8.21)

Serbia was overrun by Austro-Hungarian, German and Bulgarian forces in late 1915, and in March 1916 the Bosnia-Herzegovina *K.u.K. Militarpost* stamps portraying Franz Joseph were overprinted SERBIEN, sometimes horizontally and sometimes diagonally.(8.22) Soon afterwards the Kingdom of Montenegro was occupied and the new Franz Joseph 10h and 15h *K.u.K. FELDPOST* stamps were issued there overprinted either *Montenegro* or *K.U.K. MILIT. VERWALTUNG MONTENEGRO* (Imperial and Royal Military Administration Montenegro).(8.23)

German and Austro-Hungarian forces occupied most of Romania in autumn 1916, and in November 1917 the *K.u.K Feldpost* stamps featuring Charles were overprinted in the Romanian values BANI and LEI. Later, in March 1918, the Romanian values were incorporated into the printed design.(8.24) In June 1918 after Venetia-Friuli had fallen under Austro-Hungarian occupation the field post stamps were issued overprinted with Italian values.(8.25)

Newly designed Bosnia-Herzegovinia *K.u.K Militarpost* stamps portraying an angled portrait of Franz Joseph appeared in October 1916 just before he died. In July 1917 another new set featured Charles.(8.26)

By the Armistice Austro-Hungarian military deaths exceeded 1,200,000 and the number of wounded was estimated at 3,600,000. As Charles' Empire and Kingdom collapsed around him many issues reflected the desperate need for relief funds. Several old Bosnia-Herzegovina stamps were drafted into service. In May 1917 10h and 15h stamps featuring the deceased Franz Joseph were overprinted WITWEN UNO WAISENWOCHE 1917 (Widows and Orphans 1917), and in March 1918 the pair of 'wounded soldiers' stamps reappeared with higher surcharges.(8.27)

On 1 July 1918, however, a completely new charity set appeared picturing Charles and Zita. These were inscribed *Karlsfond* (Charles' Fund); some were also inscribed *K. und K. Militarpost* for use in Bosnia-Herzegovina, and some *K. und K. Feldpost* (Imperial and Royal Field Post) for wider use in occupied areas.(8.28) On 1 September, as chaos loomed, the 2h Mostar stamp from Franz Joseph's 80th birthday set in 1910 and the 2h Franz Joseph stamp from 1912 were hurriedly brought

8.27 1916 10h Franz Joseph K.u.K Militarpost overprinted WITWEN UNO WAISENWOCHE 1917 (pair 9 May 1917)

93

8.28 15h Zita and 10h and 40h Charles K. und K. Militarpost Karlsfond postmarked K.u.K Militarpost at Kozarac in Bosnia and dated 21.VII.18, the day after issue.

8.29 1910 2h Mostar and 1912 2h Franz Joseph K.u.K. Miltarpost overprinted 1918 (pair 1 September 1918)

8.30 Franz Ferdinand Memorial Fund (set 28 June 1917)

back into charity relief service overprinted *1918*.(8.29)

The sole set commemorating Archduke Franz Ferdinand was issued for Bosnia & Herzegovina on the third anniversary of his assassination, 28 June 1917.(8.30) It attracted a premium for the construction of a memorial church in Sarajevo featured on the 10h stamp. The two accompanying stamps pictured the archduke and, with her years of humiliation seemingly forgotten, his archduchess. At a time of crisis, it seems probable the set aimed more at blackening Serbia's name and reinforcing the dignity and continuity of the Hapsburgs than enforcing a memorial on a divided Bosnia. Many sets appeared on picture postcards showing the doomed pair being driven into Sarajevo. The church was never built, the Hapsburgs soon departed, Bosnia duly became part of Yugoslavia, and not long afterwards a museum commemorating the assassins rather than their victims opened at the site of the shooting.

As autumn 1918 and chaos and defeat approached, the US President, Woodrow Wilson, demanded that Emperor Charles acceded to the demands of ethnic minorities. Charles considered a confederation, but it was far too late as the ethnic minorities seized the opportunity to wrest themselves completely free from Vienna and Budapest. The Czechoslovak provisional government joined the Allies on 14 October, the South Slav Council declared itself independent on the 29th, and exactly a month later the new State of Slovenes, Croats and Serbs was born. On 11 and 13 November 1918 respectively Charles issued proclamations relinquishing all personal involvement in the administration of Cisleithania and Transleithania, but deliberately did not abdicate. On 12 and 16 November respectively the Republics of Austria and Hungary were proclaimed, but their fate lay not in their own hands but in those of the 'peacemakers' assembled in Paris. On 24 March 1919 Charles and his family left Austria, and on 3 April the Austrian Parliament barred him from returning.

REPUBLIC OF AUSTRIA

Signalling the dramatically changing times, from December 1918 many stamps featuring Emperor Charles and the Austrian Crown and Arms, were reissued overprinted *Deutschosterreich* (German-Austria).(8.31) Newspaper and Postage Due sets joined them

They stemmed from an abortive attempt begun in October 1918 by the 208 ethnic German deputies in the *Reichsrat* (the Cisleithanian Parliament) to establish an independent German-Austrian state that embraced not only Austria but also Bohemia, Moravia and Austrian Silesia which they were determined should not become part of Czechoslovakia. On 12 November Karl Renner, a Social Democrat, was elected provisional Chancellor, and a provisional constitution declared German-Austria 'is an integral part of the German Reich.' There was a widespread belief that union with Germany was essential as German-Austria was too weak politically and economically to stand alone, especially as Hungary now refused to sell it grain and Czechoslovakia to sell it coal.

In October 1918 a dramatically new Austrian coat of arms in modernist style had been proposed incorporating a black tower representing the people, surmounted by crossed red hammers representing industry and surrounded by golden ears of corn representing agriculture. The three colours were, deliberately, those of the German flag, but the design was widely criticized as losing all sense of nationhood, and dropped. The eventual design looked superficially like the 1915 Arms, but the eagle was clutching a hammer and sickle (for agriculture and industry, not an overt link with Communism) and the mural crown represented the republic not the Hapsburgs.

From July 1919 a new definitive set appeared incorporating *Deutschosterrreich* in the design. The four images included a posthorn from mailcoach days, the new controversial Austrian coats of arms, an allegory of

8.31 1916 6h Imperial Austrian Crown overprinted Deutschosterreich (from set December 1918)

8.32 10h Republic Arms, 25h posthorn, 50h planting a tree and 4k Parliament (from set July 1919+)

8.33 90h Mercury Newspaper (from set 1920+)

8.34 80h Austrian Republic Arms (from set 1920+)

the new republic itself in the form of a worker planting a tree, and for the higher values a picture of the Parliament Building.(8.32) Representing both continuity and dramatic change, the vast neo-Classical Parliament Building was originally the seat of both the Imperial Council and Cisleithanian legislature but now housed the republic's upper and lower chambers. In 1920 Postage Due and Newspaper stamps were redesigned incorporating the provocative inscription.(8.33) In 1920 and again in 1921 the republic's controversial new Arms reappeared on sets inscribed *Deutschosterreich*.(8.34)

However all hopes of an internationally recognized Deutschosterreich (German-Austria) had been dashed in June 1919 when the draft peace treaty revealed that the

8.35 20h Land Tirol Freimarke (Tyrol Free Province) with crowned eagle arms of Tyrol issued 1919 for use on parcels

8.36 1920 2k Austrian Republic Arms overprinted in gold Deutscher Gau Osttirol to promote the East Tyrol plebiscite October 1920

8.37 1920 2k Austrian Republic Arms overprinted Abstimmung in Salzburg 29. Mai 1921 (Plebiscite in Salzburg 29 May 1921)

Allies were totally opposed to enlarging Germany. Signed under protest on 10 September 1919 the Treaty of St Germain created the Republic of Austria which lost not only Bohemia and the Sudetenland to Czechoslovakia, but also southern Carinthia and Styria to the Kingdom of Slovenes, Croats and Serbs (later Yugoslavia). North and East Tyrol remained Austrian but South Tyrol was granted to Italy. And Austria and Germany were barred forever from uniting.

During these uncertain post-war years, several ex-Hapsburg regions – notably Tyrol and Salzburg – had engaged in unofficial plebiscites over their future. Sometimes stamps were issued to support and publicise them, but the postal authorities refused recognition.(8.35) Among them was the Austrian set overprinted in gold *Deutscher Gau Osttirol* (German Province of East Tyrol) to publicise a locally inspired plebiscite in Lienz on 17 October 1920.(8.36) The stamps were issued the previous day and sold well, but the post office and everyone responsible for deciding the region's future ignored both the stamps and the plebiscite. The plebiscites in Tyrol and Salzburg, however, revealed majorities of 98% and 99% in favour of unification with Germany.(8.37)

In October 1918, before hostilities ceased, the large region of Carinthia embracing Klagenfurt, Villach and Wolfsberg, and reaching up to Graz in Styria, was under severe pressure to join the emerging Slav Kingdom of Serbs, Croats and Slovenes to its south. However a majority on the Carinthian Council preferred to join German-Austria, and bitter fighting across southern Carinthia up to and beyond the Armistice obliged the Allies to send troops to restore a semblance of peace, award a small border section to the new Kingdom of Serbs, Croats and Slovenes, and order a plebiscite to determine the future of the rest of the province.

Both countries embarked upon vigorous propaganda campaigns, Austria enticing voters with promises of peace, brotherhood and equality, the Kingdom of Serbs, Croats and Slovenes by highlighting Slav unity and German aggressiveness. Both states issued stamps to help pay for their campaigns. Austria chose to reprint the four reassuring images from the 1919 *Deutschosterreich* set in new colours and values overprinted *Karnten Abstimmung* (Carinthia Poll).(8.38) They sold for a hefty three times face value, and no doubt targeted collectors as much as sympathetic Austrians. On 10 October 1920 a majority of 59.1% voted in favour of joining Austria. Austria kept its promises of equality, but only until the later 1930s when Nazi influences led Slovenes to be treated as second-class citizens.

Between January 1922 and December 1924 rampant

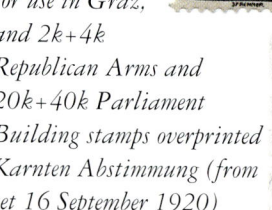

8.38 50h Austrian Republic planter overprinted Eilmarke (Express Stamp) for use in Graz, and 2k+4k Republican Arms and 20k+40k Parliament Building stamps overprinted Karnten Abstimmung (from set 16 September 1920)

8.39 30k pincers and hammers, 240k ear of corn, and 500k allegory of unity inscribed Osterreich (from set January 1922+)

8.40 60h Posthorn and 20k Parliament overprinted hochwasser 1920 (from set 1 March 1921)

8.41 5k Mozart, 7½k Beethoven and 10k Schubert (from set 24 April 1922)

River Danube.(8.40) They comprised the posthorn, planter, Arms and Parliament designs reprinted in new colours and overprinted *hochwasser 1920* (flood 1920). They sold at three times face value.

After 1920 Austria was governed by coalitions of Christian Socialists, closely linked to the Roman Catholic Church, and the right wing Greater German People's Party. The coalitions were fragile and tense, with the left wing Social Democrats of Karl Renner retaining considerable popular support, notably in Vienna. Czechoslovakia, Hungary, the Kingdom of Serbs, Croats and Slovenes and Italy maintained trade blockades, and the Allies had to provide support for the small land-locked nation. Unemployment soared, as did inflation, and the League of Nations took control of the economy, but still barred any customs union with Germany. Although a new stabilizing currency was inaugurated in 1925 with the groschen and schilling replacing the heller and krone at a rate of one schilling to 10,000 kronen, the enduring discontent encouraged the ominous growth of extremist parties of both the left and right.

Stamps, however, contributed significantly to the campaign to create a better image of Austria as well as support the economy. Most issues in the 1920s promoted charities and did so through positive portrayals of Austrian culture and cities. In 1922 seven composers featured on a set sold at ten times face value in aid of musicians' charities.(8.41) All had close connections with Austria; Joseph Haydn was born in Rohrau, Wolfgang Amadeus Mozart in Salzburg, Ludwig van Beethoven in Bonn, although he worked mainly in Vienna, Franz Schubert in Vienna, Anton Bruckner near Linz, Johann Strauss the younger in Vienna, and Hugo Wolf in Styria when it was part of the Empire.

In 1923 an artists' charity set featured historic sites in post-war Austria's nine provincial capitals.(8.42) The stamps sold at six times face value and featured Martins Tower in Bregenz, the Mirabelle Gardens in Salzburg, the ancient church at Eisenstadt, the Assembly House at Klagenfurt, the famous house with the golden roof at Innsbruck, the main square at Linz, Castle Hill at Graz, the Benedictine Abbey at Melk, and the Upper Belvedere Gardens in Vienna.

inflation disrupted the national economy and family life. In response a highly stylized and rapidly expanding set that reached 10,000 krona by January 1924 featured a hammer and pincers of urban industry, ears of corn from rural life, and a unifying allegory of science, agriculture and human endeavour.(8.39) Along with a few Newspaper stamps of December 1921, this was the first time the simple inscription *Osterreich* (Austria) appeared. Barred union with Germany, viewed by France and Italy as little better than Germany as a recent aggressor, and still the object of Czech and Hungarian enmity, Austria was turning in on itself as it struggled with its lowly status and parlous economy.

Another long set of 20 stamps appeared on 1 March 1921 in support of the victims of floods along the

8.42 (E) 120k Salzburg, 200k Innsbruck and 600k Melk (from set 22 May 1923)

8.43 500k mother and children, and 600k aid for the elderly (from set 6 September 1924)

8.44 Child Welfare set (8 March 1926)

The 1924 artists charity set highlighted the social benefits associated with successful farming and industry, generous giving and therapeutic art.(8.43) These stamps sold at four times face value.

In 1926 a Child Welfare set sought to raise funds through decidedly adult scenes from the early medieval Nibelung legends of treasure, curses, love, honour, treachery and death.(8.44) The 3g+2g recalls Siegfried who bathed in the blood of a dragon he killed and becomes invulnerable to wounds except where a leaf had fallen onto his skin. Armed with the great but cursed treasure he has stolen from the northern dwarfs, the Nibelungs, he is welcomed by King Gunther of Burgundy and falls in love with his sister Kriemhild. The 8g+2g features Gunther's voyage to Iceland accompanied by Siegfried to win the hand of its Queen Brunhild. After numerous adventures Gunther marries Brunhild, and Siegrid marries Kriemhild, but the 15g+5g pictures the growing jealousy between Brunhild and Kriemhild. As tension rises between Siegfried and Gunther, Gunther's loyal henchman Hagan treacherously kills Siegfried on a hunting trip with a spear that strikes the fatal spot, and hurls all Kriemheld's treasure to the Rhinemaidens. (20g+5g). Kriemhild had told Hagan about the leaf when he swore to be his protector, and now she swears vengeance. Many years later Rudiger (24g+6g) successfully solicits Kriemheld's hand in marriage to his overlord King Etzel of the Huns. She entices Gunther and Hagan and their court to their great hall for the Midsummer Solstice. The Huns and their ally, Dietrich of Bern await them, and in an explosion of violence (40g+10g) Gunther and Hagan, and then Kriemhild, are killed. Rendered even more famous by Richard Wagner's musical cycle *The Ring of the Nibelung*, the legends and the titanic human struggles and destinies they portrayed were to prove particularly attractive to the Nazis. In 1926, though, it was Austria that selected these Norse/Germanic myths as relevant to its national culture, and perhaps to its recent traumatic experiences.

The 1928 war orphans and invalids set took a different approach again. All six stamps portrayed Dr Michael Hainisch (1858-1940) who was President of Austria from 1920 to 1928 and did much to encourage agriculture, communications and tourism, and raise the profile of Austria's history and traditions – as reflected in stamp issues of the period.(8.45) Significantly he remained in favour of German-Austrian unity and supported the *Anschluss* in 1938.

Between 1925 and 1927 the first new definitive set using the new currency featured several values showing telehone cables spreading across the countryside. Other values featured an eagle, probably the European golden eagle, perched high in the Austrian mountains, and Vienna's oldest monastery, the *Minoritenkirche* (the Friars Minor Church).(8.46) It dated back to 1224 when the site was given to the followers of St Francis of Assissi.

By then the economy was slowly recovering, the infrastructure of the state improving, and tourism starting to prosper again. Gradually international relations eased, and old enemies such as Czechoslovakia and Italy relaxed

8.45 40g+40g Dr Hainish (from set 5 November 1928)

8.46 15g communications, 20g eagle and 1s Minorite Church (from set 1 June 1925+)

8.47 Reprinted 3k Austrian Arms in ochre overprinted FLUGPOST and 2.50k (from set 24 June 1918)

8.48 900k hawk and 1,200k Wilhelm Kress (from set 31 October 1922+)

8.49 8g airman and 30g crane and biplane from the set issued from 1 August 1925. The biplane is said to be a De Haviland DH34, but there is no evidence that Austrian Air Transport possessed one.

their guard, supplied loans and sought trade agreements.

Austria was a pioneer in air transport, and this was reflected in three Air issues. As early as March 1918 three Austrian Arms stamps were reissued in new colours for air mail, two of them surcharged, and all three overprinted 'FLUGPOST'. (8.47) On 1 April 1918 a dangerous wartime route was established from Vienna via Krakow and Lvov in Austrian Poland to Kiev in the Ukraine, then occupied by Germany.

The 1922-24 set featured the Austrian aviation pioneer Wilhelm Kress (1836-1913).(8.48) In 1901 in his *Drachen-flieger* (Dragon-flier) he attempted bravely but unsuccessfully to take off in an engine-powered aeroplane. He had, though, invented the first modern winged hang-glider as early as 1877, and almost certainly this is represented as a hawk in flight in the accompanying stamp.

Two designs featured in the 20 strong 1925-30 Air set; one is a helmeted airman by his plane, and the other a common crane flying below an aircraft.(8.49) *Osterreichische Luftverkehrs AG* (Austrian Air Transport), the precursor of Austrian Airlines, commenced operations in 1923 and invested in a series of powerful triple-engined machines throughout the inter-war years.

In the 1930s the international scene changed yet again. Austria found itself torn apart by extremist influences, but primarily those opposing and approving Nazi influences and closer ties with Germany. In 1933 Austria began its own controversial experiment with dictatorship when Engelbert Dollfus established a Fascist-style government that was continued by his successor Karl Schuschnigg. Opposing parties, including the Communists and Nazis, were banned, and revolts suppressed, but in the end Austria could not resist the remorseless pressure from Hitler's Germany, and many Austrians had no wish to do so. In 1938 it was absorbed into the German Reich.

HUNGARY: FROM DUAL MONARCHY TO REPUBLIC AND REGENCY

In 1914 the war brought mobilization and then widespread conscription and with it death, economic collapse and disillusionment on a massive scale. Giving an indication of the early slaughter and growing distress, in October and November 1914 stocks of the 1913 turul and Franz Joseph stamps with the flood relief labels (see 8.2) were re-issued overprinted *Hadi segely Ozvegyeknek es arvaknak ket (2) filler* (War aid for the widowed and orphans - two (2) filler).(8.50)

In January 1915 stamps from the 1913 reprinting of the ordinary turul and Franz Joseph set appeared with the same War Aid message printed over the main designs.(8.51) The inscriptions were carefully arranged not to obscure St Stephen's Crown or the portrait of Franz Joseph.

Only in November 1916 were specially designed Hungarian war charity stamps issued, but two images commissioned from the celebrated graphic designer Joseph Diveky were particularly striking.(8.52) The 10f featured a soldier in a trench with bayonet fixed ready to defend his position or make a charge, and the 15f showed an infantryman swinging his rifle by its barrel in hand-

8.50 1913 3f Franz Joseph Flood Relief Fund overprinted for the War Aid charities (from set 7 October 1914+)

8.51 1913 10f Turul and 2k Franz Joseph with War Aid overprint (from set 10 January 1915+)

8.52 *War Charity 10f and 15f infantrymen (15 November 1916) and 40f turul departing its lair (1 May 1917)*

8.53 *5f harvesters and 50f Hungarian Parliament (from set 1 November 1916+)*

8.54 *10f + 1k harvesters with War Exhibition overprint (15 September 1917)*

8.55 *25f King Charles and 50f Queen Zita (from set 30 August 1918)*

8.56 *10f Charles and 40f Zita overprinted KOZTARSASAG (from series 23 November 1918)*

to-hand combat. In May 1917 a third equally evocative stamp by another renowned artist, Jeno Haranghy, was added featuring an aggressive looking turul wearing the Holy Crown of Hungary, clutching a scimitar, and about to soar into battle from its mountain lair. Each stamp carried a 2f premium.

In October and November 1916 a pair of stamps that came to symbolize Hungarian philately were issued featuring a pair of harvesters cutting and binding sheaves of wheat.(8.53) Reissued several times in lengthy sets in slightly different formats during and long after the war they celebrated the essential and enduring role of rural life and agriculture. An accompanying issue in November 1916 highlighting Hungary's national identity featured the Parliament in Budapest. This, too, was reused several times. In the event, a more ephemeral 1916 issue was the pair of stamps featuring King Charles and Queen Zita on the day of their coronation, 30 December (see 8.13).

In an attempt to hold Transleithania together as civil and military unrest mounted, an extensive War Exhibition, with profits going to charities, was staged on an island in the Danube at Budapest under the auspices of the Hapsburg Archduke Joseph August, an army commander and unusually popular with his Hungarian soldiers. Two 'harvester' stamps were duly issued, one in September 1917 and another in May 1918, overprinted *Jozsef foherczeg vezerezredes hadi kiallitasa 1 korona* (Archduke Joseph Colonel General War Exhibition 1 crown). (8.54) They carried a 1k premium.

By autumn 1918 industrial strikes organized by desperately war-weary workers and Socialist and Communist agitators were common, and there was little energy or interest left in the Hungarian government to pursue the war or exercise authority over restless ethnic minorities, let alone save the Dual Monarchy or dynasty. On 30 August a new pair of stamps was issued picturing Charles and Zita wearing their Hungarian crowns, and these proved to be the last Kingdom of Hungary issues.(8.55) It was not, though, the final time these stamps were used.

On 31 October Count Mihaly Karolyi together with many army units and supporters of his new Hungarian National Council rose in revolt to seize Budapest's public buildings, force the prime minister to resign, and secure King Charles's recognition of the coup and formal appointment of Karolyi as Prime Minister. Through the flowers worn as recognition symbols by the rebels, it became known as the Aster Revolution. The union between Austria and Hungary was quickly dissolved. On 13 November Charles surrendered all authority as King of Hungary although significantly he did not abdicate, and on 16 November Karolyi became President of the new Hungarian People's Republic. On 23 November an array of wartime stamps, and, ironically, the recent Charles and Zita pair, appeared hurriedly overprinted *KOZTARSASAG*

(REPUBLIC).(8.56) The overprint was diagonal and went straight across the images.   In a further sign of the dramatic change, in January 1919 the harvester and Parliament stamps were reissued with the non-royal inscription *Magyar Posta* (Hungarian Post).(8.57)

Count Karolyi was a wealthy aristocrat turned pacifist and socialist, but sadly ill-suited to politics and post-war negotiations. He denied Hungary the future option of armed force by demobilizing much of the army, failed to dissuade the Slovaks, Romanians and Ruthenians from petitioning the Allies to break up the country, and completely underestimated the harshness of the Allies' attitude towards Hungary.   And all the while Hungary continued to endure the hardship wrought by the Allied blockade as no peace treaty, only an armistice, had been signed.

On 19 March Karolyi and all Hungary were shocked when the French ordered the remnants of the Hungarian army to retreat back from their border stations.   A little earlier Karolyi's disgruntled Social Democrat partners in government had allied with the Communists led by Bela Kun, and on 21 March they forced Karolyi to resign, and announced the new Hungarian Soviet Republic.   At the same time they affirmed that French advances and all Italian, Czech and Romanian territorial encroachments would be fiercely resisted.   On 5 May, though, the French forces holding the Arad area in the far east of Hungary pointedly issued an assortment of Hungarian harvesters, Parliament, and Charles and Zita stamps overprinted *Occupation francaise* (French Occupation). (8.58)

The disputes over the post war borders flared into open warfare, and Hungary's neighbours seized every opportunity to stake their territorial claims.   Initially crude locally applied overprints on Hungarian stamps often marked territory occupied by the Romanians and Croatians but these were soon replaced.(8.59)

During the Romanian occupation of Banat and Backsa the Temesvar postal authority overprinted an assortment of Hungarian stamps with *Banat Bacska 1919* in various styles(8.60).   In Debrecen the Romanians overprinted Hungarian stamps with a circle enclosing the inscriptions *REGATUL ROMANIE* (Kingdom of Romania) or an oval with *ZONA DE OCUPATIE 1919 ROMANA* (Romanian Zone of Occupation 1919).(8.61/8.62)   Within the overprints were the back to back 'F' monogram of King Ferdinand of Romania and the letters P.T.T. for Posts, Telegraphs and Telephone.

And in occupied Baranya the Serbs issued Hungarian stamps overprinted *Baranya 1919* in several different formats.(8.63) Often new values were added.

As early as July 1917 Serbian, Croatian, Slovenian and Montenegrin delegates had agreed they would form a new united nation, and on 1 December 1918 the Kingdom of the Serbs, Croats and Slovenes had been

8.57 3f harvesters and 2k Parliament inscribed MAGYAR POSTA (from set January 1919)

8.58 40f harvesters overprinted KOZTARSASAG and overprinted again Occupation francaise (from series 5 May 191)9

8.59 Magyar Kir. Posta 25f harvesters with locally applied Romanian Arms overprint (1918-19)

8.60 Magyar Kir. Posta 6f harvesters overprinted KOZTARSASAG and Banat, Bacska 1919, and 10k Parliament overprinted Banat, Bacska (from series July 1919)

8.61 50f Parliament overprinted REGATUL ROMANIE (from series 1919)

8.62 3f harvesters and 40f Zita overprinted ZONA DE OCUPATIE 1919 ROMANA (from series 20 November 1919)

8.63 5f harvesters and 20f Charles overprinted Baranya 1919 (from series 5 May 1919)

8.64 *5f harvesters and 20f Charles variously overprinted SHS HRVATSKA (from series 18 November 1918+)*

8.65 *Hungarian Soviet Republic: 45f Sandor Petofi, 60f Ignac Martinovics and 75f Gyorgy Dozsa (from set 14 June 1919)*

proclaimed – all of it on ex-Dual Monarchy territory. Numerous Hungarian stamps were overprinted SHS *HRVATSKA* (Serbs, Croats, Slovenes: Croatia) by a Croatian provisional assembly.(8.64)

Despite such troubles, in June 1919 a set of five Hungarian stamps celebrated the new Bolshevik era with portraits of the Communist theorists, Karl Marx and Frederic Engels, and three historic Hungarian revolutionaries.(8.65) The common thread was the struggle of the common people, and each stamp bore the inscription *MAGYAR TANACS KOZTARSAGAG* (Hungarian Soviet Republic). The Bolsheviks fully appreciated the importance of dramatic publicity.

Sandor Petofi (1823-49) (45f) was Hungary's national poet. His poem *Nemzeti Dal* (National Song) and co-authorship of the *Twelve Demands* to the Imperial government helped inspire the 1848 revolution. He joined the revolutionary army, and was either killed during its defeat by Russia at the battle of Segesvar on 31 July 1849 or captured and died in Siberia. One of his last poems, *Az Apostol* (The Apostle) is about a revolutionary who endures great suffering but fails in his objective of slaying a merciless king. His fame endured as a visionary poet and revolutionary martyr, and in 1911 his statue was erected in Pressburg (only to be destroyed soon after the area was ceded to Czechoslovakia in 1918).

Ignac Martinovics (1755-95) (60f) was a Hungarian philosopher, and former government secret agent, who became enamoured with French Revolutionary egalitarianism and was executed for attempting to stir up a peasants' revolt.

Gyorgy Dozsa (1470-1514) (75f) was a Transylvanian knight who was ordered by Tamas Bakocz, the Hungarian chancellor, to form a crusading army against the encroaching Turks. He recruited and trained some 40,000 peasants, but enthusiasm faded when supplies of food and clothing dried up, and landlords, angry at the loss of farm workers, oppressed the volunteers' families. The crusade was cancelled and the rebellious army vented its fury on the gentry; thousands were slaughtered and hundreds of castles and manors destroyed. Dozsa sympathized with, and subsequently led, the revolt. However his peasants were no match for the well-armed forces of the aristocracy that eventually won a decisive victory. Dozsa himself was executed on a red hot metal throne wearing a red hot mock crown.

In July 1919 the Soviet Republic also issued harvesters and Parliament stamps overprinted *Magyar Tanacs Koztarsasag*, but by then the radical regime was in serious difficulties.(8.66) The forced creation of collective farms rather than encouraging peasant holdings, and the requisitioning of crops by the Red Militia, soon divided the government from its key supporters. On 24 June an anti-communist coup failed, and Communist police and tribunals wreaked savage revenge – the 'Red Terror'. Long before then Bela Kun had failed to reach agreement with the Allies over border controls, and the new Hungarian volunteer Red Army had offered endless provocation but no effective opposition to determined French demands to clear the borders. Adding to the chaos, outright war had broken out between Bela Kun's Red Army and Czech and Romanian forces.

After months of fighting, the Romanians triumphed and occupied much of Hungary, taking Budapest on 4 August 1919. After just 133 days in power Bela Kun fled, the Red Army collapsed, little effective government remained, and a vengeful 'White Terror' spread across

8.66 *January 1919 6f harvesters and 3k Parliament overprinted MAGYAR TANACS KOZTARSASAG (from set 21 July 1919)*

8.67 *40f turul in lair overprinted KOZTARSASAG and overprinted again MAGYAR NEMZETI KORMANY Szeged 1919 (from series 28 June 1919)*

the country. During Bela Kun's brief regime a Conservative and Royalist counter-revolution had begun in the southern city of Szeged with the quiet connivance of the French occupying authorities. Calling itself the Hungarian National Government it had bided its time until Kun's collapse, but with French permission it had issued a wide variety of Hungarian stamps overprinted *MAGYAR NEMZETI KORMANY Szeged 1919* (Hungarian National Government, Szeged 1919).(8.67)

Led by Istvan Bethlen, a Transylvanian aristocrat, and Admiral Miklos Horthy, the former commander-in-chief of the Austro-Hungarian navy, the counter-revolution now spread across the country, hunting out and summarily executing all Communists, and many of their liberal sympathisers too. All this came on top of extensive looting by the Romanian army that refused to evacuate the country until forced by the Allies. Finally, on 16 November 1919, Admiral Horthy and his army ceremonially entered Budapest on behalf of, and indeed creators of, a new government. On the same day several harvester stamps appeared overprinted *A nemzeti hadsereg bevonulasa 1919 XI/16* (The entry of the national army 16 XI 1919).(8.68)

In January 1920 all stocks of definitive harvesters and Parliament stamps were issued overprinted with ears or sheaves of corn wrapped in a celebratory ribbon inscribed *1919*.(8.69) In a deeply symbolic as well as pragmatic act, the new black overprints overlay the red Bela Kun ones. The symbols offered hope and prosperity, and later that year Hungarians had the opportunity to vote in the country's first secret ballot election – which confirmed the right wing Horthy/Bethlen government in power.

With active opposition brutally crushed, the right wing government gradually claimed wide support. But by now, though, the Paris Peace Treaty had reduced Hungary to a territorial shadow of its pre-war self. Slovakia had gone to Czechoslovakia, and Banat, Backa

8.68 10f harvesters overprinted A nemzeti hadsereg bevonulasa 1919 XI/16 (from set 16 November 1919)

8.69 6f harvesters and 1k 40 Parliament variously overprinted with sheaf of corn ringed with the date 1919 obliterating (almost) the Soviet Republic's inscription (from series 27 January 1920)

8.70 15f harvesters overprinted NYUGAT MAGYARORAZAG ORSZVE, new value, and WESTUNGARN ORGLAND (from series October 1921+), and 1k view inscribed Lajtabansag Posta (from local set October 1921+)

and Baranya had been shared out between Romania and the Kingdom of Serbs, Croats and Slovenes with just a thin slice around Szeged staying in Hungary. In June 1920 Hungary had little choice but to formalize these losses with the Allies in the Treaty of Trianon. Many Hungarians now found themselves living in new neighbouring countries against which Hungary bore a deep grudge throughout the coming decades.

In the autumn of 1921 several Hungarian stamps suddenly appeared overprinted *NYUGAT MAGYARORAZAG ORSZVE* and *WESTUNGARN ORGLAND* (Western Hungary in Hungarian and German) and new filler and kroner values. They came from Lajtabansag, a region in the former Kingdom of Hungary not far to the east of Vienna. As its inhabitants were primarily German speakers it was awarded to Austria, but a force of Hungarian revolutionaries seized the area, and for a month, from 4 October until they were ejected on 5 November 1921, they sought to establish their own state. Stamps were a symbol of authority and time was even found to produce a specially designed set.(8.70)

Hungary had lost most of its timber resources, iron ore, industrial plants and financial institutions, and was land locked. It was led Admiral Horthy, an admiral without a port or navy, and soon it was to be a kingdom without a king. In March 1920 the National Assembly declared Hungary was still a kingdom, and Horthy was elected Regent. However, although Royalist elements twice sought to secure the restoration of Charles in 1921, and Charles himself returned to Hungary full of optimism, there was little hope of success. The Allies opposed it and so did all Hungary's neighbours, and threatened war if he neared the throne again. Probably wisely, if perhaps selfishly too, Horthy himself offered no support. Charles was ignominiously dispatched in a British destroyer to Madeira where he died on 1 April 1922.

Admiral Horthy and Istvan Bethlen, his prime minister from 1921 to 1931, created stability and a degree of national unity; gradually the economy strengthened, deals were sealed with trades unions, and international relations improved. Just one set in aid of returning prisoners of war recalled not only the horrors

8.71 *Returned Prisoners of War Fund (set 11 March 1920)*

8.72 *TB Relief Fund (set 8 April 1924)*

8.73 *500k harvesters and 2,000k Parliament (from set 1 June 1924+)*

8.75 *40k Death of Petofi, and 50k Petofi addressing the people (from set 13 January 1923)*

8.74 *5,000k Madonna and Child (from set February 1921+)*

of the world war but also the equally vicious fighting afterwards. Issued in March 1920 the set had dramatic images of a prison camp, a prisoner trudging through the snow, and a family reunion. Each one is inscribed SEGITSSUK HAZA VEREINKET (Help our people go home).(8.71)

Across Hungary, as elsewhere in Europe, tuberculosis was a major killer and 1924 saw a relief fund set centred upon folk images of a naked child of Nature, a mother rocking a cradle and a hunter teaching a youth to draw a bow. (8.72)

Between 1920 and 1924 the harvesters and Parliament stamps were reprinted with new colours and the pre-war inscription of MAGYAR KIR. POSTA (Hungarian Royal Post).(8.73) This reinforced Regent Horthy's own unusual semi-royal status, if not the return of the Hapsburgs. The high values of 1923 and 1924 additions to the set – up to 2,000k – revealed Hungary's susceptibility to the ravages of inflation until currency reforms were put in hand in 1925-26.

Several dramatically designed sets reinforced the national identity, and Hungarian culture and religion were key subjects. Between 1921 and 1925 ten stamps featured the Madonna and Child with the inscription *PATRONA HUNGARIAE* (The Patron of Hungary).(8.74)

In 1923 the national poet Sandor Petofi was commemorated in romantic and triumphant style befitting his passionate revolutionary works.(8.75) As we have seen, he had had the distinction of being honoured in Bela Kun's 1919 Bolshevik set (see 8.65) prior to this issue by Horthy's right wing government a few dramatic years later. Petofi was too potent a symbol to be left to the Communists.

In 1926 the first set with the new currency of filler and pengo adroitly used images of St Stephen's Crown, the Matthias Church in Budapest, Budapest's royal palace and the Madonna and Child.(8.76) The set maintained the fiction of the continuity of the Kingdom of Hungary; Franz Joseph and Charles had taken their coronation oaths outside the Matthias Church.

In 1927 the much revered turul returned in triumphant, but not aggressive, poses on the new Air stamps.(8.77) They replaced the unfortunate Air set of 1924 that pictured Icarus – the headstrong Greek who perished when he flew too close to the sun and his waxed

THE AUSTRO-HUNGARIAN EMPIRE, THE AUSTRIAN REPUBLIC AND REGENCY HUNGARY

8.76 (E) *8f St Stephen's Crown, 16f Matthias Church, 40f Royal Palace, 1p Madonna and Child (from set 26 March 1926+)*

 8.77 *72f soaring turul (from Air set 1 September 1927)*

 8.79 *8f Admiral Horthy (from set 1 March 1930)*

 8.78 *2,000k Icarus over Budapest (from Air set 4 April 1924+)*

wings melted.(8.78)

In 1930 Miklos Horthy himself finally featured on a set marking the 10th anniversary of the Regency.(8.79). No-one now expected a king to appear. Hungary seemed secure in its new contracted role. By then, though, depression was sweeping across Europe, and within a few years Hungary was soon to take the deceptively attractive step of closer cooperation with Hitler's Germany and be drawn inexorably into the Second World War.

Archduke Franz Ferdinand and his wife photographed in their car a few minutes before their assassination in Sarajevo on 28 June 1914. Commemorative postcard issued with set of stamps June 1917.

CHAPTER 9
Czechoslovakia

Under the Dual Monarchy established in 1867 Slovakia was part of the Kingdom of Hungary while the Czechs in Bohemia and Moravia (later to be the western half of Czechoslovakia) lay within the Austrian Empire.

This division went back to the Battle of Mohacs in 1526 when medieval Hungary, including much of Slovakia, was lost to the Ottoman Turks. However Bohemia, Moravia and western Slovakia escaped, and elected the Hapsburg Archduke Ferdinand (1503-64) as king. In 1558 he became Holy Roman Emperor, and the Imperial annexation of Bohemia and Moravia was complete.

However the Czech and Slovak languages, cultures and folk memories of historic greatness survived, most noticeably in Bohemia where powerful kings such as Premsyl Otakar II (1253-78) had, many centuries ago, dominated the region. Independence, though, remained an unfulfilled dream during the 1848-49 revolution, but the dream subsequently intensified alongside all the other nationalist aspirations disturbing Franz Joseph's Empire and Kingdom.

The Czechs envied the stunning 1867 success of the neighbouring Kingdom of Hungary. There was, though, little support for Czech aspirations within the essentially German-speaking Austrian Empire, and the Germans living in Bohemia itself were particularly hostile. The Czechs were represented on the Cisleithanian (Imperial Austrian) National Council but remained a minority bloc.

As the Turks were gradually pushed back from the later seventeenth century the Slovaks also fell under Hapsburg rule, but within the highly repressive Kingdom of Hungary they possessed fainter voices than the Czechs in Austria. They also endured - but survived - far greater attempts to crush their cultural identity and language.

From 1914 many Czechs and Slovaks within the Dual Monarchy were conscripted but they possessed little enthusiasm for fighting for their Austrian or Hungarian overlords against fellow Russian and Serbian Slavs. In contrast Czech and Slovak groups living within the Russian Empire successfully petitioned Tsar Nicholas II to allow volunteers to fight alongside his armies. A small unit was attached to the Russian Third Army as early as October 1914. The Russian government barred recruitment from the thousands of Czechs and Slovaks taken prisoners of war, but in some places the hard-pressed Russian military authorities proved more sympathetic. By the end of 1916 the Czechoslovak Rifle Brigade comprised three regiments. It achieved fame in July 1917 by seizing Austrian trenches in the Battle of Zborov during the Kerensky Offensive ordered by the Russian Provisional Government after the Tsar's abdication. After Zborov the prison camps were opened for recruitment, and by 1918 the Czech Legion had 40,000 men in two divisions, each with four regiments.

Other volunteer units of the Czech Legion were formed in France where they were heavily involved in battles around Arras in 1915, and two new regiments were created from prisoners of war and overseas volunteers in 1918. In Italy Czech and Slovak prisoners of war formed reconnaissance and propaganda units and, later, a combat regiment.

The Czech Legions were a potent publicity weapon, and gave added weight to the skilled diplomacy of Czech and Slovak nationalist politicians arguing their case in Russia, France, Italy, Great Britain and the USA. A key figure was the charismatic Milan Stefanik (1880-1919). Born in Slovakia, by August 1914 he was a renowned astronomer and astrophysicist based in France and already using his world-wide connections to promote the idea of Czech and Slovak unity and independence. He became a French General and then Minister of War within the new Czechoslovak National Council – the increasingly influential Czech and Slovak nationalist movement. He coordinated and publicised the Czech Legion, and was instrumental in bringing other key nationalists such as the future Czechoslovak Presidents, Tomas Masaryk and Edvard Benes, into constructive dialogue with key French, Italian and American politicians.

Edvard Benes (1884-1948) was a Czech academic but also an early member of the anti-Austrian resistance movement. In voluntary wartime exile in Paris he championed the independence campaign and became Secretary of the Czechoslovak National Council and Minister of the Interior and Foreign Affairs. Tomas

Masaryk (1850-1937) was also an academic, and also effectively championed independence during the war in Italy, Great Britain, Russia, the USA and France. He ensured the Czech Legions worked as closely as possible with Allied armies, and through contact with the sympathetic American President, Woodrow Wilson, he secured powerful support for the independence movement. Indeed, while the Dual Monarchy was still crumbling the Allies recognised Masaryk as head of the Czechoslovak Provisional government on 14 October 1918, and on 14 November the National Assembly in Prague elected him President of the new Czechoslovak Republic.

In early 1918 the Czech Legion in Russia found itself stranded in a vast country wracked by civil war, and the object of widespread Bolshevik suspicions. After fighting the Germans at Bakhmah in the Ukraine in March 1918, the Legion struggled eastwards, sometimes seizing trains, sometimes fighting Bolshevik units, and sometimes having to capture whole towns, before moving slowly on towards Vladivostok and, hopefully, embarkation home. The tsar and his family were executed in Ykaterinburg just a week before the Legion seized the town. The dogged, and ultimately successful, campaign lasted until September 1920 and included active cooperation with White Russian forces ranging across Siberia. Finally, though, in the face of the Red Army's relentless advance the Czech Legion had to abandon further cooperation and sail home where many battle-hardened legionnaires joined the new Czechoslovak Republican army.

From December 1919 the Legion had issued stamps for its members' use and for general sale along the Trans Siberian railway sections it controlled. Nine values featured the Lion of Bohemia; the other three pictured a church in Irkutsk (25k), the armoured train *Orlik* (50k), and a sentry (1r).(9.1) The Siberian town of Irkutsk had been a centre for exiles under the tsars, including the Decembrist rebels, and had thrived culturally. For a while it was a Czech Legion centre, and saw bitter fighting between Red and White Russian forces. *Orlik*, the heavily armoured and powerfully gunned train, had been built for the Russian army in 1916 and used in the Galicia campaign before being seized by the Red Army and then captured by the Czech Legion who gave it its name. They used it primarily as a powerful rear defence as they moved slowly eastwards.

By the time the Legion returned home General Stefanik was dead, killed in a mysterious aeroplane crash near Bratislava in May 1919 that excited great controversy as Hungarian Communist forces were still contesting this area of Slovakia with the Czechoslovak Republican army. And although the Versailles peace settlement had sanctioned an independent Czechoslovakia it simmered with widespread discontent. Despite Hungarian protests a large and discontented Hungarian minority found itself living in southern Czechoslovakia. In addition a large and discontented Sudeten German minority found itself living within western Czechoslovakia. Masaryk had been successful in persuading the Peace Conference to override the Sudetenland's overwhelming preference for inclusion in Germany or Austria. With Allied approval, he had also wrested Subcarpathian Ruthenia (in Western Ukraine) from Hungary and this now formed the far eastern province of Czechoslovakia. It had required, though, a short but vicious war against Bela Kun's Red Army to secure control.

Not surprisingly stamps from this tumultuous period glorified the birth of the new republic. In October 1918 the nascent National Government, still known as the Revolutionary Council, issued two stamps in Prague for general use, but primarily on its own mail. Featuring the two tailed crowned lion rampant of Bohemia they

9.1 25k church in Irkutsk, 50k armoured train Orlik, and 1r sentry (set January 1920).

EUROPEAN STAMP ISSUES AND THE FIRST WORLD WAR

9.2 10h National Government/Czech Scout Post (pair October 1918), and 20h Emperor Charles overprinted with Bohemian lion and CESKO SLOVENSKY STAT (from series November 1918)

9.4 10h Hradcany without rising sun and foreground tree and 300h Hradcany without rising sun but with shaded tree (from set 1919+)

9.3 1h and 3h Hradcany with the rising sun and 'white' tree but different shading and inscription styles (from set December 1918+) The 3h was issued imperforate but subsequently perforated at a local post office.

9.5 Alphonse Mucha's dove designs – the 2h Newspaper and 2h Newspaper Express stamps (from sets 1918+)

9.6 Registered cover with the Czechoslovak Legion Commemoration and First Anniversary of Independence set issued 27 October 1919 and postmarked Ober Hennersdorf in the Sudetenland dated 28 October 1919.

were inscribed *Posta Ceskych Skautu* (Czech Scout Post), signifying the method of delivery, and *Ve Sluzbach Narodni Vlady* (On the Service of the National Government). Legend has it that when the 12th century Emperor Frederick granted Bohemia a new coat of arms he ordered the lion to have two tails as he disliked the original design of a lion with its tail between its legs. Alongside these, Austrian stamps continued in use until early 1919, sometimes without overprinting but often with locally applied handstamps featuring Bohemia's lion and the key words CESKO SLOVENSKY STAT (Czech Slovakian State).(9.2)

From December 1918 a lengthy Art Nouveau set appeared featuring Hradcany (Prague Castle), the historic seat of several Kings of Bohemia and now the presidential palace and symbol of republican independence.(9.3) It highlighted the Czech city of Prague's dominance over the country, and notably over Slovakia. The Czech designer was Alphonse Mucha who explained the leaves in the upper corners represented awakening, the rising sun heralded the new day that was announced by the roosters in the lower corners, and the hearts were signs of the desire for peace. The picture was slightly amended for reissuing in 1919-20, probably for the sake of clarity, but it meant the rising sun, and its symbolism, was omitted.(9.4) Many values appeared in different shades and perforation types.

Peaceful emblems of doves by Mucha adorned the early Postage Due sets, and an Art Nouveau windhover with outstretched wings featured on Newspaper stamps.(9.5) Later on, though, ordinary definitive stamps overprinted *DOPLATIT* (TO PAY) were deemed sufficient for Postage Dues.

These early stamps were inscribed Cesko-Slovenska in tacit acknowledgement of the two distinct halves of the republic, but when the set jointly commemorating the first anniversary of the republic and the achievements of the Czech Legion appeared from 27 October 1919 the hyphen had disappeared.(9.6) The Czech Legion stamps portrayed, no doubt symbolically, a mother embracing her son. It was, though, inscribed *Sirotam Nasich Legionaru* (An orphan of our legion), and profits from sales went to the orphans. The Czech anniversary stamps pictured the two tailed lion breaking free of his chains – once more concentrating upon the Czechs rather than the Slovaks. The western-looking Czechs and eastern-looking Slovaks were finding they had little in common except the initial desire to wrench themselves free from the Austrians and Hungarians.

Stamps from the old Austrian Empire and Kingdom of Hungary were permitted for Czechoslovak mail until 15 March 1919. That December vast quantities of redundant Dual Monarchy stamps from a variety of sets were made available overprinted *POSTA CESKOSLOVENSKA 1919* in Prague's Philatelic Bureau

9.7 1917 25f Austrian Emperor Charles and 1918 10f Hungarian King Charles overprinted *POSTA CESKOSLOVENSKA 1919* (from series 12 December 1919+)

9.8 100h and 200h Allegories of the Republic (from set 1 June 1920+)

9.9 80h Hussite (from set 1 June 1920+)

for 50% over face value.(9.7) These stamps could be used for postage up to 31 January 1920, with the premium earmarked for various charities.

Further allegorical designs appeared in 1920 in a long set interspersing images of a captive breaking free of chains with a crouching figure holding open a blossoming book and clasping a sheaf of corn.(9.8) By the crouching figure a plant was entwining itself around a sword embedded in the ground. The page of the book was blank, perhaps signifying a new chapter was about to be written, and the sword was still shiny and supporting the plant, highlighting the continuing need for armed vigilance.

Two values in the set featured a medieval Czech Hussite holding a chalice, and recalled the long and bloody wars of the fifteenth century, partly fuelled by religious schism and partly by resistance to Holy Roman Empire invasions.(9.9) Coming at a time when discontented minorities abounded, and borders were barely settled, the stamps were a vivid reminder of the perils of internal dissent, but also of the nation's determination to resist outside interference.

Jan Hus, rector of Prague University, had incurred German and Roman Catholic enmity by his vocal criticisms of papal wealth and corruption, and persistent advocacy of a purer, simpler, but strictly disciplined faith based upon the Bible. Many Czechs supported him, but many Germans within and beyond Bohemia rose in

9.11 Souvenir postcard with 40h and pre-printed 50h Tomas Masaryk cancelled with a special 75th birthday first day of issue handstamp in Prague, 7 March 1925.

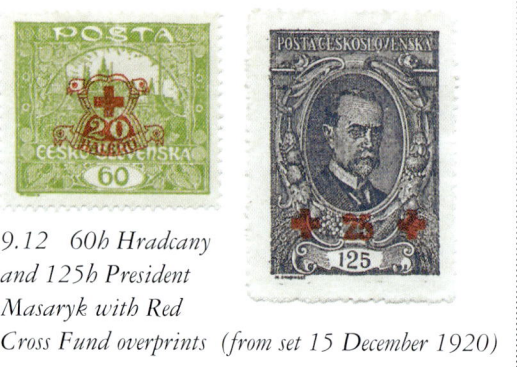

9.12 60h Hradcany and 125h President Masaryk with Red Cross Fund overprints (from set 15 December 1920)

opposition. King Wenceslas of Bohemia turned against him, largely because the monarch received a percentage of the sale of indulgences for the remission of sins, and Hus was burned at the stake for heresy in 1415.

A long and bitter religious war wracked the country, and whenever they could each side resorted to savage persecutions of its religious opponents. In 1436, with the Protestant Hussites in the ascendancy, the Compacts of Basel seemed to reconcile the Roman Catholic Church to key Hussite beliefs regarding the communion liturgy, freedom of preaching, the redistribution of church lands, and the public exposure of sinners, but the pope rejected it, thereby sparking off further decades of conflict. Bohemia finally settled down after 1485 when the Czech Catholics, well aware that the country was now largely Hussite, grudgingly accepted the Compacts.

In July 1920 Czechoslovakia and Poland finally accepted the Allied division of Eastern Silesia between them after being at loggerheads since the Armistice over their respective borders in this coal rich region (see also Poland). Amidst strikes and violence an initial agreement had crumbled, a plebiscite had been ordered but then cancelled when both Czechs and Poles decided they preferred the Allies to sort the border out. In a sure sign of the sensitivities, the new border divided the Silesian city of Teschen in two – one half became Polish Cieszyn and the other Czechoslovakia's Cersky Tesin. The solution was accepted because Poland was otherwise engaged in a war with the Soviet Union, and the Czechs were pleased to receive the invaluable industrial area. The French led Allied peace-keeping force allowed each country to issue overprinted postage stamps in permitted areas to publicise and fund the ultimately aborted 1920 plebiscite.(9.10)

President Masaryk's status as a creator of the state ensured he appeared on numerous issues from 1920 onwards.(9.11) The designs changed slightly, including the length of his drooping moustache, but most used the authoritative portrait by the famous Czech artist, Max Svabinsky.

Not surprisingly his image was chosen for several charity issues. In December 1920 one of them along with two Hradcany values were issued overprinted with a heart and surcharged 20h in aid of the Red Cross.(9.12) In October 1923 a high value set of four President Masaryk stamps inscribed *1918 28/X 1923* marked the fifth anniversary of the republic, with the premium going to the Red Cross and other charities.(9.13)

9.10 1920 6h Newspaper overprinted SO 1920 (for Silesie Orientale 1920) (from set 13 February 1920)

9.13   300h+300h President Masaryk inscribed 1918 28/X 1923 (from set 28 October 1923)

9.14   1923 200h+200h President Masaryk overprinted CONGRES OLYMP. INTERNAT. PRAHA 1925 (from set 11 May 1925)

9.15   1923 50h+50h President Masaryk overprinted VIII. SLET VSESOKOLSKY PRAHA 1926 (from set 1 June 1926)

9.16   40h National Arms (from set 10 April 1929)

In May 1925 three Masaryk stamps were reissued overprinted *CONGRES OLYMP. INTERNAT. PRAHA 1925* (INTERNATIONAL OLYMPIC CONGRESS PRAGUE 1925).(9.14) Sold at double face value, the premiums went to a Post Office employees' charity and to swell national Olympic funds. The Congress was noted for the address by Baron Pierre de Coubertin, the idealistic father of the modern Olympic Games, that sternly condemned all thoughts of professional athletes and nationalist jealousies contaminating the event.

In June 1926 four Masaryk stamps were reissued overprinted *VIII. SLET VSESOKOLSKY PRAHA 1926* (VIIIth ALL SOKOL GATHERING PRAGUE 1926).(9.15) The Sokol movement, which began in Prague in 1862, was based upon the Greek ideal of 'a sound body in a sound mind' and sought through educational courses, physical exercises and group activities to strengthen not only each participant's moral, intellectual and physical health but also that of the nation. It spread rapidly throughout Slavic countries, and periodically thousands of members participated in huge displays of marching, gymnastics, athletics and dancing called 'slets', a Czech word meaning 'the gathering of birds'. 'Sokol' itself is Czech for 'falcon'. Under the Dual Monarchy the movement developed nationalistic and even militaristic attributes and aroused strong Austrian and German opposition, and many disgruntled Sokol devotees joined the Czech Legion and preached disaffection. Both Tomas Masaryk and Edvard Benes were members, and welcomed the 'slets' as unifiers of the nation.

It would take until 1929 for the first stamps to appear featuring the republic's National Arms – the shields of Slovakia, Moravia, Carpathian Ruthenia and Silesia superimposed by the shield of Bohemia.(9.16) During and after the war the components, colours and design of the flag and arms had attracted huge attention. Little agreement was reached, so in May 1919 a white and red flag was adopted temporarily, and then Slovakia successfully agitated for the inclusion of a large blue triangle to represent it. The final all-embracing coat of arms was almost a compromise of exhaustion, and rarely used except on state occasions. Visually it represented the cultural and historic tensions that would pull the country apart rather than the ideas that united it.

The first full set promoting the country's natural beauty and historic sights did not appear until 1926 and was slowly extended until 1931.(9.17 overleaf) Several values featured castles. Karlstejn Castle (Karlov Tyn) was situated 30 kilometres south-west of Prague. Its construction was ordered by the Emperor Charles IV (1347-78), who was also King of Bohemia from 1346, to house the crown jewels of Bohemia and signify the central role of Bohemia in his domain. Pernsteyn Castle was 40 kilometres north-west of Brno; built in the later 13th century it was for several centuries the fortress home of the powerful lords of Medlov. Prague figured prominently with stamps featuring Hradcany, the statue of St Wenceslas, Bohemia's celebrated 10th century king, and Strahov Monastery founded in 1143. Just two stamps featured Slovakia. Orava Castle was constructed on a rocky outcrop above the Orava River as a fortress against the Mongols and then against the Ottoman Turks. The final image pictured the wild Upper Tatra Mountains still the home of brown bears, wolves, lynx, wild boar, deer and chamois, which bordered Slovakia and Poland.

In the 1920s Masaryk's authority went a long way to ensuring the republic's disparate ethnic groups held together and that democratic processes were followed. The republican government confiscated the estates of German and Austrian aristocrats, and partitioned them to Czech and Slovak farmers. There was investment in

9.17 (E) *1k 20 Karlov Tyn, 1k 20 Straho, 2k Hradcany and 4k Upper Tatra (from set 1 June 1926+)*

railways to ensure all major cities in the lengthy new state were well connected. Relations with Romania, Yugoslavia and even Germany improved, although they remained strained with Hungary, Poland and Austria.

In late October 1928 an eclectic set of stamps helped mark Czechoslovakia's tenth anniversary.(9.18) The populist images highlighted the nation's evolution towards democracy while dwelling on its stunning landscapes and thought-provoking historic sites. One stamp pictured President Masaryk while others featured the renowned Tatra Mountains, the massive new telephone exchange in Prague, the ancient towns halls in Levoca and Prague, the celebrated pilgrimage site of Velehrad, the wooden village of Jasina in Carpathian Ruthenia where a short-live independent republic was proclaimed after the war, Hradek Castle in Kutna Hora where the grisly bone chapel was a reminder of the Hussite Wars, and the stunning Hluboka Castle owned, and still occupied, by the celebrated Schwarzenberg family which was, though, now stripped of its aristocratic status.

By and large during the 1920s Czech political parties cooperated rather than fought, the country remained peaceful, and its prosperity increased. The 1930s were different though. Following hard upon the world depression, a combination of factors including the rise of Nazism and heightened international tension, the ethnic disunity within the country, and the enduring hostility of its neighbours, began to threaten its stability and were, within a few years, to tear it apart.

9.18 (E) *50h Telephone Exchange, Prague, 60h Jasina, and 1k Hluboka Castle (from set 22 October 1928)*

CHAPTER 10
Italy

The diminutive King Victor Emmanuel III of the Royal House of Savoy succeeded to the throne of Italy in 29 July 1900 after his father, the arch-conservative Umberto, had been assassinated by one of the many anarchists stalking the royal houses of Europe. The new king inherited a country whose territorial ambitions and desire for recognition as a 'Great Power' were boundless – despite the rural poverty, the crippling expenditure on the army and navy, and the opposition of all those seeking welfare reform.

There had been no Kingdom of Italy until 1861, merely an historic collection of small states ruled by the Hapsburgs Emperors, the Pope, and several independent dukes, counts and kings. The initiative for unification had been taken by Victor Emmanuel's grandfather Victor Emmanuel II, King of Piedmont-Sardinia, and his dynamic prime minister Count Camillo di Cavour. In the mid-nineteenth century a dramatic series of popular revolts, brief wars and depositions had witnessed the annexation of the Duchies of Modena, Parma and Lucca, the Grand Duchy of Tuscany, the Kingdom of the Two Sicilies (Sicily and Naples) and the Papal States.

The period became known as *Il Risorgimento* (The Resurrection) and the very name hinted at the reclamation of Imperial Roman glory. The charismatic warrior Guiseppe Garibaldi was its renowned champion and a gift to propagandists, especially in his stunning military successes in the Two Sicilies, but it was the canny Cavour who achieved the all-important political victory. It was he who secured the international isolation of Austria-Hungary as an ogre of repression, and soured the reputation of the Kingdom of the Two Sicilies as the final bastion of Bourbon authoritarianism. It was he who gained the timely military support of Napoleon III of France, and wider European acceptance of not only Italian unification but also Piedmont-Sardinia's suitability to be the dominant state and provide the ruling House. It was he, too, who stopped the headstrong Garibaldi from souring international opinion by marching on Rome, and ensured a referendum was held in the rebellious Papal States (the Pope's ancient temporal possessions) before accepting them into the new stare. As the nation's successive stamp issues revealed *Il Risorgimento* affected every aspect of Italian foreign policy for the next hundred years,

Victor Emmanuel II was proclaimed King of Italy on 27 March 1861.

Twice more the popular but politically naïve Garibaldi tried to take Rome but first an Italian army and then a Papal and French one barred his way. Only in 1870 when Napoleon III withdrew his forces to face Prussia did Victor Emmanuel finally enter Rome. He did so, though, as a reluctant conqueror because Pope Piux IX refused to acknowledge the legitimacy of the Kingdom of Italy after its seizure of the Papal States. Both Italy and the Papacy were to live until 1929 with the Roman Catholic nation's new capital containing a hostile Pope who considered himself a state prisoner. In practice, the king and government ruled from Turin.

In 1900 Italy remained discontented. It had been fortunate to secured Hapsburg Venetia in 1866 despite suffering a humiliating defeat after opportunistically joining Prussia in its war against Austria. Nevertheless Italy deeply coveted the Hapsburg lands around Trieste and Fiume and the deep water ports along the Dalmatian coast, and even the Ottoman Turk's semi-autonomous province of Albania.

In its attempts to be accepted as a 'Great Power' Italy continued to engage in costly colonial ventures. Well before Mussolini came to power in 1922, Italian nationalists, imperialists and businessmen dreamed of a new Roman Empire extending across the Roman Sea to Roman Africa. In the 1880s Assab and Massawa were purchased from a local Sultan, and began their development into Italian Eritrea, and land and ports leased along the Benadir coast were the beginnings of Italian Somaliland. Italy coveted neighbouring Abyssinia but in 1896 its invasion was bloodily repulsed at the Battle of Adowa. Undaunted, in 1911 Italy provoked a more successful war with Turkey and annexed Libya, where many Italians already lived, and the Dodecanese Islands in the south-eastern Aegean Sea.

Italian definitive stamps up the First World War concentrated upon the monarchy with images of Kings Victor Emmanuel II (1861-78), Umberto (1878-1900) and Victor Emmanuel III (1900-46), and the arms of the kingdom and its reigning House of Savoy.(10.1)

In addition, considerable philatelic and propaganda attention was paid to colonial issues. In 1903 stamps were issued featuring an elephant or a lion inscribed

R. POSTE ITALIANE and *BENADIR*. (10.2) After 1905 these were replaced with ordinary Italian definitive stamps variously overprinted *Somalia* or *Somalia Italiana*.

From 1893 some Italian stamps were overprinted *Colonia Eritrea*. In 1910 the first Eritrean pictorial stamp showed the Government Palace in Massawa, with the

10.1 10l Victor Emmanuel III definitive (from set 1 November 1910)

10.2 1903 Benadir 1b elephant overprinted 2c in January 1907 and then 3b in July 1923

10.3 1914 Eritrea 5c peasant ploughing (from set 1 March 1910+)

10.4 20c Victor Emmanuel III overprinted Libia (from set December 1912+)

10.5 2c Arms of Italy and 5c, 15c and 40c Victor Emmanuel III overprinted Patmos, Piscopi, Stampalia and Cos (from series 1 December 1912+)

10.6 5c Garibaldi (from pair 15 April 1910) and 5c Southern Plebiscite (from pair 1 November 1910)

10.7 Jubilee of the Kingdom of Italy (set 1 May 1911)

second four years later being a rare Italian colonial stamp of this period showing local life – a peasant ploughing.(10.3)

In 1901 an Italian Post Office had opened in Libya and used Victor Emmanuel III definitives overprinted BENGASI. Italian stamps had been available at the Tripoli consulate since 1869, but the first that were overprinted *Tripoli di Barberia* (Tripoli in Barbary) appeared only in 1909. From December 1912, after annexation, Victor Emmanuel III issues overprinted *Libia* in various scripts dominated the colony.(10.4)

On 22 September 1912 the 25c and 40c Victor Emmanuel III stamps of 1908 appeared overprinted *EGEO* (AEGEAN) for use in the Dodecanese Islands. From that December until September 1921 each island gradually received stocks of Italian definitive stamps overprinted with their names – Calimno, Caso, Cos, Karki, Leros, Lipso, Nisiros, Patmos, Piscopoi, Rodi, Scarpanto, Simi and Stampalia.(10.5)

Just prior to the First World War Italy issued several anniversary sets. In April 1910 two stamps featuring the iconic figure of Garibaldi marked the forthcoming 50th anniversary of the unification plebiscites held in Sicily and Naples. They were inscribed merely *1860* and *1910*; there was no need to name the famous bearded figure. In November two further stamps were issued featuring Garibaldi to reinforce the significance of the 'southern plebiscite' – the final stage in annexation after the Bourbon royal family had fled after briefly challenging Garibaldi's Red Shirts in the summer of 1860. The inscription read *ITALIA E VITTORIO EMMANVELE* (ITALY AND VICTOR EMMANUEL) and *PLEBISCITO MERIDONALE 1860 21 OTTOBRE 1910* (SOUTHERN PLEBISCITE 1860 21 OCTOBER 1910).(10.6)

In 1911 the Kingdom of Italy's Jubilee was commemorated with four large stamps strengthening the connection with Ancient Rome. They featured symbolic representations of Rome and Turin (2c), the fight for freedom (5c), the Genus of Italy (Apollo and Pegasus at Delphi) (10c), and the Glory of Rome epitomized by a mason inscribing *DEA ROMA* (GODDESS OF ROME) on a monument (15c). Each stamp included the words *CINQVANTENARIO DEL REGNO D'ITALIA ROMA E TORINO 1911* (FIFTIETH ANNIVERARY OF THE KINGDOM OF ITALY: ROME & TURIN 1911).(10.7)

The state celebrations included the start of the construction of the vast white marble neo-Classical *Altare della Patria* (Altar of the Fatherland) and *Monumento Nazionale a Vittorio Emmanuele II* (National Monument to Victor Emmanuel II) a short distance from the forum of Ancient Rome.(10.8) In the centre is an equestrian statue of the king, and the goddess Victoria rides a four horse chariot at the top of each wing. No-one could doubt the Kingdom of Italy's ambitions.

The other stamps issued before Italy entered the First World War were the 1912 pair celebrating Venice's rebuilding of the ancient Campanile (Bell Tower) of St Mark's Cathedral after its collapse a decade earlier.(10.9) They also highlighted the famous city's incorporation into the kingdom.

In August 1914 Italy's refusal to support Germany and Austria-Hungary and its eventual decision to join the Allies said a great deal about its attitude to international affairs. And the consequences of its decisions were long lasting.

Membership of the Triple Alliance with Germany and Austria-Hungary did not oblige Italy to join them in an aggressive war, and by 1914 Italy believed no amount of support for Austria-Hungary, its major nineteenth century enemy, would secure the territories Italy sought – Trieste, Istria and Dalmatia. After fraught negotiations with both sides, Italy did a deal with the Allies who blithely promised it Trentino and South Tyrol, huge swathes of the Austrian mainland and islands east of the Adriatic down to Dalmatia, and parts of Germany's African colonies.

Italy declared war on Austria-Hungary on 23 May 1915, Turkey on 21 August 1915, Bulgaria on 19 October 1915, and finally Germany on 28 August 1916. Italian troops fought Austro-Hungarian forces in Albania, and in 1917 were in control of much of the country. The annexation of Albania was one of Italy's key aims. However, the greatest, and bloodiest, battles were fought around the mountainous Austrian border with vast frontal assaults costing hundreds of thousands of lives interspersed with hideous trench warfare with troops striving to exist and fight dug into rocks, crevices and even glaciers. Twelve huge and costly battles occurred between June 1915 and November 1917 around the Isonzo River and its surrounding mountains. They afforded little strategic advantage, but the stream of casualties incited considerable domestic alarm and despondency. Not surprisingly, surcharged Red Cross stamps were issued in November 1915 and February/March 1916. One featured the Banner of the Kingdom of Italy, and three others the eagle arms of the House of Savoy.(10.10)

Italy has the distinction of producing the first two Airmail stamps, although they were limited souvenirs not general issues. On 20

10.9 5c St Mark's Campanile (from pair 25 April 1912)

10.8 Postcard of the National Monument to Victor Emmanuel II sent from Rome to Paris in December 1921. The building was not completed until 1925.

10.10 10c+5c National Banner and 15c+5c House of Savoy Arms (from set 20 November 1915+)

10.11 25c Express Letter overprinted for the Turin-Rome flights (20 May 1917)

10.12 40c Express Letter overprinted for the Naples-Palermo flights (27 June 1917)

10.13 1916 40h Austrian Arms overprinted Regno d'Italia Trentino 3 nov 1918 (from series 11 November 1918), and 1906 5c Victor Emmanuel III overprinted Venezia Tridentina (from series 20 December 1918)

10.14 1917 15h Emperor Charles badly overprinted Regno D'Italia Venezia Giulia 3. XI. 18 (from series 14 November 1918+), and 10c Victor Emmanuel III overprinted Venezia Giulia (from series 6 December 1918+)

10.15 1901 1c and 1l Italian definitives overprinted for use in all occupied Austrian territories (from series January 1919+)

May 1917 the 1903 Express Letter stamp appeared overprinted *ESPERIMENTO POSTA AEREA MAGGIO 1917 TORINO – ROMA * ROMA – TORINO* (EXPERIMENTAL AIR MAIL MAY 1917 TURIN – ROME * ROME – TURIN).(10.11) On 20 May Mario de Bernardi, an officer and test pilot with the Pomilio Aircraft Company flew 400 miles from Turin to Rome in a Pomilio biplane in four and a quarter hours carrying over 300 pounds of mail. Bad weather delayed his return flight for a week.

More significantly perhaps, in June a new 40c Express Letter stamp appeared overprinted 25 cents and *IDROVOLANTE   NAPOLI – PALERMO – NAPOLI* (SEAPLANE   NAPLES – PALERMO – NAPLES). (10.12) This marked an experiment to offset the dangers Austrian submarines were posing to Italian mail boats. Seaplanes proved the imaginative answer to carrying mail from Naples to the island of Sicily.

In October 1917 Italy endured a particularly humiliating defeat at Caporetto and had to retreat to the Piave River where the lines eventually held. However when the Austro-Hungarians failed to break through in the Battle of the Piave in June 1918, their exhausted armies began to disintegrate. Strengthened with British, French, Czech and American divisions, Italy's attack across the Piave near Vittorio Veneto in October was decisive, not least because many demoralized Austrian units simply refused to counter-attack and melted away. A formal armistice was signed on 3 November.

Italy was quick to celebrate the situation and stake its territorial claims. On 11 November 1918 Austrian stamps of the reigns of Franz Joseph and Charles appeared overprinted in Trentino with either *Regno d'Italia Trentino 3 nov 1918* (Kingdom of Italy Trentino 3 November 1918), or *Venezia Tridentina* which included the two regions of Venezia Trentino and Venezia Alto Adige. And from 20 December Italian definitive stamps were issued overprinted *Venezia Tridentina*.(10.13)

In Venezia Giulia (the Austrian Littoral comprising the Istrian Peninsula, and Trieste and Gorizia and their surrounding areas), which was also occupied by Italian forces, Austrian stamps appeared from 14 November 1918 hurriedly, and often badly, overprinted *Regno D'Italia Venezia Giulia 3. XI. 18.* They were replaced from 6 December by Victor Emmanuel III issues overprinted *Venezia Giulia* but without any date.(10.14)

For a few months in 1919 Italian stamps were used in all these occupied areas with overprints confirming the Austrian values in Italian, such as *5 centesimo di corona* (5 cents of a krone or crown).(10.15) Postage Due and Express Letter stamps were similarly overprinted. There seemed little concern that the overprints obscured the reigning monarch's head.

Debt ridden, exhausted and shattered by casualties amounting to 600,000 dead and 950,000 wounded, Italy at least hoped the territorial agreement with the victorious Allies would be honoured. However its

10.16 *1 lira Occupazione Italiana Castelrosso (from set January 1923)*

diplomats were out-manoeuvred at the Paris Peace Conference, and afterwards Italy bore a lasting grudge at its humiliating treatment – something Mussolini carefully exploited. Britain and France proved reluctant to abide by their 1915 agreement and now considered Italy with its repeated wartime failures to be over-demanding, arrogant and greedy. Most important of all, the American President, Woodrow Wilson, had not been party to the original agreement and much preferred the voluntary creation of the Slavic Kingdom of Serbs, Croats and Slovenes and an independent Albania to pandering to Italian Imperialist ambitions.

Italy's claims to African territory were largely ignored, although Great Britain and France threw the Italians a few bits adjoining Libya, and grave doubts surrounded Italy's chance of holding on to the Austrian Littoral, Fiume, the Dalmatian coast and its ports of Zadar and Sebenico. Italy also sought the Albanian port of Vlore and its hinterland. Italy rejected all thoughts of compromise with the emerging Kingdom of Serbs, Croats and Slovenes, but its case was not helped by stories of its brutality towards the Slavs in areas it occupied under the Armistice and stubbornly held on to during the Paris Peace Conference.

The Treaty of St Germain that settled Austria's fate on 10 September 1919 finally awarded Italy South Tyrol, Trentino, the Austrian Littoral and some Dalmatian Islands. In August 1920 the Allied Treaty of Sevres with the remnant of the Ottoman Empire confirmed Italy's *de facto* possession of the Dodecanese Islands. Ordinary Italian stamps soon replaced the overprinted Italian issues, but not on the island of Castelrosso off the Turkish coast. Here a series of Italian definitive and commemorative stamps were used overprinted CASTELROSSO. In January 1923 the island enjoyed its own specially designed set featuring a map, the Italian flag and an inscription highlighting the Italian occupation.(10.16)

However Fiume (modern Rijeka in Slovenia) and the exact border with the Kingdom of Serbs, Croats and Slovenes were omitted from the treaties, creating jealousies and tensions that would last a generation. A modest port south of the Istrian peninsula with a mixed Italian and Slav population, Fiume's fate became Italy's symbol of bitterness towards its seemingly treacherous Allies.

A charismatic Italian soldier-poet now sprang into prominence. Gabriele D'Annunzio (1863-1938) had achieved renown as a mystical writer and fervent nationalist before the war and as a daring pilot and torpedo boat commander during it. On 12 September 1919 he led around 2,500 Italian volunteers into Fiume forcing out the America, British and French forces. He sought annexation to Italy but the Italian government refused and D'Annunzio declared Fiume an independent state – the Italian Regency of Carnaro, named after the nearby Gulf. He wrote a constitution that was proto-Fascist in its proclamation of himself as *Duce* (Leader) and its establishment of an array of corporations and courts to control and develop every aspect of the economy and community life. Social welfare was high on D'Annunzio's agenda, but so was social control. He was a master of emotion stirring speeches, theatrical parades and quasi-religious rallies, and also the use of black shirted squads to suppress dissent and enforce active participation in the creation of his version of Utopia.

On 12 November 1920 Italy signed the Treaty of Rapallo with the new Kingdom of Serbs, Croats and Slovenes. Italy received most of Upper and Inner Carniola (in modern Slovenia), the Dalmatian city of Zadar (Zara), the islands of Lastovo and Palagruza, and was confirmed in the Austrian Littoral with the important exceptions of Fiume that was designated a Free City and the island of Krk. Around half a million Slovenes and Croats found themselves living in Italy, and treated as second-class citizens. D'Annunzio ignored the treaty, and bizarrely declared war on Italy. Soon afterwards an Italian warship appeared and fired a few shots at Fiume, and then troops were dispatched to occupy the city on Christmas Eve 1920 and eject D'Annunzio and his men. D'Annunzio retired without trial or imprisonment to Italy, and was ennobled by the King in 1924. It was probably no coincidence that in 1924 Fiume ceased to be a Free City and was ceded to Italy under another international treaty. Italy might have felt obliged to obey international law in 1919 and 1920 but for many Italians, including Mussolini, D'Annunzio's dash and daring had represented the spirit of the nation.

The dramatic events in Fiume were tracked by a flurry of stamp issues. Fiume had been a Hungarian port, and on 3 December 1918 superannuated Hungarian harvesters, Parliament, war charity, Charles and Zita, and Postage Due stamps were issued overprinted *FIUME* by hand or by machine.(10.17)

Between January and April 1919 there were three printings of a set of four special stamps. Two images were symbolic of Liberty and Revolution, and two

10.17 *1916 40h Hungarian harvesters overprinted FIUME (from set 3 December 1918+)*

10.18   25c Revolution and 30c Harbour (from set 28 January 1919+)

10.20   25c+2corona Dr Grossich (20 September 1919)

10.21   45c Revolution overprinted FRANCO 10 (from series 10 October 1919+)

10.19   15c Romulus and Remus, and 45c Venetian war galley (from set 18 May 1919)

10.22   1919 1cor+5l Venetian war galley overprinted Valore globale (from series 5 February 1920)

10.23   25c Gabriele D'Annunzio (from new currency set 12 September 1920)

featured Fiume's harbour and clock tower flying the Kingdom of Italy's flag.(10.18)   These stamps were inscribed *FIUME,* although a later printing in July preferred *POSTA FIUME.*

On 18 May 1919 a set of twelve stamps from Fiume marked the 200th day of peace since the Battle of Vittorio Veneto ended on 18 October 1918. They featured the statue of the wolf suckling Romulus and Remus, a thirteenth century Venetian war galley, and St Mark's Square; all harked back to Ancient Rome or the medieval Venetian Republic that controlled all the territory around the head of the Adriatic and along the Dalmatian coast that Italy now claimed.(10.19)   They were inscribed *PRO FONDAZIONE STUDIO* (FOR THE EDUCATION FUND) along with the date *30.X.1918* and a five lira premium

A spate of stamps and overprints between 12 September 1919 and 24 December 1920 tracked D'Annunzio's dictatorship, and fall. The first, a single stamp issued on 20 September, featured Dr Antonio Grossich and carried a premium to promote his Medical Foundation.(10.20)   A distinguished surgeon in Fiume's City Hospital, Grossich pioneered the use of iodine as a rapid sterilizing agent, especially on the battlefield. He was also an ardent nationalist and headed the Italian Council of Fiume in 1918.

Between October 1919 and March 1920 the pictorial stamps featuring Liberty, Revolution and Fiume's clock tower and harbour were reissued crudely overprinted *FRANCO* with surcharges for local (but unspecified) charities.(10.21)

From December 1919 to February 1920 the Dr Grossich stamp and the Education Fund set also appeared overprinted with varying degrees of intensity *Valore globale* (global or general value) together with the original postal value of the stamp.(10.22)   In other words, the overprint cancelled the charity premium and rendered the stamp an ordinary postage one.

On September 1920, the first anniversary of the takeover of the city, a set of 14 values in cents and liras was issued featuring the head of Gabriele D'Annunzio and the Latin inscription *HIC MANEBIMUS OPTIME* (perhaps best translated as HERE WE SHALL STAY – THE VERY BEST). They sought to highlight the civic virtues and benefits offered by his bizarre socialist dictatorship – something the young Benito Mussolini had not failed to notice.(10.23)

In the same month a more blood-chilling set designed from drawings by D'Annunzio himself celebrated the anniversary.(10.24) They said much about the self-styled *Duce's* perception of his role and ideals. The stamps were primarily for use by his *Arditi* - the war veterans, adventurers and nationalists that made up his polygot army.   They featured the severing of the Gordian

10.24 First anniversary (set 12 September 1920)

Knot (resolving the problem of the ownership of Fiume) (5c), the city's Coat of Arms of blood pouring out of a vase (10c), the Crown of Thorns (signifying the sacrificial acceptance of international rejection) (20c), and a series of hands clenching daggers (reinforcing the willingness to fight on) (25c).

On 20 November 1920 the set was overprinted *Reggenza Italiana del Carnaro* (The Italian Regency of Carnaro) to highlight D'Annunzio's response to Italy's rejection of his intended annexation, and his creation of the new despotic socialist constitution.(10.25) Some of the stamps were overprinted 'Arbe' or 'Veglia' for use on two nearby islands deemed part of Carnaro. On the reverse of several values was the *Arditi's* badge of stars encircled by a snake swallowing its head that symbolized Eternity swallowing Rome, the Eternal City.

On Christmas Eve 1920 the Regency of Carnaro came to a shuddering end, and on 2 February 1921 the celebratory set featuring D'Annunzio's head was ignominiously reissued overprinted *Governo Provvisorio* (Provisional Government).(10.26) The stamps had a new ochre coloured background suggesting they were specially reprinted to reinforce Fiume's dramatic change of ownership.

On 21 March the education fund set from May 1919 was also reissued with the images obliterated and new values as Postage Due labels.(10.27)

10.25 10c Arms of Fiume overprinted 15c and Reggenza Italiana del Carnaro with (cancelled to order) Posta Militare postmark

10.26 5c D'Annunzio overprinted Governo Provvisorio (from set 2 February 1921)

10.27 1919 20c Romulus and Remus overprinted Valore globale Cent. 20 additionally overprinted with obliterating fan design and 0.06c value as a Postage Due label (from set 21 March 1921

10.28 1919 60c+5l Venetian war galley overprinted Costituente Fiumana 24-IV-1921 (from set 24 April 1921)

10.29 1919 80c+5l Venetian War galley with the additional 1922 overprint (from set 12 April 1922)

Under the Treaty of Rapallo Fiume and its neighbouring port of Susak was declared a Free City. Although neither Italy nor the Kingdom of Serbs, Croats and Slovenes had ownership, Fiume remained completely reliant upon Italian diplomatic, financial and economic goodwill and Italy lost little time in pressurizing the internally chaotic Kingdom of Serbs, Croats and Slovenes for its complete annexation.

On 24 April 1921 the education fund set was reissued overprinted diagonally with *Costituente Fiumana* (Constitution of Fiume) and above this inscription the date *24–IV–1921*.(10.28) It marked the meeting of the first new constituent assembly.

However, Fiume's new moderate government did not last long. A year later, on 12 April 1922, the second assembly reissued the set with the same overprint but with the additional date *1922*.(10.29) 1922 was a small addition and it might have seemed a surplus issue, but in fact it marked an important Fascist coup in the city

10.30 5c medieval ship, 25c Roman archway, 1l St Vitus, and 5l boats and column from the Tarsatic Principia (from set March 1923)

that predated Mussolini's seizure of power in Italy itself later that year. In March 1923 the new regime produced a set of stamps that in true Fascist style harked back to the city's days as a prosperous medieval port and as the late Roman fortified settlement of Tarsatica.(10.30) Three values pictured a medieval ship, three a Roman archway, three a Roman column, and three a portrait of St Vitus, who was thought to be a Roman martyred during the reign of the Emperor Diocletian in 303AD. He became the city's patron saint. Later in March two Express Letter stamps featured the sixteenth century walled city.(10.31)

On 22 February 1924, under a new treaty signed the previous month, Fiume was finally incorporated into Italy while nearby Susak was annexed by the Kingdom of Serbs, Croats and Slovenes. On that same day the previous year's set was reissued overprinted with a decorated tablet enclosing the Italian Arms and the inscription *REGNO d'ITALIA* (KINGDOM OF ITALY). On 1 March they appeared again, this time inscribed with the date *22 Febb 1924* or *22 Febbraio 1924* and a decorated tablet enclosing the Arms and the clearest possible inscription *ANNESSIONE ALL'ITALIA* (ANNEXATION TO ITALY).(10.32) As we shall see, the Slovenes and Croats continued to loath the Italians.

The Kingdom of Italy had celebrated the formal annexation of Venezia-Giulia, although bereft of much of Dalmatia, with a set of three stamps in June 1921.(10.33) They featured the ancient seal of the commune of Trieste, the region's capital. The set came at a critical time of post-war disillusionment, civil unrest and rising nationalism, and aimed at restoring some pride in Italian achievements and perhaps curbing the widespread criticism of the government's failure to wrest more concessions from the Allies.

In this it was supported by a striking set issued on 1 November 1921 to mark the third anniversary of the Italian victory at Vittorio Veneto. The stamps featured the celebrated Winged Victory of Brescia and are inscribed *VITTORIO VENETO XXIV OTTOBRE MCMXVIII*.(10.34) The bronze cast statue dated from around 250BC, and the stamp showed it with the temporary nineteenth century additions of the traditional shield honouring the victor and a helmet under the figure's foot.

Inbetween these two issues a set appeared on 28 September commemorating the 600th anniversary of the death of Italy's most celebrated poet, Dante Alighieri (c1265-1321).(10.35 overleaf) Beset by his burning love for the unobtainable Beatrice and sentenced to permanent exile from his beloved Florence during a time of bitter factional rivalry, Dante wrote the *Divine Comedy* describing his journey through Hell, Purgatory and Paradise guided first by Vergil and then by Beatrice until he looks into the face of God. The title *Divine Comedy* upheld the concept of an ordered universe in which God's will guides all things and everyone, however unhappy and confused like Dante himself, to an ultimately good ending.

10.31 2l Express Letter walled city (pair 23 March 1923)

10.32 20c Roman archway overprinted *REGNO d'ITALIA* (from set 22 February 1924) and *ANNESSIONE ALL'ITALIA 22 Febb. 1924* (from set 1 March 1924)

10.33 40c union of Venezia Giulia with Italy (from set 5 June 1921)

10.34 15c Victory (from set 1 November 1921)

10.35 15c eagle and Divine Comedy, 25c Italy and Divine Comedy, and 40c Dante (from set 28 September 1921)

10.37 50c Victor Emmanuel III with De Montel and Singer advertising labels (from series November 1924+)

10.36 1906 Victor Emmanuel III overprinted IX CONGRESSO FILATELICO ITALIANO TRIESTE 1922 (from set 4 June 1922)

10.38 25c sword and fire, 40c portrait of Mazzini (set 20 September 1922)

The set embraced several features dedicated to enhancing contemporary pride in Italian history, culture and language. The 15c featured an eagle holding LA DIVINA COMMEDIA encircled by the inscription *Che sopra gli altri com'aquila vola* (He who is above all others as the eagle soars). The 25c featured the figure of Italy crowned with a laurel wreath displaying to the nation a volume inscribed DA DC (for Dante Alighieri and Divina Commedia). The surrounding inscription read *Onorate l'altissimo poeta* (Honour to the greatest poet). The 40c pictured the seated Dante talking about his work. The inscription reads *Mostro cio che potea la lingua nostra* (He shows us what our language can achieve). Each stamp also possessed the initials S.N.D.A. that stood for the *Societa Nazionale Dante Alighieri*, a cultural and nationalist organization dedicated to the promotion of the Italian language at home and abroad. Earlier in 1921, in honour of the anniversary, Pope Benedict XV had issued an encyclical calling Dante one of 'the many celebrated geniuses of whom the Catholic faith can boast.' The set, perhaps, was a timely issue in the fraught church-state relationships.

To complement the post-war issues getting into their stride as an arm of state propaganda, the Ninth Italian Philatelic Congress was held in Trieste in June 1922. Four overprinted Victor Emmanuel III definitive stamps commemorated the event.(10.36)

The ubiquitous nature of stamps and their capacity to publicise events and ideas – and raise funds - came together in 1924 with the introduction of advertising labels to the most common definitive values – 25c and 50c. For a time King Victor Emmanuel became somewhat incongruously attached to advertisements ranging from Campari to Columbia and De Montel lamp bulbs to Singer Sewing Machines.(10.37) There were no easy-tear perforations between the stamps and the labels.

In September 1922 another set harked back to a national hero, this time marking the 50th anniversary of the death of the revolutionary leader and writer Guiseppe Mazzini (1805-1872).(10.38) The young Mazzini was a member of *La Giovane Italia* (Young Italy), a secret society dedicated to fomenting a popular revolution, especially against Austrian overlordship. In 1834 he fled to London where further societies were created and plots hatched, but all failed. Although he enjoyed brief power as a leader of the republic established in Rome in 1849, his later attempts at uprisings failed and gradually Cavour, Garibaldi and Victor Emmanuel II assumed greater prominence. His last years were ones of bitterness that Italy was a kingdom and not a republic, and he refused loyalty to the ruling House of Savoy. However his abiding hostility to Marxism, his preference for a society based upon collaboration rather than a class struggle, and his retention of the Christian faith, made his vision of an Italy united under a humanitarian Roman Catholic government very appealing to Benito Mussolini and the Fascists who were about to seize power. One stamp in particular – the 25c image of a sword inscribed *JVS* (RIGHT) being burnished in a flame springing from a Classical altar adorned with the word *AMOR* (LOVE) – firmly related Mazzini's life and writings to post-war Italy's continuing battle for a prominent place in the international sun.

Some years before Italy joined the Allies the young Mussolini had become a prominent Socialist opposed to the war, but then he perceived participation as the means of liberating Italians still living under Austro-Hungarian rule and paving the way for Italy to achieve greater international influence. Ejected by the Socialist Party, in 1915 he formed a new political party, the *Partito Fascista Rivoluzionario* (Fascist Revolutionary Party) whose members became known as *Fascisti* (Fascists). Fascism became a philosophy advocating class collaboration not egalitarianism, aggressive nationalism not international socialism, and an education and welfare system dedicated to producing a nation healthy in body and mind and united in its sense of civic service and readiness to wage war.

The Fascists also advocated overseas expansion and promoted them with arguments of racial superiority over the Africans and Slavs. At a time of civil unrest and post-war depression Mussolini's heady revolutionary nationalism proved immensely popular, especially with the army, farmers and industrialists, and was avidly promoted through theatrical rallies, partisan newspapers, and the daunting presence of squads of Fascist Blackshirts. In 1921 the growing party was renamed the *Partito Nazionale Fascista* (National Fascist Party). On the night of 27/28 October 1922 30,000 uniformed Blackshirts massed in Rome and King Victor Emmanuel III, fearing civil war and seeing Mussolini as essentially a deep-died traditionalist, offered him the Prime Ministership.

Over the next few years Mussolini consolidated support largely by legislation favouring the agrarian and industrial elite, and in June 1923 secured the passage of the Acerbo Law that ensured any party getting at least 25% of the vote received two-thirds of the seats in Parliament. The 1924 election, which the Fascists won amidst widespread stories of intimidation and corruption, was the last one until 1946. On Christmas Eve 1925 a law made Mussolini 'Head of Government' rather than merely 'President of the Council of Ministers', and he became *de facto* dictator responsible only to the king.

On 24 October 1923 the first anniversary of the Fascist march to Rome was celebrated with a set of six stamps.(10.39) The 10c, 30c and 50c featured the fasces – the ancient Roman symbol of state authority and now the Fascist emblem of power. The 1l and 2l pictured a winged eagle and wreath resting on a fasces, and the 5l pictured warplanes flying over a smoking industrial scene flanked by two fasces.

On 29 October 1923 three surcharged stamps appeared raising funds for the Blackshirts.(10.40) On 1 February that year the Fascist *squadristi* had been transformed into the M.V.S.N – the *Milizia Volontaria per la Sicurezza Nazionale* (Volunteer Militia for National Security). The Fascists represented themselves as inheritors of the glory of ancient Rome, and the stamps showed new members dressed as Romans swearing the oath of allegiance over an altar. The scene is made to look like the reverse of a Roman coin. The inscription reads *CASSA PREVID CAMICIE NERE* (MONEY DONATED TO THE BLACK SHIRTS).

Funds were enhanced further through a colourful surcharged set on 26 October 1926.(10.41) The frames comprised the fasces, eagle and wreath, and the dates I.II.MCMXXIII and I.II.MCMXXVI – the former recalling the creation of the M.V.S.N. and the latter its third anniversary. The inscription read *PRO OPERA PREVIDENZA M.V.S.N.* (FOR THE WORK OF THE FORCES OF THE M.V.S.N). The central images harked back to ancient Rome, featuring the site of the Emperor Hadrian's tomb in the Castle of St Angelo (40c+20c), the huge Claudian Aqueduct that brought water into the city (60c+30c), the fifteenth century version of the ancient Porta de Popolo gateway on the Via Flaminia (1l 25+60c), and the mix of Renaissance buildings and temple remains on the Capitoline Hill (5l+2l 50). The set was reissued in 1928 and 1930 with different colours, values and dates.

No opportunity was lost to heighten national pride. On 27 August 1923 an Italian general and several officials working on the island of Corfu on a League of Nation's commission to settle a boundary dispute between Greece and Albania were murdered. With no evidence, the Greeks were blamed and after Greece refused to admit guilt Mussolini ordered the island to be bombarded and occupied. On 20 September eight Italian definitive stamps featuring King Victor Emmanuel III were issued overprinted CORFU, and a few days later several more followed overprinted with Greek values.(10.42) Few were used commercially, but the propaganda effect was all that mattered. Hostilities loomed between Greece and Italy, and at Mussolini's insistence the affair went to the international Conference of Ambassadors for resolution. In the event Italian power and threats to leave the League

10.39 50c fasces, 2l eagle, wreath and fasces, and 5l fasces and warplanes (from set 24 October 1924)

10.40 1l Fascist Black Shirt Fund (from set 29 October 1923)

10.41 (E) First National Defence (M.V.S.N.) set (26 October 1926)

10.42 50c King Victor Emmanuel III overprinted Corfu (from set 20 September 1923)

of Nations triumphed. Greece had to investigate the murders, arrange full military honours for those murdered, salute the Italian fleet, apologise to the British, French and Italian ambassadors, and lodge 50 million lira as a guarantee. After the Italians left on 27 September surplus stocks of overprinted stamps were available for collectors in Rome. Italy was overjoyed at the outcome, although Mussolini may well have hoped to retain Corfu.

Mussolini had inherited rather than created Italy's vision of a new Roman Empire, and indeed in 1921, just before he gained power, Italian Libya received a set firmly associating the modern conquest with Imperial Rome's dominance of north Africa.(10.43) It eschewed any thought of local life, much preferring images of a Roman legionary, the Goddess of Plenty, a galley leaving Tripoli and an allegory of Victory.

Once in power, though, Mussolini ensured he received maximum publicity from Italy's colonial development and, notably, settlement by Italian families. Throughout the 1920s most Italian stamps were overprinted ERITREA or SOMALIA ITALIANA for use overseas. Between 1927 and 1934 Libya was divided into Tripoli and Cyrenaica, but from 1923 the two provinces were flooded with Italian commemorative sets overprinted Tripoli or Cyrenaica and also with sets specially designed for each of them. Among the latter were sets giving a highly favourable view of colonial life and by implication justifying Italy's 'right' to the region.(10.44)

In 1929 a set honoured the king's visit to the chief Dodecanese island of Rhodes.(10.45) One stamp featured the famous medieval windmills, while several others highlighted Rhodes' combative Christian heritage with images of the heroic Knights of St John who defended the island against the Ottoman Turks until finally defeated in 1522. Afterwards the Knights settled in Malta where they continued to defend the Mediterranean from Turkish naval onslaughts.

Mussolini fully appreciated the need to attract the support of the Roman Catholic Church and its local congregations. Several stamp issues publicized key anniversaries prior to the final 1929 Concordat that ended nearly sixty years of antipathy after Italy seized the Papal States. Under it, Italy recognised the independence of the Vatican City, guaranteed Roman Catholicism as the state religion, and promised to protect the honour and dignity of the Pope. In return the Roman Catholic Church recognised the Italian state.

Several years before the Concordat, on 11 June 1923 four large stamps were issued featuring Jesus blessing followers to mark the tercentenary of the *Sacra Congregatio de Propaganda Fide* (the Sacred Congregation for the Propagation of the Faith).(10.46) Founded by Pope Gregory XV in 1622 the Congregation sought to

10.43 5c Roman standard bearer and 50c Roman galley leaving Tripoli (from set July 1921)

ITALY

10.44 (E) 1l 25+20c camel riders and 2l 55+50c Tripoli (from Second Tripoli Trade Fair set 20 February 1928)

On 24 December 1924 the Holy Year of 1925 was marked by a set of six stamps with the premium devoted to the expenses in dealing with the influx of pilgrims to Rome. Four of the stamps contained detailed images of the Church of St Mary Major (20c+10c), the Church of St John Lateran (30c+15c), the Church of St Paul-outside-the-Walls (50c+25c) and St Peter's (60c+30c). During Holy Year the Pope and selected cardinals ceremonially opened the great doors of these four churches as a sign that pilgrims were welcome. The final two stamps pictured the Pope opening the Golden Door of St Peter's (1l+50c), and closing it again at the end of the year (5l+2.50l). (10.48)

Pope Boniface VIII had instigated the first Holy Year in 1300, and every pilgrim who reached St Peter's received a full remission of sins. Further Holy Years were proclaimed at various intervals of 25, 33 or 50 years, and especially at times of particular peril, and were highlighted as periods of penance, forgiveness, reconciliation and

10.45 Rhodes 25c fasces and knight defending Christianity (from set 19 May 1929+). The set was sold in all the islands.

10.47 10c lakeside scene from I Promesso sposi (from set 29 December 1923)

10.46 50c Sacred Congregation for the Propagation of the Faith (from set 11 June 1923)

champion Roman Catholic missionary work in Muslim eastern Europe, and in Africa and Asia in the face of Protestant colonial expansion by the British and Dutch. A portrait of Pope Gregory XV appeared at the top left corner and in each stamp a different unnamed convert was featured at the top right. Significantly, the Arms of the House of Savoy appeared in the bottom left corner.

Soon afterwards, on 29 December 1923, the 50th anniversary of the death of the poet and novelist Alessandro Manzoni (1785-1873) provided an opportunity for a set of six stamps to celebrate his work, and notably his masterpiece *I Promesso sposi* (The Betrothed).(10.47) Embracing a host of adventures and colourful characters this story of love, power and treachery centred on the truly Christian attitudes, emotions and lives of the heroine Lucia, Friar Cristoforo and Federigo Borromeo, the Cardinal-Archbishop of Milan.

10.48 (E) 60c+30c St Peter's, 1l+50c Opening Golden Door, and 5l+2.50l Closing Golden Door (from set 24 December 1924)

10.49 20c vision of St Francis, 40c St Damian's chapel, and 60c Basilica in Assisi (from set 30 January 1926+ with TRIPOLITANIA overprints)

renewal. One planned for 1848 was aborted due to the revolution, another in 1875 was held but the doors were not opened as Rome was occupied by Italian troops, and in 1900 the Holy Year served to highlight the Pope's self-imposed captivity. By 1925 relations had eased, and the doors were opened without overt controversy. Pope Pius XI dedicated the year to the work of missions and world peace.

During 1926 a set of stamps commemorated the 700th anniversary of the death of St Francis of Assisi (c1181-1226), the co-patron saint of Italy with St Catherine of Sienna.(10.49) Born the son of a wealthy silk merchant, Francis enjoyed the high life of a wealthy young man until he experienced a mystical vision of Jesus Christ in the little chapel of St Damian outside Assisi (40c). He forsook all wealth and wandered through Umbria quickly attracting followers through his preaching and charisma. With Papal approval, in 1210 he founded the Franciscan Order, and then the female Order of Poor Clares and the lay Order of the Brothers and Sisters of Penance. With Francis's emphasis upon joyful worship, a perception of the natural world as the mirror of God, and the difference an individual can make to it, the Orders spread rapidly across western Europe. In 1224 Francis experienced a vision of the Cross in the mountains of Varna, and his hands, feet and side received the stigmata of the crucifixion (20c). He died in 1226, and was canonized in 1228 when Pope Gregory IX laid the foundation stone of the Basilica of St Francis in Assisi (60c). In 1927 work started on the complete refashioning of his tomb, and this set was a politically shrewd move.

King Victor Emmanuel III did nothing to stem Mussolini's swift moves towards autocracy. It is reasonable to assume he, in common with most capitalists and traditionalists, preferred the order the Fascists brought to the country to the spectre of Communism. In 1925 his Silver Jubilee was marked with due ceremony and a set of three new portrait stamps.(10.50) Several new values were added later in the 1920s.

In 1928 an unusual set of ten stamps mixed images of the celebrated warrior Emmanuel Philibert, Duke of Savoy (1528-80) to mark the 400th anniversary of his birth with those of a modern soldier to commemorate the tenth anniversary of victory in the Great War.(10.51) The duality of the issue, however, contained a significant message about Italian political and cultural ambitions. Against considerable odds, the redoubtable Duke had forced the French out of Savoy, secured further territory from his Hapsburg relations, and replaced Latin with Italian as the official language. Modern Italy still thought it was engaged in a struggle, and had much to prove.

Monarchy and Fascism combined in April 1929 in the so-called Imperial Series of definitive stamps. (10.52) Some values featured the king while others recalled past glories and dreams of a new Roman Empire with images of Julius Caesar, the Emperor Augustus, the wolf feeding Romulus and Remus, an allegory of Italia, and Italy's fascist coat of arms. The fasces now appeared on all definitive stamps. And as the 1930s advanced, so did international tensions, and when the Axis agreement was made with Hitler's Germany Fascist aggression was given full and largely disastrous rein in Ethiopia and the Balkans.

10.50 1l 25 Royal Jubilee of King Victor Emmanuel III (from pair 1925+ with ERITREA overprint)

10.51 50c modern soldier and statue, and 1l 25 statue of Duke of Savoy in Turin (from set 27 July 1928+)

10.52 2c Fascist Arms, 15c Italia, 50c King Victor Emmanuel III and 1l 75 Emperor Augustus (from Imperial Series 21 April 1929+)

CHAPTER 11

Serbia, Montenegro and Emergence of the Kingdom of Serbs, Croats and Slovenes (Yugoslavia)

SERBIA

The independent Principality of Serbia was progressively overcome by the Ottoman Empire when Smederevo was captured in 1459, Belgrade was seized in 1521, and Vojvodina finally fell in 1540. It regained internal autonomy after two revolts in 1804 and 1815 at a time of upheaval within the Ottoman Empire, and in 1817 it was granted *de facto* independence although Ottoman garrisons remained until 1867.

After success in the Russo-Turkish War of 1877-78 Serbia received international recognition as an independent principality along with Romania and Montenegro. In 1882 it declared itself a kingdom. It remained, though, wary of its mighty neighbours, Imperial Russia and Austria-Hungary, and its relations with the emerging states of Bulgaria and Romania were riven with jealousies. Its large standing army did little to ease local tension.

Serbia particularly resented Austria-Hungary being granted administrative rights over Bosnia in 1879, and its grudge was to strain relationships until 1914. And in 1885 its anger at Bulgaria declaring unification with Eastern Rumelia, a semi-autonomous Ottoman province, boiled over into a costly war and humiliating defeat. But it was Serbia's bizarre internal affairs that confirmed its reputation as the epitome of Balkan aggression, instability and immorality.

King Milan Obrenovic suddenly abdicated in 1889 surrounded by sexual scandals and deeply unpopular after the disastrous Bulgarian war and accompanying heavy taxation. And in 1903 his son King Alexander and Queen Draga were brutally murdered by army officers repulsed by Draga's dubious sexual reputation, convinced she was plotting her unpopular brother's promotion to heir-presumptive, and angry at the king's suspension of the constitution and purge of officers suspected of disloyalty. Europe was beguiled by rumours that a secret army group known as the Black Hand led by the mysterious 'Apis' (Dragutin Dimitrijevic) had carried out the assassination.

11.1 25p Prince, later King, Milan Obrenovic (from set 1 November 1880), and 5p his son King Alexander Obrenovic (from set 5 November 1894+)

11.2 25p King Alexander Obrenovic with portrait obliterated by Serbian Arms (from set 25 June 1903)

Several different stamps bearing Alexander's portrait had been issued during his reign, and the last set was ready for distribution just before his death.(11.1) It was still issued that June but with his portrait obliterated with the Kingdom of Serbia's coat of arms – a white cross on the breast of a double-headed eagle surrounded by an open mantle topped by the crown.(11.2) It continued in use for well over a year.

Queen Draga's brother was killed, other murders ensured the Obrenovic dynasty was exterminated, and Peter Karageorgevic from the Obrenovic's rival ruling family readily accepted the throne. During Serbia's convoluted history Karageogevics had ruled from 1804 to 1813, and from 1842 to 1858, with Obrenovics inbetween – usually with violent depositions marking the change of families.

11.3   15p King Peter Karageorgevic and Djordje Petrovic and 5st Djordje Petovic and insurgents (from set 8 September 1904)

Peter's accession proved popular within Serbia, although several nations, including Great Britain, severed connections with Serbia when it failed to punish the conspirators. Peter was crowned in Belgrade on 21 September 1904, and on 8 September a set of eight large stamps had appeared to mark the occasion and, pointedly, highlight the centenary of the Karageorgevic dynasty. Indeed the coronation was deliberately delayed until the exact anniversary. One design featured Peter alongside Djordje Petrovic, the first Karageorgevic *Gospodar* or Leader of Serbia between 1804 and 1813. The other pictured Djordje Petrovic amidst his insurgents in 1804.(11.3) Only Bulgaria and Montenegro sent representatives to the coronation.

In October 1912 a Balkan League comprising Serbia, Bulgaria, Greece and Montenegro seized upon an increasingly promising Albanian revolt to join in the war against the crumbling Ottoman Empire. King Peter's call to arms preached the brotherhood of all Christian and Muslim Albanians and Serbs, but in reality Serbia coveted Kosovo, Albania was wary of Serbian intentions and the Serb army displayed little sympathy with Albanian communities. The Balkan League won the war, but in June 1913 Bulgaria attacked its erstwhile allies Serbia and Greece for failing to hand over parts of Macedonia they had occupied, as agreed prior to the war. Serbia and Greece, later joined by Romania, totally crushed Bulgaria, and the ensuing Treaty of Bucharest greatly expanded Serbia to the south and south-west. It was also the pre-eminent military force in the Balkans. However, the cost of the two wars across the Balkans had been hundreds of thousands of casualties and appalling atrocities. The ruthless use of heavy artillery bombardments, the recourse to disease-ridden trench warfare, and the mass advances ordered into hails of machine gun fire presaged the greater war soon to come.

The years 1904 to 1915 saw two different definitive sets portraying Peter in uniform. They highlighted his military prestige without emphasizing the suffering.(11.4) As 1914 approached Serbia bathed in the approbation of Croatian, Slovenian, Bosnia-Herzegovinian and Dalmatian Slavs, and Peter himself was feted for his kingdom's relatively free press and political freedom. An unusual set in 1911 raised money for the Serbian Union of Journalists. Just possibly the robed figure represents Ozwiena, the Slav goddess of the voice. (11.5) Initially the stamps were merely fund raising labels with no postal validity, but later they were accepted as postage on newspapers for most of 1912. Many others were cancelled to order for collectors.

Austria-Hungary, though, was greatly perturbed at Serbia's Balkan ascendancy and readiness to interfere in other country's affairs. In 1903 Russia had been quick to acknowledge Peter as king, and Serbian relations warmed with Russia and cooled with Austria-Hungary. A prolonged customs dispute with Austria-Hungary in 1906 was followed by angry protests at Austria-Hungary's annexation of Bosnia in 1908. In 1914 Dragutin Dimitrijevic ('Apis') was now Head of Serbian Military Intelligence and still the leader of the Black Hand Society dedicated to the union of the south Balkan Slavs under Serbian leadership in a new country they would call Yugoslavia.

Archduke Franz Ferdinand, heir to Emperor Franz Joseph, became the target of Black Hand assassins not only because of his Hapsburg lineage but also because of his ideas, however vaguely expressed, on turning the Dual Monarchy into a Triple Monarchy with a third crown covering the southern Slav provinces. This was anathema to those seeking complete autonomy and especially to Serbians who saw their own dynasty, not the Hapsburgs, as the rightful monarch. Franz Ferdinand, of course, envisaged creating a strong bulwark against Serb aggression.

Conspiracy theories abound about his assassination in the Bosnian city of Sarajevo on 28 June 1914, but Gavrilo Princip was one of five Serbs and a Bosnian trained and armed by Apis's colleague Major Vojislav Tankosic with the attack being coordinated by Danilo Ilic, the Black Hand's representative in the city. In addition, overall security was suspiciously slack and the police on duty few in number. Seizing the chance to quash Serbia, Austria-Hungary issued it with a totally

11.4   2p King Peter (from set 29 June 1911+)

11.5   5p Serbian Union of Journalists (from set 1 December 1911)

SERBIA, MONTENEGRO AND EMERGENCE OF THE KINGDOM OF SERBS, CROATS AND SLOVENES (YUGOSLAVIA)

11.6 (E) 15p King Peter on the battlefield (from set 15 October 1915)

11.7 40c French Olivier Merson handstamped POSTES SERBES for use by Serbian exiles in Corfu (from series 1916-18)

11.8 3h Franz Joseph Bosnia-Herzegovina K.u.K. Militarpost overprinted SERBIEN (from series 6 March 1916+)

11.9 10p King Peter and Prince Alexander (from set 1 October 1918+)

unacceptable ultimatum, and war was declared on 28 July 1914.

Serbia planned a defensive campaign until Russian armies arrived. Initially Serbia had some success in forcing back a hurried Austro-Hungarian attack through Bosnia, and even advanced across the Sava river into Syrmia. However further Austro-Hungarian attacks forced a Serbian retreat, and after several weeks of bitter fighting Belgrade was lost in December. Serbia had suffered 170,000 men killed, wounded or captured, and the Austro-Hungarians nearer 215,000. The fighting dragged on and Belgrade was recaptured, but in September 1915 Bulgaria became an enemy again, and German forces bolstered a new Austro-Hungarian campaign. Belgrade was lost once more, and Bulgaria won the battles of Morava, Ovche Pole and Kosovo. A set of Serbian stamps was issued on 15 October that year featuring King Peter on a battlefield, and it seems that although the elderly king played no military part in the campaigns he did visit the troops to boost morale.(11.6) Quite possibly in the chaos many values were used as currency.

In the same month of October a general Serbian retreat was ordered in which Peter himself participated. Struggling through the freezing mountains of Albania to the Adriatic sea during harsh winter conditions around 100,000 soldiers and accompanying civilians died, but early in 1916 the survivors were met at the coast by Allied ships and transported to Corfu. The island became King Peter's seat of government in exile until he returned home on 13 October 1918. A Serbian post office was established in Corfu alongside the Greek civilian one and British and French field post offices. The Serbians used French stamps that were handstamped with the inscription POSTES SERBES.(11.7)

On the mainland only the Serbian territory around Monastir in Macedonia in the far south remained in Serbian and French hands as part of the grindingly slow Allied advance northwards from Greece. From March 1916 the Austrian armies occupying the rest of Serbia introduced a range of Bosnia-Herzegovina *Feldpost* stamps featuring the Emperor Franz Joseph carefully overprinted SERBIEN well away from the portrait.(11.8) The *Feldpost* issues remained in use until the Allies finally broke out of Macedonia in September 1918.

After all the misery, on 24 November 1918 Serbian dreams of Southern Slav unification came true when Peter was elected King of a new country officially termed the Kingdom of Serbs, Croats and Slovenes. On 3 October 1929 it became Yugoslavia although most people, including diplomats, used the far shorter name much earlier. The last stamps from Serbia (until 1941) were issued in several printings on various papers with various perforation types in October 1918 and used into 1920. They featured King Peter silhouetted with Prince Alexander, his son and heir, who had taken over many of his father's duties just before and during the war.(11.9) He acceded to the throne on 1 August 1921.

MONTENEGRO

In 1914 Montenegro was a small mountainous country squashed between the Adriatic Sea to the west, Serbia to the east, Albania to the south and Austria-Hungary to the north. Historically the coastal area had been under Venetian control for several centuries and much of the inland area under Ottoman suzerainty although the warlike tribal communities in Montenegro's heartlands were next to impossible to completely subjugate. Indeed, early in the sixteenth century the Ottoman Empire ceded *de facto* authority within the Sanjak of Montenegro to a locally elected Vladika (a prince-bishop with both religious and secular authority) but even so the region was wracked by vicious blood feuds, internal revolts, and wider rebellions against Ottoman authority.

In the eighteenth century the position of Vladika became hereditary within the Petrovic Njegos family. A century later, however, instability and violence were still much in evidence. In 1858 Montenegro routed an Ottoman army at Grahovac, and this celebrated victory led to significant territorial acquisitions and international recognition of Montenegro's *de facto* independence. Although Danilo II Petrovic Njegos (Vladika 1851-52, Prince 1852-60) was the victor, his Francophile sympathies soon alienated Russia and the many Russian sympathisers within Montenegro. It was, though, a blood feud with a rival tribe over Danilo's taxation that led to his murder in 1860.

His nephew Nicholas succeeded him. Although educated in France, he resisted its allure and greatly preferred Russia and its financial support. As a successful participant in the 1877-78 war against the Ottoman Empire Montenegro almost doubled in size and gained an important Adriatic seaboard. The country prospered with Russian money encouraging communications, schools and military expansion, although generally speaking Nicholas himself still behaved, like Danilo, as though the country, and much of its income, was his personal property and fiefdom. However he achieved international stature, attending Tsar Nicholas II's coronation in 1896, and visiting Queen Victoria at Windsor in 1898.

Stamps featuring Prince Nicholas first appeared in May 1874.(11.10) From 25 July 1893 many appeared overprinted with the dates *1493* and *1893* and a Cyrillic inscription celebrating the four hundredth anniversary of the introduction of printing into Montenegro.(11.11) Ironically, many shades of colour and shifts of place occurred in the overprinting.

In 1896 the first specially designed commemorative set was issued to mark the bicentenary of the dynasty. Vladika Danilo I Petrovic Njegos had been elected in 1696. The stamps featured the Serbian Orthodox Monastery at Cetinje which Danilo I had rebuilt and made the centre of the prince-bishop's spiritual, political and cultural life.(11.12)

Unusually Montenegro had no currency of its own

11.10 15n Prince Nicholas (from set 1898)

11.11 25h Prince Nicholas overprinted 1493 and 1893 and printing anniversary inscription (from set 25 July 1893+)

11.12 30n Monastery near Cetinje (from set 1 September 1896)

11.13 50h Prince Nicholas (from set 12 July 1902)

11.14 1h Prince Nicholas overprinted Constitution 1905 (from set 5 December 1905)

11.15 5k Prince Nicholas (from set 1 June 1907)

until 1909, and at various times it had used Venetian, Turkish and Austro-Hungarian coinage, and in daily life often mixed them. As its stamps reveal, early in the twentieth century it changed from *novcic* and *florins* to *hella* and *krona* with the new currency on a definitive set in July 1902 featuring an older looking Nicholas.(11.13) In 1907 the main currency changed again to *para* and *krone*, but more significantly the previous year Prince Nicholas had ordered the first national coins in nickel and bronze, and, later, silver and gold. They were based on the medieval Serbian Empire's *perper,* and, just possibly, the idea had emanated from his ambitions of regional unification, hopefully under his leadership.

With the murder of King Alexander of Serbia in 1903 it would have been surprising if Nicholas, now well-established and respected, did not think the unification of the southern Slavs might be achieved under his authority rather than the Karageorgevics. Although somewhat reluctantly, in 1905 he had granted Montenegro its first constitution, formalized a western European style criminal code and permitted greater press freedom. In 1905 stamps were overprinted *Constitution* in Latin and Cyrillic script and the date *1905*.(11.14)

On 1 June 1907 a portrait of Nicholas diplomatically adorned in the historic Serbian/Montenegrin cap appeared on a set of definitive stamps.(11.15) Three years later a set of twelve stamps featuring Nicholas at various ages, and with his wife Milena, were issued on 28 August 1910 –

SERBIA, MONTENEGRO AND EMERGENCE OF THE KINGDOM OF SERBS, CROATS AND SLOVENES (YUGOSLAVIA)

11.16 1pa Prince Nicholas as a youth 1855, 5pa on a charger in the year of his accession, 2pa and 20pa King Nicholas and Queen Milena in 1860 and 1910 (from anniversary set 28 August 1910)

11.17 2per King Nicholas (from set 1 April 1913)

11.18 15h Franz Joseph K.u.K. Feldpost with K.U.K. MILIT VERWALTUNG MONTENEGRO overprint (from pair 1 March 1917) with a first day cancellation from the capital city of Cetinje, and unissued 15h with Montenegro overprint

the day he celebrated the fiftieth anniversary of his reign and assumed the title of king in response to a well timed petition from the national assembly.(11.16)

King Nicholas was an enthusiastic member of the Balkan League that waged war against the Ottoman Empire in 1912-13. He gained the small neighbouring Turkish region of Pljevlja but the Great Powers dominating the peace talks forced him to cede Shkodra to Albania. Montenegro's siege of this well-fortified key city had lasted from 28 October 1912 until 23 April 1913, and cost 10,000 lives. The final definitive set of the Kingdom of Montenegro was issued on 1 April 1913 when victory seemed in sight, and once again featured Nicholas in the Serbian/Montenegrin cap.(11.17) By then the death toll, and humiliation at having Shkodra snatched from his grasp, had cost Nicholas much of his popularity.

In July 1914 Montenegro hastened to support Serbia in its struggle against Austria-Hungary, and for a time it was supported with supplies by France through the port of Bar until it was blockaded by Austro-Hungarian warships. In 1914 and early 1915 Montenegrin forces enjoyed some success in bombarding Kotor and taking Budva, and helping resist attacks on Serbia.   However by December 1915 Austro-Hungarian, German and Bulgarian armies finally overrun Serbia, and in January 1916 Montenegro was occupied too.

King Nicholas fled first to Italy and then established a government-in-exile in Bordeaux. Austrian stamps dominated Montenegro. The 10h and 15h *K. .u K. Feldpost* stamps picturing the Emperor Franz Joseph were issued overprinted on the left side *K. U. K. MILIT. VERWALTUNG* (IMPERIAL & ROYAL ARMY SERVICE) and on the right *MONTENEGRO*. The two values were later overprinted just *Montenegro*, but too late to be used.(11.18) Numerous Franz Joseph and Charles stamps without overprints were available to the civilian population.

King Nicholas would never return to Montenegro, and in November 1918 his kingdom ceased to exist. It had been annexed by Serbia. In the brutal arena of Balkan politics he had been trumped by the Karageorgevics. Nicholas died in France in 1921, still claiming the throne of the Kingdom of the Croats, Serbs and Slovenes.

YUGOSLAVIA

Very soon after the liberation of Montenegro by Allied forces in early November 1918 two seemingly opposing events occurred in the region soon to be known as the Kingdom of Serbs, Croats and Slovenes, and later Yugoslavia. The first was the avid lobbying of the victorious Allies by various Slav politicians for the unification of the southern Slavs in Bosnia-Hercegovina, Croatia, Slovenia, Carinthia and Dalmatia with Serbia and Montenegro. The second was the utter chaos spreading across these war-torn provinces and countries as the Austro-Hungarian Dual Monarchy collapsed, its armies disintegrated, and Serbian and Italian forces sought to claim territory by right of occupation.

Confusing the situation even further, not every southern Slav politician wanted unification, and not every Slav desired unification under the Serbian monarchy. Croats and Serbs might be Slavs but they detested each other, and many Slovenes, Carinthians and, indeed, Croats, had dutifully and sometimes enthusiastically fought in the Austro-Hungarian armies against Serbia and Montenegro. And religious and tribal loyalties cut deeply into any thoughts of greater integration and racial harmony with, for example, most Serbs being Eastern Orthodox Christians using Cyrillic script while most Croats were Roman Catholic and used the Latin alphabet. And Serbia made little secret of its hatred of Bosnia's Muslims despite its loud public criticisms of Austria-Hungary's historic ill-treatment of the province's Slavs.

The key American, British, French and Italian members of the Paris Peace Conference only got round to seriously considering the region's future in February 1919, and then were confronted with nearly a hundred representatives from the assorted countries and provinces. With varying degrees of enthusiasm most Conference members accepted that the establishment of large new country was preferable to any return to Austro-Hungarian overlordship or the creation of several new small countries that would end up susceptible to pressure from much larger ones.

There were, though, major danger signs, but these were never resolved by the Allies or by members of the new country. They blighted Yugoslavia's development and contributed to its vicious fragmentation in 1941. No-one had any clear idea where the borders of the new united country would be, or exactly which provinces and countries would be integrated into it. Italy detested the thought of a large strong Slav nation across the Adriatic Sea challenging its claims to Istria and Dalmatia, while Serbia sought to ensure the new country stretched as far as possible north and east into ex-Hungarian lands. Serbia had little genuine interest in the fate of the Carinthians and Slovenes, and they knew it.

Nikola Pasic, Serbia's aged Prime Minister, played the diplomatic game well. Fundamentally he sought the union of all Serbs, including those over the border in Austria-Hungary, and cared little for other Slavs. However while he, King Peter, and Prince Alexander saw the end of the war as the moment for all their wartime aspirations of expansion to be fulfilled, so did influential and fundamentally rival politicians in Croatia, Montenegro and Bosnia-Hercegovina.

Both Pasic's Serbian National Radical Party and the independent Yugoslav National Committee in London headed by a Croat, Ante Trumbic, preached Balkan liberation and unity. And both organisations received enthusiastic support from Slav communities, especially in the USA, and in July 1918 Pasic and Trumbic finally agreed on the unification of Serbia, Croatia and Slovenia under the Serbian monarchy. It was a tactical decision to secure international agreement, but personally both men hated the marriage of political convenience. They never resolved between them the key issues of borders or whether the country should be a federated or unitary state.

Events moved dangerously fast. In the euphoria of impending victory, on 29 October 1918 a National Council of Croats, Serbs and Slovenes met in Zagreb, Croatia's capital, to declare independence from Austria-Hungary but beyond this there remained deep divisions regarding union with Serbia or the creation of several autonomous countries. However at this time the Serbian army was advancing north, east and south across Austro-Hungarian territory, and the French army allowed it free rein as France favoured a strong Yugoslavia to hold Italy's Balkan ambitions in check. And while this was happening Nikola Pasic encouraged, and indeed pressurised, the self-elected and supposedly representative assemblies in Bosnia-Herzegovina, Montenegro and the three former Kingdom of Hungary provinces of Baranja, Backa and the Banat to vote for union with Serbia. Baranja, Backa and the Banat had enjoyed a very brief period of post-war independence, but Serbian arguments and threats proved irresistible. And with Italian forces advancing to seize the northern Adriatic ports, Zagreb's National Council, with no army at its disposal and with chaos looming, had little choice but to cooperate with Serbia. On 1 December 1918 Prince Alexander of Serbia proclaimed the Kingdom of Serbs, Croats and Slovenes with his father as monarch. And thus King Nicholas of Montenegro found himself without a throne.

In November and December 1918 each major component of the new country commenced issuing an array of stamps with hurriedly applied overprints marking and publicising the event. In and around Sarajevo stocks of pre-war and wartime Bosnia-Herzegovina stamps featuring the Emperor Franz Joseph, his 1910 birthday, the War Invalids and Emperor Charles reappeared overprinted *1918 DRZAVA S.H.S 1918 Bosna i Hercegovna* (1918 COUNTRY OF SERBS, CROATS & SLOVENES 1918 Bosnia and Herzegovina).(11.19) Others appeared with the same inscription in Cyrillic. Slightly later, similarly overprinted Postage Due and Newspaper stamps appeared, although without the date.

Significantly, in March 1919 the overprinted inscription changed to KRALJEVSTO S.H.S. or Srba, Hrvata i Slovenaca (KINGDOM OF SERBS, CROATS &

11.19 1910 80th birthday of Franz Joseph and 1918 War Invalids Fund overprinted in Cyrillic and Latin script 1918 COUNTRY OF S(ERBS), C(ROATS) & S(LOVENES) Bosnia and Herzegovina 1918 (from series November 1918+)

SERBIA, MONTENEGRO AND EMERGENCE OF THE KINGDOM OF SERBS, CROATS AND SLOVENES (YUGOSLAVIA)

11.20   1912 Franz Joseph K.u.K. Feldpost overprinted with obliterating square and KRALJEVSTO S.H.S. (from series March 1919)

11.23   40f Hungarian turul in his lair overprinted HRVATSKA SHS and NAROD VIJECE (from set November 1918)

11.21   20h Mostar and 40h Mail wagon overprinted KRALJEVSTO S.H.S. Srba, Hrvata i Slovenaca in Latin and Cyrillic script with surcharges for the War Victims' Fund (from set March 1919)

11.24   10h 'Freedom of Croatia' represented as a kneeling figure above the Arms of the old Kingdom of Croatia-Slavonia (from set 29 November 1918)

11.25   3f angel of peace, 10f sailor, standard and falcon, and 1k falcon (from set 15 January 1919)

11.22   1k Hungarian Parliament overprinted HRVATSKA SHS and KRUNA (from set 18 November 1918+)

SLOVENES) in Latin or Cyrillic script. (11.20)   Several stamps had surcharges for charities supporting the countless victims of the war.(11.21)   Postage Due and Newspaper stamps were also overprinted, and these were often permitted for ordinary postage in these tumultuous times.

In Croatia a range of Kingdom of Hungary stamps – including those featuring the harvesters, the turul, Parliament, and Charles and Zita – were used with variously designed overprints partially obliterating the images and inscribed *HRVATSKA SHS* (CROATIA : SERBS, CROATS, SLOVENES).(11.22)   Some had the additional popular inscription *NAROD VIJECE* (THE PEOPLE'S COUNCIL).(11.23)

On 29 November 1918 a specially designed stamp portraying an allegorical Freedom of Croatia was issued.(11.24)   This was followed in January 1919 by a distinctive set featuring an Angel of Peace, a falcon symbol of Liberty, and a sailor with a falcon and national standard.(11.25)   In the light of the prevailing tensions, it was significant that the design of these later sets boldly incorporated the name *HRVATSKA* (CROATIA) as a title as well as either *DRZAVNA POSTA* or *DRZ SHS POSTA* (STATE POST or STATE OF SERBS, CROATS & SLOVENES POST).

Slovenia was also quick off the mark with specially designed stamps that seemed to portray the sense of optimism at impending Slav unity.   From 3 January 1919 it issued a set of stamps featuring a man breaking the chains binding him, a cherubic herald of peace treading on skulls, an allegory of Yugoslavia with three falcons (the main regions), and a portrait of King Peter. The inscription read *DRZAVA SHS* (COUNTRY OF SERBS, CROATS & SLOVENES).(11.26)   Such was the

11.26   20v chainbreaker, 50v allegory of Yugoslavia, 1k herald of peace, and 5k King Peter (from set 3 January 1919+)

11.27 Redesigned 10p chainbreaker and 2d King Peter (from set 9 June 1920)

11.28 4v Newspaper (from set 1919)

11.29 1919 Newspaper overprinted 1920 KGCA and 25p/50p surcharges (from set September 1920+)

11.30 15p Prince Alexander (from set 16 January 1921) and 5d King Alexander (from set 1 September 1931)

kingdom's government; indeed many Serbs saw the new country primarily as an enlarged Serbia. Thus in February 1919 when the Paris Peace Conference eventually found time to consider the issues, the situation seemed, at least superficially, to have resolved itself. Great Britain and France still recognised Nicholas as King of Montenegro, but were not prepared to support him even though there was a brief, but unsuccessful, uprising on his behalf in Montenegro. The main discussions centred on the borders, not the creation, of the new country. The Treaty of St Germain in September 1919 formally recognised the the Kingdom of Serbs, Croats and Slovenes, and the Treaty of Trianon in June 1920 attempted to settle at least some of the border issues. The new kingdom successfully acquired the small north-western regions of Medjumurje and Prekomurje from Hungary, or, rather, had its occupation of them formally confirmed. It was also awarded most of defeated Bulgaria's Macedonian territory. The ex-Hungarian provinces of the Banat, Backa and Baranja had opted for union with Serbia, although pointedly keeping their provincial assemblies, but the Treaty of Trianon stored up future trouble by dividing Backa and Baranja between Hungary and the Kingdom of Serbs, Croats and Slovenes, and the Banat between both these two countries and Romania.

Founded in political confusion and amidst exaggerated stories of Slav harmony, the Kingdom of Serbs, Croats and Slovenes spluttered into life riven with jealousies and surrounded by enemies. Italy was especially aggressive in its claims for Istria, Fiume and Dalmatia, and many Croats and Slovenes never forgave the mainly Serbian government for finally signing away Istria and parts of Dalmatia in 1920.

Carinthia lay in the unresolved post-war borderland between German-Austria and the Kingdom of Serbs, Croats and Slovenes. Despite its provisional assembly rejecting Slovenia's claims, on 5 November 1918 Serbian forces occupied the southern half but met with stiff opposition. The Allies intervened, forced the occupiers to leave and the Treaty of St Germain gave a small slice to Slovenia but ordered a plebiscite in the main southern half. The north (Zone B), which was mainly German-Austrian, did not need a plebiscite and was duly awarded to Austria. In September 1920 two of the cherubic Slovenian Newspaper stamps were issued with a heavy premium and various eye-catching overprints with the initials *K G C A* (Karinthian Governmental Commission Zone A) to support the campaign and assist Carinthians to return home to vote.(11.29) However Zone A (the south) returned a majority of 59.1% in favour of Austria.

During the 1920s the new kingdom enjoyed some positive growth in its economy, but not in political stability. Much of the time the National Assembly was boycotted by angry political groups and at other times it

chaotic state of supplies and production that the issue had several printers, types of paper, perforation sizes, shades of colour and clarity of image.

In June 1920 the chain breaker, allegory and King Peter images were used again in new formats when the province converted from Austro-Hungarian krona to the Serbian currency of dinars that assumed supremacy throughout the new kingdom. The inscription now read KRALJEVSTO SHS (THE KINGDOM OF SERBS CROATS & SLOVENES.(11.27) Slovenia, in common with Croatia, also used its own designs for Postage Due and Newspaper stamps – the latter showed a cherub with a backpack of newspapers.(11.28)

Although the Croat Ante Trumbic became Foreign Minister, from the outset Serbs dominated the new

11.31 (E) Disabled Soldiers' Fund (set 30 January 1921)

resounded with vitriolic speeches denigrating the integrity of opposing politicians and accusing them of subversive regional bias. The attempts made by politicians and parties to present a more united front against the Serbs invariably failed to survive the deeper ethnic and religious divisions separating them. The repeated issuing of stamps featuring Alexander as Prince and then King (1921-34) in 1921, 1924, 1926, 1931 and 1933 reinforced national unity for the Serbs but only confirmed Serbian dominance for others.(11.30)

On 30 January 1921 a set of three surcharged stamps for the Disabled Soldiers' Fund once again highlighted essentially Serbian themes – as well as the continuing human suffering from the war.(11.31) The 10p+10p was taken from a celebrated painting of a Serbian maiden searching for her betrothed on the Kosovo battlefield of 1389. However a dying soldier to whom she stopped to give wine and bread pointed sadly towards her dead lover lying amidst his friends. The 15p+15p showed a wounded soldier on the Serbian retreat through Albania in late 1915, and the 25p+25p contained a representation of national unity in the form of a Serb, Croat and Slovene holding aloft the royal crown of Serbia, now the crown of the greatly extended kingdom.

Political life literally exploded on 19 June 1928 when a Serb delegate shot at five Croat members in the National Assembly, killing three of them. In the tense and chaotic aftermath King Alexander suspended the constitution on 6 January 1929, banned political parties, assumed executive power and formally renamed the country Yugoslavia. Although a thorough-going Serb and comfortable with dictatorial powers, Alexander sought to balance tight control of the country with some concessions to Croatian aspirations by granting them more local autonomy.

One small sign of the modest change was the set of three in November 1929 belatedly marking the millenary of Croatia.(11.32) The 3d pictured Tomislav who was raised from duke to king in 925 and held much of what is modern Croatia against Hungarian and Bulgarian invaders. The 50p featured Duvno Cathedral that in medieval times was in the Kingdom of Croatia. In 1929 King Alexander changed Duvno's name to Tomislavgrad, but possibly clouding the honour for Croatians was the fact that Alexander had named his own son Tomislav. The 1d pictured the medieval King Tomislav facing the modern King Alexander. Although highlighting King Tomislav, the set could easily be interpreted as Serbia and the Karageorgevics inheriting Croatian power and prestige. The lower inscription read TISUCGODISNJICA HRVATSKOGA KRALJEVSTVA 925-1925 (A THOUSAND YEAR OLD CROATIAN KINGDOM 925-1925) but the one at the head read KRALJEVINA SRBA, HRVATA I SLOVENACA (The Kingdom of the Serbs, Croats and Slovenes).

In the 1930s violent extremists such as Ante Pavelic, the ruler of Croatia under the Nazis, and the Macedonian Revolutionary Organisation seeking autonomy, found ready refuge in Mussolini's Italy where they plotted the downfall of Alexander and Yugoslavia. It was a Macedonian who fired the shots that killed him in Marseilles in 1934. By then Yugoslavia was being courted by Nazi Germany and gratefully accepting Hitler's offer of a trade deal and diplomatic support, and all the while Italy was encouraging those hoping to fatally damage its fragile internal stability. In 1941 Yugoslavia finally shattered into warring factions and Axis puppet states.

11.32 Millenary of the Kingdom of Croatia (set 1 November 1929)

CHAPTER 12
Romania

Romania gradually emerged as a country in the nineteenth century. It comprised the two ancient principalities of Wallachia and Moldavia, the former lying between the lower Danube and southern Carpathian Mountains and the latter between the Dneister River and eastern Carpathians. Both principalities succumbed to the Ottoman Turks in the 15th centuries, and for several centuries were wracked by internal feuds between the boyars (nobles) interspersed with abortive revolts against their Ottoman overlords. When the Ottoman grip began to loosen in the later eighteenth century the Russia and Hapsburg Empires were eager to expand their influence and territory in this strategically significant region. Indeed, in 1774 Bukovina, a small region north-east of Transylvania, was seized by the Hapsburgs, and after defeating the Ottoman Turks in 1828-29 Russia secured Bessarabia, a region bounded by the River Dneister to the east and River Prut to the west giving access to the Danube in the south. Russia also secured the right to occupy Wallachia and Moldavia to protect, and in practice exploit, their trade. The scene was set for conflict and controversy lasting well into the twentieth century.

Greater prosperity and loosening Ottoman overlordship fuelled the agitation for complete independence, and both Wallachia and Moldavia agreed this could be best achieved through united action. Gradually the generic name Romania, harking back to the Roman province of Dacia, came into use. Great Britain, France and the Ottoman Turks were victorious allies in the Crimean War against Russia (1853-56), and agreed that a strong internally autonomous united Romania would be a buffer not only against Russian but also Austrian expansion. Russia was obliged to return southern Bessarabia to Romania.

In 1859 the Allies confirmed the local choice of Alexander Cuza, a minor Moldavian prince, as ruler of both principalities that were still nominally subject to Turkish overlordship. Unfortunately his mishandling of agrarian reform angered the boyars who lost their feudal rights and also the peasants who found their plots inadequate to make a living and, as a result, were rendered helpless victims of the boyars once again. As we shall see, he left a legacy of class bitterness for generations to come, and this in turn affected political stability.

When Cuza was ousted in 1866 Romania selected another constitutional monarch acceptable to the Great Powers as well as Turkey, and Prince Carol of Hohenzollern-Sigmaringen, a branch of the Prussian royal family, was duly installed.

A few years later the balance of power was upset again. After the combined Russian, Romanian, Bulgarian, Serbian and Montenegrin victory over the Ottoman Turks in 1878, the total independence of Romania, Serbia and Montenegro was assured. Romania also gained north Dobruja, a valuable region bounded by the curving Danube to the north and west and the Black Sea to the east. However the post-war Congress of Berlin laid the seeds of further conflict. Romania resented having to return southern Bessarabia to Russia, and Bulgaria coveted north Dobruja as it already possessed the south.

Not long afterwards, on 15 March 1881 the Romanian parliament proudly made the country a full monarchy and Carol was crowned king on 10 May. He appeared on numerous sets of stamps.(12.1) Possessing a Germanic love of grandeur, he built a grand palace and delighted in the army, and yet remained popular in the essentially backward country he ruled for forty eight years. To avoid deposition and, indeed, assassination in the Balkans for so long were notable achievements. The new kingdom developed economically over the next thirty years, but widespread poverty and the unresolved land issue led to a firmly suppressed peasants' revolt in 1907 and an estimated 11,000 deaths.

Special pictorial sets started to appear early in the new century reinforcing the positive roles of King Carol and Queen Elisabeth, notably their concern for the poor and

12.1 5b King Carol (from series 1893+)

12.2   15b Four-in-hand mail coach (from set 1 May 1903)

12.5   5b+10b Queen of Romania nursing wounded soldier inscribed 'The wounds dressed and the tears wiped away' (from set 10 March 1906)

12.3   10b+10b Queen of Romania spinning inscribed 'God guide our hand' (from set 1 January 1906)

12.6   10b+10b Welfare Fund inscribed 'But glory, honour and peace to all who do good' (from set august 1906)

12.4 (E) 15b+10b Queen of Romania weaving inscribed 'Woman weaves the future of the country (from set 5 March 1906)

12.7 (E)   3b+7b Angel guides poor family to Crown Princess Marie (from set January 1907)

sick, and close association with national developments. In 1903 two closely linked sets featured Bucharest's prestigious new Post Office and dramatic images of a speeding four in hand mail coach.(12.2)   1906 was a bumper year for issues.   Two welfare fund sets that January and March featured Queen Elisabeth attired in rural costumes spinning and weaving.   In her own handwriting the former is inscribed *God guide our hand*, and the latter *Woman weaves the future of the country*.(12.3/12.4)

A third set, also in March 1906, featured Elisabeth tending a wounded soldier; its inscription read *The wounds dressed and the tears wiped away*.(12.5)   A fourth welfare set in August pictured an angel, possibly the Queen herself, and the all-embracing inscription *But glory, honour and peace to all who do good*.(12.6)   All four had the logo *Timbre de Binefacere* (Postage and Charity) and were sold at a premium.   Elisabeth was a renowned writer and poet under the name Carmen Sylva; she had worked as a nurse during the 1877-78 war and remained fully engaged in educational and charitable throughout her life.

In January 1907 a fifth welfare set extended the royal connection by picturing an angel guiding a poor family towards help offered by Crown Princess Marie and her children. (12.7) Formerly Princess Marie of Edinburgh, she was married to the future King Ferdinand of Romania and became immensely popular for her charity work, especially during the First World War, and for her vigorous post-war campaign for international recognition of a larger Romania.

12.8   50b 25th Anniversary of the kingdom (from set June 1906)

King Carol, too, had his share of carefully crafted philatelic publicity.   In June 1906 a set featuring the Latin motto NIHIL SINE DEO (NOTHING WITHOUT

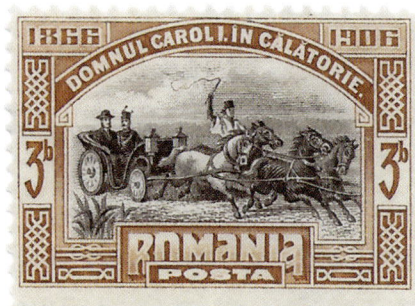 

12.9 (E) King Carol's 40th anniversary 3b, 5b, 40b and 2l (from set July 1906)

12.10 10b Angel supporting peasant ploughman, and 25b Exhibition Hall (from Jubilee Exhibition set 29 October 1906)

GOD) with an angel facing the king's portrait celebrated the 25th anniversary of the kingdom with an adroit combination of pride, service and humility.(12.8)

Amidst all these issues, in July 1906 a set of ten dramatic images marking Carol's fortieth year as monarch highlighted key events from his life, and most notably his role in the 1877-78 war.(12.9) Among the images was Prince Carol in a carriage (3b), probably the one in which he was met at the Romanian border by Ionel Bratianu, his future prime minister in 1866. Owing to the war between Germany and Austria, Carol, a German prince, had travelled across Hapsburg lands incognito. Another (5b) featured Carol at the Battle of Calafat in 1877 when Romanian forces replied to Turkish shelling by bombarding Vidin across the River Danube. The 40b showed Carol's triumphant return to Bucharest in 1878. He had been an active commander of both Romanian and Russian forces. The 2l jumped to the King and Queen's ceremonial visit to a Shrine of St Nicholas, possibly at Brasov, in 1904.

In October 1906 a set of eleven stamps inscribed *EXPOZITIA GENERALA* were sold at the national and royal JUBILEE EXHIBITION in Bucharest.(12.10) The lower values featured the exhibition building, a rural farmhouse, and an angel watching over a peasant ploughing; the higher values portrayed the royal family's pavilion, Carol on horseback, and Elisabeth in royal attire. Not all was peace and harmony though as the following summer the peasants' revolt swept the country.

After this flurry, special issues dried up for several years. In their stead King Carol appeared on three slightly different definitive designs between 1908 and his death in October 1914.(12.11)

Throughout these decades Romania remained squashed between the potentially aggressive Austro-Hungarian, Ottoman and Russian Empires, and bordered by resentful neighbours. As the twentieth century dawned Russia still wanted access to the Mediterranean, and Great Britain, France and Italy still sought to prevent it. Propping up the Ottoman Empire was one way to do it, and keeping the Balkan states stable and independent was another.

In late 1912 what is known as the First Balkan War broke out. In search of territorial expansion Greece, Serbia, Bulgaria and Montenegro allied against the Ottoman Empire. However Romania stayed neutral in return for Bulgaria's promise to cede its strategic border fortress of Silistra. The Balkan allies were victorious, but

12.11 3b King Carol (from set 1909+)

soon fell out when Serbia and Greece reneged on their commitment to allow Bulgaria most of Macedonia. In June 1913 Tsar Ferdinand of Bulgaria invaded Serbia and Greece in the Second Balkan War but soon reeled under their counter-offensives. Ever eager for easy pickings, Montenegro and the Turks then attacked Bulgaria, and Romania joined them when Bulgaria stubbornly refused to cede Silistra.

The subsequent Treaty of Bucharest revealed that jealousies among the Great Powers matched those swirling around the Balkans. Albania achieved independence at the insistence of Italy and the Dual Monarchy, both of whom had designs on it. Macedonia was carved up between Serbia and Greece with a small slice for Bulgaria, and Romania received southern Dobruja. Russia's move toward the Mediterranean was thwarted once again, and its only friend was Serbia.

Romania was reasonably satisfied though. On Christmas Day 1913 a set celebrated the acquisition of south Dobruja with images of the Romanian crown shining over a Danube fortress, allegorical figures of Dobruja clasping Romania, views of troops crossing the Danube, the port of Constanta and a provincial church and school.(12.12) A final stamp pictured King Carol with Prince Mircea the Great who ruled Wallachia at its greatest extent, including all Dobruja, between 1386 and 1418.

12.12 *3b Crown of Romania over Danube fortress, 1b Dobruja clasping Romania, 5b troops crossing the Danube, 10b Constanta, and 15b King Carol and Prince Mircea (from set 25 December 1913)*

12.13 (E) *Silistra Commemoration Committee PEO (1913)*

Around the same time an unusual and carefully designed stamp appeared inscribed *Scutit Posta Ordinul 23466-913* (Postage Exempt Order 23466-913) for use by the Silistra Commemoration Committee.(12.13) In the centre was an allegory of Romania carrying the national flag along a Danube causeway. In the background was Romania's huge Anghel Saligny railway bridge built across the Danube between 1890 and 1895 to connect Muntenia with northern Dobruja. Assertive patriotic inscriptions read *Voeste si vei putea* (To want and you shall be able) and *Dreptul nostru* (Our right).

Romania faced a dilemma when war broke out again in August 1914. It coveted Transylvania in the Kingdom of Hungary and Bessarabia in Russia. It had important links with France, but was well aware of the dangers when Austria-Hungary defeated Serbia, and when Bulgaria and Turkey joined Austria-Hungary and Germany. Very quickly all trade down the Danube and through the Dardenelles was blocked. And very quickly Bucharest was full of competing diplomats and agents from the warring Great Powers seeking an alliance.

Romania stayed neutral until the fateful summer of 1916 when General Brusilov's massive Russian offensive forced a chaotic Austro-Hungarian retreat. With Transylvania uppermost in mind, and with Franco-British assurances that their forces landing in Salonika would soon be attacking the Bulgarians in Macedonia, Romania joined the Allies that August. For several weeks Romanian armies poured into Transylvania and seized strategic Carpathian passes, but then everything turned horribly wrong. A Bulgarian and German offensive in Dobruja overran Romanian defences around the Danube, and the Germans and Austro-Hungarians broke the Romanians in Transylvania, and advanced on Bucharest. Ferdinand, king only since October 1914, and his ministers fled to Iasi in the far north-east and the Germans imposed martial law on the occupied parts, including Bucharest. A quarter

12.14 10b King Carol overprinted TIMBRU DE AJUTOR (from pair 11 January 1915)

12.15 10b Queen weaving inscribed TIMBRU DE AJUTOR (from pair 1916)

12.16 80 BANI K.u.K Feldpost (from set 1 March 1918+)

12.17 20pf Germania overprinted with M.V.i.R. tablet and 25 Bani (from set 1 June 1917)

12.18 30pf Germania overprinted with Gothic M.V.i.R. and 40 Bani (from set 2 July 1917+)

12.19 10pf Germania overprinted Rumanien and 10 Bani (from set 1 March 1918)

12.20 10b Romanian TIMBRU D'AJUTOR and 20pf Germania overprinted Gultig 9. Armee (from sets 10 March 1918+)

of a million Romanian soldiers had died.

The Allied Salonika offensive had some success but far too late to help, and to Romania's fury France and Britain could offer no further assistance except some food supplies via a tortuous route through Russia. And when Lenin pulled Russia out of the war in December 1917, Romania's residual resistance ended in February 1918 in the face of overwhelming German numbers and half a million dead. It was a country defeated, occupied, hungry and bitter. Late in 1918, though, belated Allied successes on the Salonika front, the defeat of Bulgaria, news of German retreats in the west and the chaos within the Dual Monarchy gave renewed heart to Romania, and its military forces regrouped just in time to take advantage of the post-Armistice confusion and its opportunities.

Stamp issues reflected the pendulum swings of fortune. From January 1915 a variety of special postal tax stamps were introduced to raise money for national relief funds. Initially these included supplies of 5b and 10b King Carol definitive stamps overprinted TIMBRU DE AJUTOR (AID STAMP), but in 1916 an image of the Queen weaving was used with the inscription as part of the design.(12.14/12.15) The figure was viewed from the back and probably represented Queen Marie as the dowager Queen Elisabeth died that March. The purchase of postal tax stamps was made mandatory at various times, and any failure to attach them to mail incurred hefty Postage Due charge

In the autumn of 1916 German and Austro-Hungarian forces occupied the country south and west of the River Sereth. In Austro-Hungarian areas *K. u. K. Feldpost* stamps with Romanian bani values in red were used from 1 November 1917, and values in black from 1 March 1918.(12.16)

In June 1917 the German military administration started using the 15pf, 20pf, and 40pf Germania stamps overprinted with bani values and a tablet reading M.V.i.R. (*Militarverwaltung in Rumanien* Military Administration in Romania).(12.17) In July the overprint was simplified and designed wholly in Gothic script, and a 10pf Germania stamp was added.(12.18) And in March 1918 the M.V.i.R. logo was replace by *Rumanien*. (12.19)

In March 1918 some 10pf, 15pf, 20pf and 30pf Germania stamps were overprinted with the boxed logo *Gultig 9. Armee* (Valid 9th Army). Romanian TIMBRU D'AJUTOR and fiscal stamps were similarly overprinted for army use.(12.20) The German 9th army had been reformed specifically for the Transylvanian campaign, and remained in Romania until hurriedly dispatched to the hard-pressed Western Front in September 1918, thereby easing the pressure on Romania itself.

Bulgarian forces occupied Dobruja in 1916, and ensured overprinted Bulgarian stamps marked the achievement.(12.21)

Increasingly Romanian issues were limited to Iasi and the unoccupied north east, and resort was made to overprinting older stocks – and raising revenue. In May 1918 some stocks of 1b King Carol stamps reappeared overprinted as a postal tax issue with the surcharge '25 BANI', and the 5b and 10b appeared overprinted *1918* for the same purpose.

Some time in 1918 as Romania desperately reorganized itself, dies of King Carol stamps from 1893 and 1908 were used to produce a set of eight definitive stamps in new colours.(12.22) By then he had been dead for nearly four years, but at least some Romanian stamps could be provided for the unoccupied parts of Moldavia, and later the whole country.

On 31 October 1918 the Aster Revolution brought Count Karolyi to power in Hungary, and he ordered the army to disarm. Hungary was in no effective position to contest the decision of the National Council of Romanians in Transylvania to declare for union with Romania. Despite Hungarian protests, the Romanian army, with the Allies approval, advanced across Transylvania towards Cluj and Sighet in the face of the hostile but confused and disbanding Hungararian army. However outright war broke out in April 1919 after Bela Kun seized power, and after initial Hungarian success the Romanian counter offensive entered Budapest and ended the Hungarian Soviet Republic. In June 1919 the Treaty of Versailles formally ceded Transylvania and Bukovina to Romania and further treaties in 1919 and 1920 defined the exact border with Hungary. Bessarabia had wrested itself free from Russia after the 1917 revolution and also united with Romania. In 1922 Ferdinand and Marie were finally crowned King and Queen in Alba Iulia Cathedral.

After the Treaty of Versailles numerous Hungarian stamps found lying in Transylvanian post offices and warehouses – the 1913 flood relief, war charity, harvester, Parliament, Charles and Zita, Postage Due and Newspaper sets – were overprinted Bani or Lei and a double circle surrounding the inscription *Regatul Romaniei* (Kingdom of Romania).(12.23) In the centre of the circle the mirror image 'F' refers to Ferdinand, and small letters 'P. T. T.' to 'Posts, Telegraphs, Telephones'. Some areas received the King Carol definitive stamps overprinted with King Ferdinand's monogram.(12.24)

In January 1920 the first definitive stamps featuring King Ferdinand were issued.(12.25) Various papers and perforation combs were used, and slight design variations

12.23 80s Hungarian Parliament with Kingdom of Romania overprint (from series 26 July 1919)

12.24 1908 5b King Carol overprinted with King Ferdinand's monogram (from set 1919)

12.25 1b King Ferdinand (from set January 1920+)

12.21 Bulgarian 25st Tsar Ferdinand overprinted Military Post in Romania (from set 1916+)

12.22 Souvenir cover postmarked Iasi, dated 9 August 1918, with 1918-19 King Carol reprints in new colours – the 1890s 25b, and 1908 10b overprinted 1918, 1b overprinted 25 BANI, and 15b.

occurred in the value tablets. Not surprisingly after the tumult and distress of war, new postal tax stamps were in frequent use during the early 1920s. They featured a mother embracing an elderly man and young child.(12.26)

In due course during the 1920s special pictorial sets appeared celebrating the monarchy and the nation's past and present achievements. The first, on 15 October 1922, celebrated the coronation and featured Alba Iulia Cathedral (5b), King Ferdinand wearing a military steel helmet (25b and 3l), Romania's Coat of Arms (50b), Queen Marie (1l and 6l), and King Ferdinand and Michael the Brave (2l).(12.27)   Michael (1558-1601) was a national hero for his successful wars that briefly united Wallachia, Moldavia and Transylvania before his assassination by a jealous rival.

12.26   25b (Asistenta Sociala) Charity/Welfare Postal Tax (from series 1921+)

12.27   5b Alba Iulia Cathedral, 1l Queen Marie and 3l King Ferdinand (from coronation set 15 October 1922)

All ten stamps in the second set on 1 July 1926 featured the king to mark his 60th birthday. The third set on 15 March 1927 ostensibly honoured the 50th anniversary of the Romanian Geographical Society but its five heavily surcharged stamps created strong links between the present monarch, his greatly enlarged country and his illustrious predecessors.(12.28)   The 1l+9l proudly featured 'Greater Romania', and the 5l+5l Kings Carol and Ferdinand. The 6l+4l featured the monument erected by the Roman Emperor Trajan to mark his decisive defeat of the Dacian ruler Decebalus at Adamclisi in Dobruja in the winter of 101-102AD. The 3l+7l pictured Michael the Brave, and the 2l+8l Stephen

12.28   Romanian Geographical Society (set 15 March 1927)

12.29   5l Hotin Fortress and 10l Cetata Alba Fortress (from 10th Anniversary of Annexation of Bessarabia set 29 April 1928). Hotin became Khotyn and Cetata Alba became Bilhorod-Dnistrovskyi in Ukraine SSR after the Second World War and remain in Ukraine today.

12.30   5l Bran Castle and 10l King Ferdinand with cheering crowds and inscription SERBARILE UNIREI ARDE ALULUI (Celebrating the Forged Union) (from Union with Transylvania set 10 May 1929) Bran Castle was Queen Marie's favourite retreat, and long thought, erroneously, to be the origin of Dracula's Castle.

the Great whose long reign as Prince of Moldavia from 1457 to 1504 was fraught with wars, more successful than not, against the Poles, Turks and Hungarians, and ensured his status as a national hero in future centuries.

As the 1920s drew to a close Romania had reason to compare the last twenty years favourably with the great rulers of the past. Three pictorial sets in 1928 and 1929 celebrated the 10th anniversary of the annexation of Bessarabia, the 50th anniversary of the acquisition of Northern Dobruja and the 10th anniversary of the union with Transylvania.(12.29/12.30)

However not all these territories were to stay Romanian very long, and Romania itself would undergo another revolution as the Second World War ended. The fraught 1930s and 1940s were not far away.

CHAPTER 13
Bulgaria

After briefly dominating the Balkans during the reign of the brilliant Tsar Ivan Assen II (1218-41) Bulgaria weakened during the internal disputes and civil wars of his successors and was unable to withstand the onslaught of the Ottoman Turks as they advanced north in the later fourteenth century. In 1393, the Turks captured Veliko Turnovo, the capital city, and after the Battle of Nicropolis in 1396 they subjugated the whole country. In 1444 a joint Hungarian-Polish crusade to free the Balkans was crushed at the Battle of Varna. Bulgarian castles were demolished, and the Bulgarian Orthodox Church largely subordinated to the Patriarch in Constantinople. However, the outcome of these desperate battles, the fate of the great castles, and the perilous survival of Ohrid as a Bulgarian Orthodox centre, remained in Bulgarian folk memory until their pictorial revival in early twentieth century stamp issues seeking to restore national pride and unity.

In the 1870s the struggle for political liberation was formalized through the Bulgarian Revolutionary Central Council led by fervent revolutionaries such as Vasil Levski and Hristo Botev, the former betrayed and executed in 1872 and the latter killed during an abortive revolt in 1876. Both became national heroes, and honoured by stamps issues fifty years later. At the time, however, Turkish atrocities and intransigence gave Russia the opportunity to extend its territorial influence and in April 1877 in a blaze of righteous indignation it led its Balkan allies into war against the Ottoman Empire.

The combined Russian and Balkan armies defeated the Turks at Shipka Pass and Pleven, and in March 1878 the Treaty of San Stefano created a Principality of Bulgaria that was *de jure* under Turkish suzerainty but *de facto* free to rule itself independently. And under the treaty it was greatly enlarged to embrace much of medieval Bulgaria's lands in Macedonia, Rumelia, Thrace and Moesia (a province south of the Danube).

However the thought of a huge new Balkan country under the thumb of Russia appalled Great Britain, France, Austria-Hungary and Italy who had their own interests in the Eastern Mediterranean and Balkans. The Congress and Treaty of Berlin in the summer of 1878 cut down the size of Bulgaria by 60%, and the resulting resentment shaped the aggressive foreign policy of Bulgaria for half a century, including its involvement in several further wars. Southern Dobruja was ceded to Romania, Macedonia returned to Turkey, and Eastern Rumelia allowed autonomy under Turkish sovereignty.

In 1879 Bulgaria accepted Russia's nomination of Prince Alexander of Battenberg as its ruler, but his disenchantment with Russian influence caused his deposition by a group of pro-Russian Bulgarian army officers in 1886. Western influences, however, ensured Prince Ferdinand of Saxe-Coburg and Gotha, an Austro-Hungarian army officer, replaced Alexander in July 1887. He proved an effective ruler, and encouraged ministers to improve agriculture, extend education, and develop factories, partly through extensive loans and investment from France. He did, though, encourage militarization and his abiding aim was the reversal of the Treaty of Berlin. Growing in confidence and military power, in 1908 Ferdinand broke the final *de jure* links with the Ottoman Empire, proclaimed Bulgaria a kingdom but preferred to call himself Tsar in a deliberate link with the country's exalted medieval past. The Declaration of Independence was proclaimed with due respect for Bulgaria's main religion and history in Veliko Turnovo's Forty Martyrs Church built to celebrate a military triumph by Ivan Assen II over Byzantine Epirus in 1230.

13.1 30st National Arms (from set May 1889+)

Ferdinand's early stamps reinforced key historic links, and sought to heighten national pride. From 1889 a series of stamps featuring the nation's coat of arms were issued, and then in 1901 a curious pair picturing a cannon made out of cherry wood commemorated the 25th anniversary of the 1876 uprising. (13.1/13.2) Cheaper and simpler to

13.2 (E) 15st 25th Anniversary of 1876 Uprising (pair 20 April 1901)

manufacture and transport than metal guns, 52 of these fragile and generally ineffective weapons had been used against the Turks. Soon afterwards they achieved iconic propaganda status.

In 1902 a set of three identical stamps marked the 25th anniversary of the Battles of Shipka Pass between August 1877 and January 1878.(13.3) At the aptly named Eagle's Nest in the Bulgarian Mountains, 2,500 Russians and 5,000 Bulgarians had held off repeated attacks by 40,000 Turks; the stamps featured the savage fighting.

From 1901 Prince Ferdinand, himself an enthusiastic philatelist, appeared on both definitive and special sets.(13.4) A lover of uniforms and medals he was usually featured wearing them. In 1907 the stamps marking the 20th anniversary of his accession portrayed him as he was in 1887 and 1907.(13.5)

In 1911 an impressive set of twelve stamps featured a confident king in a country resplendent with historic sights and natural beauty. Five featured Ferdinand himself in various uniforms and his coronation robes.(13.6) The 1st pictured Asen's Tower perched on a cliff high above the Asenita River. It was a great

13.3 5st Fighting at Shipka Pass (from set 29 August 1902)

13.4 15st Prince Ferdinand (from set 1 October 1901+)

13.7 (E) 1st King Assen Tower and 3st Veliko Turnovo (from set 14 February 1911)

medieval border fortress extended by Ivan Assen II but later largely destroyed by the Ottoman Turks. The 3st pictured the old capital, Veliko Turnovo that became the centre of several uprisings against the Turks.(13.7) The 21 featured the ancient Orthodox Monastery at Veliko Turnovo whose church was completely restored in 1846-7 during the religious and nationalist revival. The 30st pictured another celebrated monastery, St Ivan's in Rila. Both monasteries had survived as centres of Bulgarian culture under Ottoman rule. Rila also achieved fame as a hiding place for revolutionaries, including Vasil Levski. The 15st featured the River Isker flowing through a rocky gorge, and the 31 pictured the Greek, Roman, Byzantine, Ottoman and now Bulgarian port of Varna on the Black Sea.(13.8)

Early in 1912 Bulgaria signed a secret treaty with Serbia, Greece and Montenegro agreeing the partition of Turkish controlled Macedonia and Thrace between them. Citing continuing Turkish abuses, and choosing a time when the Turks were fighting the Italians in Libya, the four countries declared war in October and were soon victorious on land and sea. That August three large eye-catching stamps with the dates '1887-1912' had celebrated Ferdinand's Silver Jubilee.(13.9) Everything seemed to be going well.

The First Balkan War, though, was quickly followed the Second when the victors fell out over the spoils. Serbia refused to surrender any territory it occupied in northern Macedonia, saying Bulgaria had required Serbian help to secure Adrianople, and Greece proved equally intransigent.

13.5 20th Anniversary of Ferdinand's Accession (from set 14 August 1907)

13.6 5st Ferdinand in uniform and 1l Ferdinand in coronation robes (from set 14 February 1911)

13.8 (E) *2l Monastery at Veliko Turnovo and 3l Varna (from set 14 February 1911)*

13.9 *25st Tsar's Silver Jubilee (from set 2 August 1912)*

13.10 *2st Ferdinand and 15st River Isker with War of Liberation overprints (from set 6 August 1913)*

13.11 (E) *30c 1911 Rila Monastery (from set 7 November 1915)*

Incensed, in June 1913 Bulgaria invaded Serbia, but both Serbia and Greece counter-attacked successfully. Then Romania invaded Bulgaria from the north, and the bruised Ottoman Empire sought revenge by advancing from the south-east. With 58,000 men dead and 100,000 wounded, and enemies encroaching on all sides, Bulgaria sued for peace.

By the Treaty of Bucharest in August 1913 Bulgaria lost most of the territory it occupied after the First Balkan War; much of Macedonia was shared between Serbia and Greece, the Ottomans kept Adrianople and eastern Thrace, and Bulgaria had to cede southern Dobruja to Romania. Bulgaria did get a little extra territory – part of western Thrace giving access to the Aegean Sea. Seven stamps from 1911 pictorial set overprinted in Cyrillic 'Liberation War 1912-1913' appeared in the same month the treaty was signed.(13.10) Unfortunately most of the liberated areas were not in Bulgaria's hands.

With the Balkans a tinderbox of bitter rivalries, in the summer of 1914 Ferdinand and his ministers were far more inclined towards friendship with Germany and Austria-Hungary than with Russia, the protector of Serbia. Ironically this meant working in alliance with Turkey when it opted to ally itself with Germany and Austria-Hungary. Bulgaria had little interest in the global aims of the major warring powers; its targets were Serbia along with Greece and Romania.

Bulgaria had suffered badly in terms of casualties, financial debt, economic dislocation and national pride as a result of the Balkan Wars, and Ferdinand appreciated his popularity had diminished. Initially his government adopted a popular policy of strict neutrality, but Bulgaria's strategic position, and still considerable military might, ensured agents and diplomats of all the warring nations flocked to Sofia to tempt it into alliance with promises of territorial gains at its neighbours' expense.

In 1915 Russian defeats in Galicia, Italy's failures against Austria-Hungary, and British ineffectiveness in Gallipoli caused Ferdinand, who in fact had no particular familial feelings for Germany, finally to think that Germany and Austria-Hungary might be the best options to secure everything that had been lost in 1913. Germany and Austria-Hungary readily agreed, believing Bulgaria could cut Russia off from her allies, crush Serbia, and open up routes to Turkey. On 14 October 1915 an enthusiastic king, but a sullen nation, declared war on Serbia.

With German and Austro-Hungarian support in the north, Bulgarian forces pushed into southern Serbia and seized Skopje and Nis. Fighting stubbornly the Serbs were forced into a difficult retreat through hostile Albania. The Bulgarians also pushed back the French and British forces that had landed at Salonika aiming to occupy parts of Macedonia. On 7 November 1915 as Bulgarian royal and military confidence soared seven images from the 1911 pictorial set, four of them picturing Ferdinand, were re-engraved and reissued in new colours.(13.11)

13.12 3st Red Cross Fund overprint (9 March 1916)

13.13 Liberation of Macedonia 5l Arms, 15st Peasant, 25st Soldier (from set 14 August 1917)

By December Bulgaria had achieved all its immediate war aims, and Serbia was crushed. The following year Romania entered the war on the Allied side, and after heavy fighting, especially around the fortress city of Tutrakan, Bulgaria seized and occupied Romania's coveted province of southern Dobruja.

Ferdinand, however, was caught in a dilemma. Ambitious by nature, he saw the chance of creating a Bulgaria dominating the Balkans from the Black Sea to the Adriatic. Yet he knew the peasantry, who comprised the bulk of the population, hated the suffering and hardship of the war, and greatly preferred Slavic Russia to Teutonic Germany. The presence of many Germans in the country served only to confirm their antipathy. Peasant unrest rose and the Agrarian National Union and Socialist parties won further seats in the National Assembly. In March 1916 a stamp raising funds for the Red Cross used a 1889 Coat of Arms issue upon which to overprint a surcharge rather than any issues that might overtly link the distress with Ferdinand himself.(13.12)

In the summer of 1916 Bulgarian forces supported by a few German and Austro-Hungarian divisions faced British and French forces, supported by Czech and Greek units, along the Macedonian front centred on Salonika. Battles raged, casualties mounted, and parts of the front line shifted a few miles from time to time, but no-one achieved outright victory. Nevertheless in August 1917 the Bulgarians felt they had occupied enough to issue a set of seven stamps marking the liberation of Macedonia. With total victory seemingly in sight, Ferdinand's personal coat of arms rather than Bulgaria's adorned the 5st. The 15st dutifully honoured the peasants with a picture of one rather dismally leading an ox cart. The 25st honoured the soldiers with an image of one advancing through the mountains.(13.13) The 30st featured the town of Nis long coveted by Bulgaria but ceded to Serbia in 1878 and since November 1915 occupied by Bulgaria. The 50st pictured the town and lake of Ohrid that were taken from the Ottoman Turks by Serbia in November 1912 and held by them until Bulgaria seized the area in November. The 2l, not issued until 1919, featured the stunning River Varda gorge at Demir Kapija, now in Bulgarian hands. Its location as the summer home of previous Serbian kings added force to the image. The 3l pictured Gevgelija, a Macedonian town on the River Varda near the border with Greece, seized briefly from the Turks in the Balkan War of 1912 and at last back in Bulgarian hands.(13.14)

Pride knew no bounds. In 1918 and 1919 three more stamps celebrated the liberation of Macedonia. One featured Veles in central Macedonia, and another St John's Monastery in Ohrid, a reminder that the city had been briefly (990-1018) the Bulgarian Empire's capital. The peasants obliged to do most of the fighting were remembered in a stamp featuring a ploughman.(13.15)

However, the Bulgarian army, mainly composed of peasants, grew increasingly reluctant to fight as the spring of 1918 turned into summer. Austria-Hungary was fracturing, the Ottoman Empire imploding and the Germans retreating on the Western Front. When the Allies broke through on the Macedonian Front many Bulgarian units dissolved in mutinies. Under intense popular and political pressure Ferdinand sued for peace. He secured an Armistice on 30 September 1918, but with revolution threatening he abdicated on 3 October and hurried into exile. A few months earlier, in July

13.14 Liberation of Macedonia 30st Nish, 50st Ohrid, 2l Varda Gorge, 3l Gevgelija (from set 14 August 1917)

13.15 Liberation of Macedonia 1l Veles, 5l Ohrid and 1l Ploughman (from set 1918+)

1918, a set of four stamps featuring Ferdinand commemorated the 30th anniversary of his accession; the dates on them, though, were *1915 - 1917* and recalled the transitory triumphs of those years.(13.16)

Ferdinand's elder son became King Boris III – the title Tsar was consigned to history. He was to have a turbulent reign. The humiliating Treaty of Neuilly in November 1919 returned Dobruja to Romania, granted all Macedonian territory except Petrich to the new Kingdom of the Serbs, Croats and Slovenes, and reserved western Thrace for Greece thereby removing Bulgaria's access to the Aegean Sea. Huge reparations had to be paid to Romania and the Kingdom of the Serbs, Croats and Slovenes, and thousands of Bulgarian refugees from Macedonia had to be absorbed.

Boris was also faced with the ascendancy of Alexander Stamboliyski and his reforming Agrarian National Union party. As prime minister Stamboliyski crushed Communist inspired strikes, organized public reconstruction projects and forced social reforms through parliament but his authoritarianism, anti-monarchist sympathies, dismissive attitude towards the middle classes – army officers, businessmen, professionals – and contempt for the dispossessed Bulgarian Macedonians eventually led to a successful coup in June 1923. The Internal Macedonian Revolutionary Committee was heavily involved; it detested Stamboliyski for signing the Treaty of Neuilly, and sought to inspire a new war of 'liberation'. Stamboliyski was executed, and his party suppressed. The new right wing government led by Alexander Tsankov had the full support of Boris, and several years of brutal 'white terror' effectively banished any thoughts of power, although not agitation and atrocities, by republicans and Communists.

These years saw a flurry of stamp issues. On 3 October 1919, when Stamboliyski was establishing his personal authority and Boris largely a figurehead, two sets reflected the trappings rather than the current reality of power. The first pictured Sofia's parliament building, and the second

13.16 Cover with the Tsar Ferdinand set issued on 1 July 1918 with a Sophia postmark dated 3 October 1918, the day of his abdication.

13.17 1st Parliament Building (from set 3 October 1919) and 10st King Boris First Anniversary (from set 3 October 1919+)

13.19 1l Ivan Vazov, 50st Borimechkata (from set 24 October 1920)

13.18 15st King Boris and 2l Varda Gorge overprinted FOR OUR CAPTIVES (from set 22 June 1920)

13.20 1l King Boris and 2l Peasant girl (from set 23 March 1921+)

King Boris to mark his first year of his reign.(13.17)

The realities of war, though, were to the fore the following June when stocks from several sets old and new were reissued variously overprinted FOR OUR CAPTIVES.(13.18) The stamps were sold at their original face values; the overprinted values referred to the 50% going to the charity leaving the remaining 50% available for postage. Interestingly in the light of the dramatically changing circumstances, the stamps included ex-Tsar Ferdinand in his coronation robes from the 1911 set and two views from the 1917 and 1919 Liberation of Transylvania sets as well as recent King Boris definitives.

In 1920 a set resonating with the post-war world marked the 70th birthday of the celebrated national writer, Ivan Vazov (1850-1921).(13.19) Born under Ottoman rule, for a time Vazov lived and plotted amongst exiled Bulgarian revolutionaries, including the charismatic Hristo Botev, a fellow poet who inspired his revolutionary vision and writings, notably *Bulgaria's Sorrows* published in 1877. After independence Vazov published *Epic of the Forgotten* and, much later in 1893, the novel of Ottoman oppression *Under the Yoke*. Significantly *Epic of the Forgotten* eulogises the heroic if doomed figures of the past in the light of what Vazov believed to be Bulgaria's moral decline after independence. *Under the Yoke* is a story of a deceptively quiet village seething with aspirations for freedom but also riven with internal differences and even betrayal. The curious figure on the 50st was Borimechkata (the Bear Fighter). His real name was Ivan Tankov, a peasant rebel fighter from Klissoura who died in the April 1876 uprising and was immortalized in *Under the Yoke*.

Alexander Stamboliyski, and indeed many other Bulgarians, favoured renewing links with Russia, and a set issued in stages from March 1921 reflected this. Alongside patriotic images of Boris, a peasant girl harvesting, Veliko Turnovo, Asen's Tower and Rila Monastery are stamps featuring the neo-Byzantine Alexander Nevski Cathedral in Sofia (10st), the huge Alexander II Monument, also in Sofia (20st), and Shipka Pass Monastery (75st) where the Russians and Bulgarians held the Ottoman Turks at bay in 1877-78. (13.20/13.21) Nevski Cathedral was planned in 1879 as a tribute to Russian soldiers who died in the 1877-78 war against the Ottoman Turks, although it was not started until 1882 and not completed until 1912. Its name had been changed to Saints Cyril & Methodius when Russia was the enemy in 1916, but diplomatically changed back again in

13.21 (E) 10st Alexander Nevski Cathedral, 20st Alexander II Monument and 75st Shipka Pass Monastery (from set 23 March 1921+)

in 1920. Alexander Nevski (1221-63) was the Russian Prince of Novrogod famous for his victories over the invading Swedes and Germans. Alexander II (1855-81) was the Russian Emperor instrumental in liberating Bulgaria from Ottoman control.

In June 1921 a set of stamps originally designed in 1915 to celebrate the occupation of Macedonia was suddenly issued. Two featured Tsar Ferdinand, one of them with a map of Macedonia, and the other three local views.(13.22) Not surprisingly they provoked an immediate protest from the Kingdom of Serbs, Croats and Slovenes, and after three days the stamps were withdrawn. Bearing in mind Stamboliyski's renowned lack of interest in Macedonia and, indeed, his intention of negotiating a friendship treaty with the new Kingdom, it is more likely this issue was a mistake rather than a deliberate provocation. Possibly the shortage of stamps, especially definitives, had contributed to the diplomatic blunder. Four of the five stamps in the set had the common 10st values.

13.22 10c Tsar Ferdinand and map and 20c Soldier guarding St Clement's Monastery (from set 11 June 1921)

13.23 1l James Bourchier and 10st Bouchier in Bulgarian costume (from set 30 December 1921)

In December 1921 a set honoured James Bourchier (1850-1920), the renowned Bulgarian correspondent of *The Times* who died the previous year.(13.23) Born in Ireland, Bourchier lived in Sofia between 1892 and 1915 and championed Bulgarian interests throughout this troubled period. His reports and articles criticized the draconian Treaties of Bucharest and Neuilly as unreasonably humiliating and incitements to future wars. He became a trusted advisor to Tsar Ferdinand, and was buried near Rila Monastery. He was proved right as throughout the inter-war years the Internal Thracian Revolutionary Organisation and Internal Macedonian Revolutionary Organisation, both based in Bulgaria, sought renewed wars of liberation, partly through provocative terrorist attacks across the border.

13.24 St Nedelya's Cathedral after the explosion (2 June 1926)

13.25 1919 15st King Boris overprinted THRACE OCCIDENTALE (from set 19 April 1920)

13.26 10st Arms and 1l Nevski Cathedral (from set 1925+)

On 16 April 1925 a huge explosion tore apart the roof of St Nedelya's Cathedral in Sofia during the funeral of General Georgiev, killing 150 people and injuring 500 others. The Communists had killed the general and also carried out the bombing. Boris escaped as he was at a different service for victims of a separate attack. Martial law was imposed, the Communists were suppressed and several hundred executions carried out – some reports say several thousand – many without trial. In 1926 a single stamp featured the badly damaged cathedral.(13.24)

Relations with neighbouring countries remained at breaking point. Certainly Bulgaria was dilatory in withdrawing from Macedonia. In Western Thrace the temporary French occupying force issued Bulgarian stamps overprinted *Thrace Interalliee* and *Thrace Occidentale* while the Allies hesitantly considered its future.(13.25) It was granted to Greece in May 1920, although the border remained perilous. In October 1925 the League of Nations had to intervene when Greek troops advanced on Petrich, the tiny part of Macedonia remaining in Bulgaria, when, allegedly, a Greek soldier was shot dead by a Bulgarian border guard as he crossed the border in search of his lost dog. Reports suggested between 50 and 100 people were killed before calm prevailed.

In 1926 Boris secured a more moderate government that lasted until 1934, despite the mounting resentment of right wing political and military groups. Many stamps featured the Tsar, some harked back to ancient Bulgaria, notably the return to the rampant lion coat of arms on the first Bulgarian stamp of 1879, and others did not forget the peasants or the Church. Alexander Nevski Cathedral was a notable feature.(13.26) The importance of

13.26 10st Arms and 1l Nevski Cathedral (from set 1925+)

13.27 1l Postal Workers Rest Home Varna (from Sunday Delivery set 1 September 1925+)

telephone and postal workers was signalled by sets of stamps that had to be attached to mail alongside the normal postage to ensure its delivery of Sundays.(13.27) The premium went towards a proposed rest home and sanatorium for employees.

Salient figures in Bulgaria's tumultuous history were never forgotten. In May 1929 a particularly eclectic set commemorated the 50th anniversary of liberation. They included portraits of the revered Tsar Alexander II of Russia, the cultural historian Father Paisii Khilendarski (1722-73), known as the 'Father of the National Revival', and Konstantin Miladinov (1830-62) who collected and popularized Bulgarian folk songs.(13.28) Three figures were from the distant past including tenth century Tsar Simeon who fought the Serbs, Croats and Byzantines to forge a Bulgarian Empire, and St Clement of Ohrid (840-916) who reputedly invented Cyrllic script and the Slav language. The set was completed with several members of the militant, yet idealistic, nineteenth century Bulgarian Revolutionary Central Committee – Lyuben Karavelov, Georgi Benkovski, Georgi Rakovski, and the iconic Vasil Levski.(13.29)

In 1934 a dramatic set marked the unveiling of the memorial at Shipka Pass where Bulgaria's victory over the Turks had brought about its freedom.(13.30) Images of the desperate fighting and a widow showing the memorial to her children highlighted the human 'face' of the achievement. The set also featured an armed veteran by the memorial, symbolising Bulgaria's constant need to guard its borders as well as treasure its achievements.

However revolutions were far from over. A right wing military coup in 1934 established a dictatorship and reduced Boris to a puppet king only for him to stage a successful counter-coup a year later and remain the key figure in government until his death, in mysterious circumstances, in 1943. By then Boris had been both pressurised into an alliance with Hitler, and Bulgaria had regained control of south Dobruja, most of Macedonia and western Thrace. All too soon, though, – on 16 September 1944 - the Red Army entered Sofia.

13.28 6l Tsar Alexander II, 1l Father Khilendarski and 15st Konstantin Miladinov (from set 12 May 1929)

13.29 2l Tsar Simeon, 10c St Clement and 4l Vasil Levski (from set 12 May 1929)

13.30 1l Defending the Pass, 4l veteran, and 14l widow and children (from set August 1934+)

CHAPTER 14
Albania

A western Balkan area abutting the Adriatic Sea fell to the Ottoman Turks after the Battle of Savra in 1385 and became the Sanjak of Albania. Intermittent revolts followed with their defeats followed by savage repression. However one rebel leader became a political and military icon who centuries later inspired a national revival and eventual independence, and featured on many Albanian stamps. His name was George Kastrioti who for a time was a renowned Janissary in the Turkish army with the name of Iskandar Bey or, more popularly, Skanderberg. In 1443 he deserted and started a rebellion that he led for 25 years. Forging a formidable army with the support of native lords and princes he broke many Turkish sieges and won many battles against superior numbers. At his death, though, the alliance crumbled and by 1479 Ottoman rule was as firm as ever.

Over the centuries many Albanians converted from Christianity to Islam, not least because it eased careers and commerce. Some tribal chiefs became powerful regional rulers under Ottoman suzerainty. Although many Albanians sought independence, many others did not as they possessed a vested interest in the status quo and feared the repercussions of a successful revolt as much as a failed one. Albanian tribes continued to feud, and although some united in abortive revolts Albania was the last Balkan state to achieve independence.

In October 1912 the First Balkan War broke out during which Serbia, Greece and Bulgaria saw the ostensibly Turkish Sanjak of Albania as fair game. On 28 November, with Ottoman forces reeling, the rebel Provisional Government of Albania declared its independence, but already Serbia had occupied territory along Albania's Adriatic coast, and its army was committing numerous atrocities while claiming credit for a war of liberation. In addition Greece had overrun parts of the south, and in 1913 Montenegro took Shkodra in the north-west.

The ensuing Conference of London recognised Albanian independence, but the settlement left around half of the ethnic Albanians in Serbia, Montenegro and Greece. With their hopes of totally partitioning Albania dashed, Serbia, Montenegro and Greece needed repeated demands from the major Powers before they withdrew their forces back to the new international borders.

14.1 Epirus: early 1l handstamped skull and eagle (from set 10 February 1914), 25l tribesman (from pair 5 March 1914), and 10l Arms (from set 24 August 1914)

14.2 Turkish 1pi overprinted with Albanian eagle and SHQIPENIA (from set 16 June 1913) and 10g Albanian Temporary Government (from set 25 October 1913+)

Conversely the Greeks left within southern Albania soon rose in rebellion in February 1914 and created the Republic of Northern Epirus. Its autonomy within the Albania principality was agreed by Albania, and until overtaken by greater wartime events it used overprinted Turkish and Greek stamps as well as issuing several of its own.(14.1) They were produced as much for propaganda as for postage.

Stamps record the perilous emergence of Albanian independence. In the summer of 1913 Turkish stamps gradually appeared overprinted with the Albanian double-headed eagle and *SHQIPENIA* (ALBANIA or more colloquially Land of the Eagle) with varying degrees of clarity. Soon afterwards the eagle appeared

14.3 2g Anniversary of Independence (from set 28 November 1913)

14.4 2q Skanderberg (from set 1 December 1913)

14.5 2q Skanderberg overprinted 7. Mars 1461 RROFTE MBRETI 1914 (from set 7 March 1914)

14.6 5q Skanderberg overprinted in red 19. MARS. 1914 KUST. I NGRITJES FLAM KOMBETAR NE FORTESE SHKODRE and then 10 PARAS (from set 19 March/2 April 1914+) and unadorned 5q stamp overprinted 10 PARAS (set 2 April 1914+)

February 1914, and on 7 March the Skanderberg stamps were reissued overprinted *7. Mars 1461 RROFTE MBRETI 1914* (7 March 1461 LONG LIVE THE KING 1914).(14.5) It referred to the German Prince William of Wied, a nephew of Queen Elisabeth of Romania, who had accepted the offer by the Great Powers (Austria-Hungary, France, Germany, Great Britain, Italy and Russia), which subsequently had been confirmed by a delegation of Albanian notables, to reign over the fraught new principality. The date 1461 recalled Skandenberg at the height of his powers after uniting the tribes, signing an advantageous treaty with the Turks, and completing a successful campaign in mainland Italy. There was an irony about the historic Italian connection as in 1914 Italy was already eyeing up Albania as a potential acquisition. As with many early Albanian overprints they conveyed a hurried look – perhaps understandable as the stamps appeared on the same day William formally accepted the throne – 7 March.

It was a classic poisoned chalice. Many Albanians welcomed the strengthening of the Albanian Orthodox Church, but many others were Muslims who detested the interference of western Christian powers. Muslim revolts broke out, and on top of this Greece sent in troops to reinforce the independence of Northern Epirus. In addition an opportunistic senior minister, Essad Pasha, was found to have accepted money from Italy to stage a coup. He was exiled, and lucky to escape execution.

In 1913 Essad Pasha had been a hero. Then a senior officer in the Ottoman Empire's Albanian army, he had led the determined defence of the fortress of Rozafa and city of Shkodra (or Shkoder) in the mountainous northern Tarabosh region against Montenegrin and Serbian forces until forced to surrender. A year later an attempt was made to mark the first anniversary of Albania's flag flying over Rozafa by diagonally overprinting the 1913 Skanderberg stamps with the rousing inscription *19. MARS. 1914 KUST. I NGRITJES FLAM KOMBETAR NE FORTESE SHKODRE* (19 MARCH 1914 THE RISE OF THE NATIONAL FLAME IN THE FORTRESS OF SHKODER).(14.6) In 1913 Albania had changed its currency from *paras* and *grosh* to *qints* and *francs,* but in a reverse – and perhaps perverse - move in April 1914 Shkodra overprinted stocks of the new Skanderberg stamps with *para* and *grosh* values. However overall the *qints* and *francs* survived until 1947.

When the First World War broke out on 28 July Austria-Hungary demanded Albanian support, and cut off Prince William's financial support when he refused. Amidst the confusion, and indeed anarchy, William departed the country in despair on 3 September 1914 never to return, but never finally abdicating. He was gone before a set of stamps with his portrait could be issued.(14.7)

Albania descended into chaos. Troops from Albania

handstamped within a double circle that contained the inscription *Posta e Qeverries se Perkoheshme* (Temporary Government's Post).(14.2) This dramatic form of the eagle was of Byzantine origin and had been adopted by the rebel hero Skanderberg.

On 28 November 1913 more crudely printed Albanian stamps marked the first anniversary of independence – at least in the enclaves that were still free from occupation. The double headed eagle was encircled with the inscription *POSTAT E QEVERIES SE PER DHESHME TE SHQIPENIES* (POST OF THE GOVERNMENT OF ALBANIA).(14.3) Three days later a far higher quality stamp (printed in Turin) was issued portraying Skanderberg wearing his famous white metal helmet adorned with a circle of gold and topped with the bronze horned head of a goat.(14.4)

Albania was formally declared a principality on 21

14.7 25q Prince William of Wied (unissued – example probably from looted wartime stocks)

14.8 6p Central Albania inscribed Tarabosh 1913 with Turkish crescent overprint (from set 10 February 1915)

14.9 2c KORCE VETQEVERITARE SHQIPERIE (from set January 1917)

14.10 5c KORCE REPUBLIKA SHQIPETARE (from set May 1917)

and Epirus started cross border fighting and in October 1914 Northern Epirus welcomed Greek occupation. A little earlier Serbia and Montenegro forces had moved into northern Albania, but reeling under Austro-Hungarian assaults in late 1915 the Serbian army retreated in vast straggling columns across Albania to exile in Corfu and other Greek islands. Many fell victim to marauding Albanian guerillas.

For a time Bulgaria rivaled Austria-Hungary for influence in Albania, and allowed Ahmet Muhtar Zogolli, an ambitious local Albanian governor, much of a free hand in the province of Elbasan. As we shall see he took full advantage of the situation. Officially Austria-Hungary and Albania were not at war, and Austria-Hungary promoted the occupation as friendly and undertaken largely to frustrate Italian ambitions. To confirm this illusion Albanian schools and culture were left largely alone and most local officials remained in place.

In January 1915 Essad Pasha, the disgraced ex-minister, returned from exile with Italian and Serbian backing to carve out a short-lived Republic of Central Albania. He had time to issue his own stamps that reflected this freebooter's previous time in the area during 1913. They comprised the 1913 Skanderberg stamps together with hitherto unissued pictorial and fiscal stamps inscribed *TARABOSH 1913*, the scene of his heroic defence, overprinted with his Turkish crescent logo and inscription.(14.8) In February 1916, however, Essad Pasha was forced out of his ramshackle republic and Austria-Hungary took control.

Soon Albania was divided into several distinct parts. In 1916 French and Italian armies appeared in Albania. In May the Italians occupied southern Albania, and in November the French occupied the south-eastern region centred on Korce, the former Greek Epirus, which became the Autonomous Province of Korce. In retaliation, in January 1917 Austria-Hungary declared the north and centre to be an independent state under its protection. In June Italy did the same in the south, and went on to add slices of northern Greece and western Macedonia to its new protectorate.

In 1916 and 1917 Korce issued its own stamps. Initially these were Epirus issues overprinted with a three or four winged double-headed eagle to give a semblance of Albanian legitimacy, but from January 1917 rather crudely designed special stamps were used inscribed, first, *KORCE VETQEVERITARE SHQIPERIE* (KORCE: ALBANIAN SELF GOVERNMENT) and later *KORCE REPUBLIKA SHQIPETARE* (KORCE: REPUBLIC OF ALBANIA).(14.9/14.10) There were many errors, including misspellings. The pretence of Korce's independence ended in February 1918 when it became French occupied territory until 1920.

In September 1918 the multi-national Allied forces on the Salonika Front finally broke through Austro-Hungarian lines north of Thessaloniki and forced a gradual Austro-Hungarian retreat from Albania. When the war ended in November Italy occupied most of Albania, but Serbia held the far north, Greece a slice in the south and France retained Korce and Shkodra. The immediate post-war issue was whether the secret clauses of the 1915 Treaty of London would be honoured. These promised Italy the Vlore region and a protectorate over Albania in return for joining the Allies, along with significant northern parts going to Serbia and Montenegro and parts of the south, notably Epirus, to Greece.

Within Albania widespread fear and anger existed at the likely partition of the infant country. Initially the Paris Peace Conference preferred partition, and in January 1920 an outraged Albanian National Assembly threatened armed resistance. In March President Woodrow Wilson blocked the decision, Allied occupying forces began to leave, and in December the League of Nations recognised Albania as a sovereign country. Its borders, though, remained uncertain and highly volatile, and it needed a brief war to force Italy to withdraw, and even then it retained Saseno Island. Although Greece received both northern and southern Epirus in 1919, international pressure by Italy secured the northern part for Albania in 1924, but as we shall see Italy was being far from altruistic.

During this restless period Albania's overprinting of stamps continued apace. With the Allied commanders agreement, the provisional government under Turkhan Bey used stocks of Austro-Hungarian fiscal issues produced for occupied Albania overprinted with values in qint and frank and the inscription *POSTA e Shkodres SHQYPNIS.* (POST of Shkodra ALBANIA).(14.11) Some had the additional overprint, *XV I MCMXIX* (15 January 1919), the date Shkoder's post office reopened.

On 16 January the stamps received yet another overprint in the form of a red or green blazing comet with a curving tail; in February a straight tailed comet appeared.(14.12) For centuries comets were thought to be harbingers of dramatic change, either bad or, one assumes in this case, good.

In June 1919 stocks of Austro-Hungarian fiscal stamps appeared with an overprint applied in Durres saying *POSTAT SHQIPTARE* (ALBANIAN

14.11 Austro-Hungarian Fiscal overprinted POSTA e Shkodres SHQYPNIS, new value and XV I MCMXIX (from set 15 January 1919)

14.12 Fiscal similarly overprinted but with comet replacing date (from set 16 January 1919)

14.13 Fiscal overprinted POSTAT SHQIPTARE and new value (from set 5 June 1919)

14.14 Unissued 10q Prince Wiliam of Wied with obliterating eagle and SHKODRA overprint (from set 16 February 1920) and 25q Skanderberg handstamped 1gr and SHKODER 1919 (1919)

14.15 1f Skanderberg with SHKODRA obliterated by a posthorn (from set 1 April 1920)

14.16 1f Skanderberg with SHKODER overprinted with BESA (from set 1921)

POST).(14.13) Durres was the capital city from 1914 until replaced by the more centrally sited Tirana in 1920. It had been occupied by Italy in 1915, and after that by Austria-Hungary until late 1918.

Early in 1920 a regency was established in an attempt to find a generally accepted national leader capable of restoring unity and stability. Despite William of Wied's own ambitions, there was no chance of the Allies permitting the restoration of the exiled German prince who had subsequently joined the German army. Indeed, in February 1920 stocks of unissued stamps featuring his portrait were brought into circulation with his face obliterated by the double headed eagle. The overprint also contained the word SHKODRA, the key northern city that was the headquarters of the International Military Administration until March 1920. In 1919 the old 1913 25q Skanderberg stamp was reissued handstamped 1gr and SHKODER 1919. (14.14) However, in April 1920 a new stamp featuring Skanderberg was issued but now in the name of unity with SHKODER obliterated with a posthorn overprint.(14.15)

In 1921 the Skanderberg stamp appeared again, this time with the letters *BESA* (an acronym for Oath of Peace) obliterating the city's name.(14.16) Across the tribes of Albania the blood feud remained a constant factor in local and national affairs; an insult, raid, robbery or murder rendered the perpetrator liable to savage retaliation. The Oath of Peace allowed for a truce in the feud, and this stamp publicized a general truce ordered by the government, not least because government ministers themselves, and notably the rising politician Ahmed Muthar Zogolli, were potential victims as well as the perpetrators of blood feuds. The issue was repeated in 1922 with a slightly different overprint. They might have publicized a tentative move towards modern democratic processes, but they had little practical effect upon national politics.

The 1920s saw the tortuous rise of Ahmed Muthar Zogolli from a family of beys or provincial chieftains to government minister in 1920, President Ahmed Zogu in 1925 and finally King Zog I in 1928. With the support of many conservative beys, merchants and industrialists,

14.17 (E) 2q Gjirokaster, 10q Berat, and 25q Vizier's Bridge *(from set January 1923)*

14.18 (E) 50q Rozafa Fortress, 1f Korce, and 2f Durres *(from set January 1923)*

and using all the Albanian traditions of repression and execution, he formed a government between 1922 and 1924 only to be wounded by an assassin, blamed for the murder of an opponent, and fall victim to a left wing coup by Fan Noli, a populist left wing politician and founder Bishop of the restored Albanian Orthodox Church. However Noli failed to consolidate support for social reforms, notably the abolition of feudalism, or to eliminate Zogolli's key supporters. On 13 December 1924 Zogu and a small military force from the Kingdom of the Serbs, Croats and Slovenes crossed back into Albania and reasserted control on Christmas Eve. Noli and his ministers were wise to flee to Italy.

In January 1923 the first set of Albanian views appeared, all of which embraced political messages. Gjirokaster Castle in the far south had been part of the Greek breakaway region of Northern Epirus in 1913. Berat in central Albania, had played an important part in the nineteenth century national revival and the 1878 League of Prizren, one of the first movements aiming at complete independence. The 15th century Venetian style Vizier's Bridge crossed the Drin River near Prizren itself.(14.17) Other stamps pictured the celebrated fortress of Rozafa near Shkodra in the far north-west, Korce in the south-east, and Durres on the Adriatic coast.(14.18)

In 1924 and 1925 the set was reissued no less than six times with overprints that tracked national events and the rise of Ahmed Zogu to the presidency. On 21 January 1924 they appeared with the inscription *Mbledhje Kushtetuese* above a diamond lozenge enclosing TIRANE KALLNUER 1924 (Constitutional Assembly TIRANE JANUARY 1924).(14.19) It was this new Assembly that opened up the bitter conflict between parties of the right and left, and Ahmed Zogolli and Fan Noli.

On 5 March 1925 the set was reissued overprinted *Triumf' i legalitetit 24 Dhetuer 1924* (Triumph of Legality 24 December 1924) to celebrate and legitimize Zogu's coup and position as Prime Minister.(14.20)

By 5 March, however, Zogu was already President having been elected to that post by the Constitutional Assembly on 21 January 1925. On that day, too, the Regency had been formally terminated, and any lingering thoughts of a monarchy banished - temporarily. The pictorial set was duly reissued on 11 April 1925 with an overprint saying *Republika Shqiptare 21 Kallnduer 1925* (Republic of Albania 21 January 1925).(14.21) Unfortunately one stamp on each sheet had the date 1921, not 1925. On 20 May the set appeared yet again with *Republika Shqiptare* in larger

14.19 50q Rozafa overprinted *Mbledhje Kushtetuese* TIRANE KALLNUER 1924 *(from set 21 January 1924)*

14.20 2q Gjirokaster overprinted *Triumf' i legalitetit 24 Dhetuer 1924* *(from set 5 March 1925)*

14.21 10q Berat overprinted Republika Shqiptare 21 Kallnduer 1925 (from set 11 April 1925)

14.22 5q Kanina overprinted Republika Shqiptare (from set 20 May 1925)

14.23 5q Kanina overprinted with Red Cross and surcharge (from set December 1924)

14.24 1925 25q Air overprinted REP. SHQYPTARE Fluturim' I I-ar Vlone-Brindisi 21. IV. 1928 marking the inauguration of the Vlore to Brindisi air service as part of closer Albanian-Italian relations.

letters printed diagonally across the stamps.(14.22) Hurriedly done, many stamps had spelling mistakes.

Interspersed with these issues the Views set appeared overprinted, first with surcharges and then with a cross and surcharges, on behalf of the Red Cross.(14.23)

Although President Zogu initiated reforms eroding serfdom and brigandage, and creating sufficient law and order to encourage rural development Albania was a police state and the merest hint of opposition invited savage reprisals. With the economy still largely functioning at subsistence level in most rural areas, he relied on huge grants and heavy interest loans from Mussolini to fund major projects – and his grandiose buildings. Gradually Mussolini bribed and pressurised Zogu into allowing Italy a greater say in Albanian affairs and thereby inexorably limiting the president's autonomy.

The stamps, of course, told a different story with pictorial and overprinted issues in 1925, 1927 and 1928 highlighting air mail and passenger services, and a set in December 1925 highlighted Zogu himself.(14.24/14.25)

In 1927 his portrait set appeared again with an overprinted wreath of triumph and the letters A Z (Ahmed Zogu) marking his second year as president.(14.26)

In August 1928 the National Assembly declared Albania a kingdom and President Zogu became King Zog I who then ensured the Assembly voted for its own dissolution. New stamps featuring the President appeared edged with the overprint *Kujtim I Mbledhjes Kushtetuese 25.8.28* (In Memory of the National Assembly 25.8.28.).(14.27) They sold at a premium of 25 per cent.

Hard on their heels on 1 September the set appeared again with arched Gothic overprints announcing *Mbretnia Shqiptare ZOG I 1.IX.1928* (The Kingdom of Albania ZOG I 1. IX 1928).(14.28)

Zog had risen from tribal leader to national monarch, but he had played into Mussolini's hands and in 1939 proved powerless against annexation by the Italian dictator.

The royal family fled to Great Britain with much of the National Bank's gold.

14.25 2q President Zogu (from set 24 December 1925)

14.26 1925 10q and 3f President Zogu with wreath and A Z overprint (from set 1 February 1927)

14.27 5q Zog overprinted Kujtim I Mbledhjes Kushtetuese 25.8.28 (set August 1928)

14.28 2f Zog overprinted Mbretnia Shqiptare ZOG I 1.IX.1928 (set 1 September 1928)

CHAPTER 15
Greece

The southern part of modern Greece fought its way free from Ottoman Turk control in 1832 after a long revolutionary war in which romantic ideals of liberty and self-determination co-existed with tribal jealousies among the Greeks and appalling massacres by both sides. But for the involvement of Great Britain, France and Russia on the side of the Greeks, the largely uncoordinated and frequently feuding rebel forces scattered across the Peloponnese, central Greece, Macedonia and Crete would have been overwhelmed. The total defeat of the Ottoman fleet as it sought to sail from Alexandria to Greece in October 1827 by a combined Allied fleet under Admiral Sir Edward Codrington at Navarino ensured Allied control of the Mediterranean and sent a clear signal to the Ottoman Empire that it fought on at its peril. This victory, and also the high profile support of the Romantic poet Lord Byron who died of fever at Missolonghi while preparing to attack Lepanto, were long remembered. Both Codrington and Byron were celebrated a century later in Greek stamps by which time the struggle for independence had been transformed into national mythology.

An education steeped in Classical texts, such as Byron received, ensured many western Europeans saw modern Greeks as far more worthy of inheriting the country than the Ottoman Turks, but European statesmen, however much steeped in Greek culture, also saw the revolution as the moment to exert their influence over the emerging country that occupied such an important strategic position in the eastern Mediterranean. Although the Treaty of Constantinople in May 1832 created an independent Greece up to the border with Thessaly, Great Britain and France were also concerned to keep the Ottoman Empire reasonably intact elsewhere as a buffer to Russia. Greece, though, quickly became obsessed with the aim of freeing all Greeks still living under Ottoman rule. It was called the *Megali Idea* (the Great Idea) and was kept alive through regular insurrections in Thessaly, Macedonia and Crete.

For the next century Greece sometimes benefited from, but frequently had cause to regret, the British, French, German and later Italian involvement in its affairs. As the 'Great Powers' selfishly pursued their foreign policies in the region – whether it was containing Russian encroachments, propping up the Ottoman Empire or seeking to avoid any over-mighty Balkan state – so Greece's frequently unstable monarchy and governments were rendered even more volatile by often irresistible outside pressures. The result was that from time to time the country exploded into rioting and revolution, and the deposition and sometimes the assassination of kings and prime ministers.

In 1833 the Great Powers obliged Greece accept the young, and hopefully malleable, Prince Otto of Bavaria as King. He was too malleable and the Greeks deposed him in 1866. His reputation had plummeted when he made only token protests at the blockade of the key port of Piraeus by British and French warships during the Crimean War. They were there to stifle the Greek revolts in Thessaly and Epirus when the Ottoman Empire was, briefly, a French and British ally,

A Danish prince was tried next. He became King George I whose fifty year reign ended in assassination in 1913. In 1864 a new constitution introduced universal male suffrage amidst a largely illiterate population. This provided endless opportunities for corruption, and introduced a new populism and even greater volatility into Greek politics. Great Britain ceded the Ionian Islands as an initial token of goodwill, and this was well received, but British friendship did not extend to allowing Greece a free hand in the further erosion of Ottoman territory. As a result the Cretan revolt of 1866-69 against Ottoman overlordship remained unsupported despite the brutality with which it was suppressed. Britain and France also prevented Greek involvement in the Russo-Turkish War of 1877-78 despite George's Russian Queen fervently desiring it. Greece's reward for enforced neutrality was the acquisition of Thessaly in 1881, but not Epirus or the island of Crete.

In 1897, however, Greece ignored all international warnings. Fearful of Bulgarian intentions towards Macedonia, still an Ottoman province but riven with discontent, Greece forces advanced into the region only to suffer humiliating defeat. The Great Powers intervened, the war ended, Macedonia remained Turkish and the aspirations of others in the Balkans held at bay. However the continuing revolts and recent Turkish massacres in Crete led the island to be placed under international

157

15.1 British Zone (Candia) 20pa (from pair 3 December 1898)

15.5 20l 'Crete Enslaved' (from Cretan set 5 October 1905)

15.2 Russian Zone (Rethymon) 1m trident with Russian eagle control handstamp (from set 8 June 1899)

15.6 (E) 1l wrestlers and 60l chariot race (from set 25 March 1896)

15.3 1l Hermes, 20 Hera, goddess of women and marriage, and 25l Prince George (from Cretan set 1 March 1900+)

15.4 2l Rhea, the mother of Zeus who brought him up in Crete (from Cretan set 9 February 1905)

15.7 1896 1d Acropolis and stadium overprinted A.M. and 5l (set December 1900+)

administration in late 1898. British, French, Italian and Russian troops were stationed in four separate zones in Crete, and for a brief period specially designed British and Russian stamps were in use.(15.1/15.2)

However unrest in Crete was pacified only in 1899 by appointing Greece's Crown Prince George as its governor. His period of office until 1906 saw two major sets issued in 1900-01 and 1905.(15.3/15.4) They included his portrait on one value while the others celebrated Cretan and Greek mythology with images of gods and goddesses and views of Minos and Mount Ida. Another revolt in favour of Greek annexation failed in 1905 during which local stamps picturing King George and a striking allegory of *Crete Enslaved* were briefly in use.(15.5)

The 1890s shone some international limelight on Greece for events other than unrest, murders and wars. In 1893 France built the Corinth Canal to cut the voyage from Piraeus to the Adriatic Sea by 150 miles. And in 1896 the Olympic Games were revived with Athens the obvious choice as host despite internal controversy over the likely cost. In the event the idea caught the public imagination, with Georgios Averoff, a wealthy shipowner, making a lavish contribution. In addition a set of twelve stamps raised an impressive 400,000 drachmas (twice the amount of ticket sales).(15.6) They embraced values up to a costly 10 drachmas. Crown Prince George was a popular chairman of the organising committee and the king presided over the opening ceremony in Athens. The elaborately designed and Classically inspired Olympic set featured wrestlers, a discus thrower, chariot racing, the Acropolis and Olympic stadium, and statues of Hermes and Victory.

In 1900, however, several ordinary definitive Hermes stamps along with some Olympic stamps were overprinted *A M* for *Axia Metalike* (Gold Metal) and surcharged.(15.7) As the Greek currency was so unstable after the recent costly and disastrous war with the Ottoman Turks the postage on all foreign parcels had to be paid for at the gold rate.

It is probably indicative of the parlous state of Greece's national finances that in 1901 a lengthy set incorporating three different designs featuring Hermes was issued, possibly prompted by the Nordic Games in Stockholm (the precursor of the Winter Olympic Games).(15.8) And in 1906 philatelic profits were almost certainly behind another set of fourteen Classically inspired stamps linked to the Second Olympiad in Paris.(15.9) The images featured a discus thrower, wrestlers, runners, a jumper along with Daemon (the god of the Games), a sacrificial offering, Hercules wrestling Antaeus to the death, and Hercules tricking Atlas in order to steal the Apples of the Hesperides.

A few years later, in 1911 the international popularity of Classical Greece was exploited even further with a long set based upon five designs, three featuring Hermes, one Iris (the Goddess of the Rainbow), and one Arcas who grew up to be a great hunter and King of Arcadia.(15.10) Higher values were added over the next dozen years and all values were printed in different ways (recess and lithograph), and in different colours and with different perforation sizes.

Despite Classical Greece's reputation as the cradle of democracy and philosophy, its real-life politics – in common with the legendary lives of its pantheon of gods – were volatile, aggressive and frequently merciless. In 1908 an aspiring Cretan politician, Eleftherios Venizelos, stirred up support for a declaration of union with Greece, but British and French hostility and fears of war with the Ottoman Empire meant the government failed to respond positively, much to general disgust, especially from the armed forces. Few were satisfied with Greece being permitted administrative control of Crete but debarred union. In 1908 and 19090 a host of Cretan stamps appeared overprinted *Greece* to highlight the islanders' aspiration – and frustration.(15.11)

In 1909 a Military League of dissatisfied officers forced an election, and after some political skirmishing Venizelos became Greek prime minister. At first King George and Venizelos worked well together with their military, social welfare and land reforms proving successful and generally popular.

In 1912 Greece, Bulgaria, Serbia and Montenegro formed the Balkan League and in a brief but exceptionally bloody war defeated the Ottoman armies on all fronts. The victors seized as much territory as they could with Greece occupying Thessaloniki and much of Epirus, and also landing troops on Crete. From October 1912 many stamps from the 1901 and 1911 sets were reissued overprinted *Hellenic Administration* for use in the newly occupied territories.(15.12) In 1912 the Bulgarians had occupied Kavalla, a port in Eastern Macedonia, but the Greeks forced them back in June 1913 and overprinted captured Bulgarian stamps with Greek values and the inscription *Greek Administration*.(15.13)

15.8 30l and 5d Hermes (from set 1 July 1901+)

15.9 25l Hercules and Antaeus, and 2d Racing (from set 25 March 1906)

15.11 1900 10l Prince George overprinted Greece (from Cretan set 21 September 1908), and 1901 20l Hera overprinted Greece and Provisional (from Cretan set 1909)

15.10 1l Hermes and 2l Iris (from set 1911+)

15.12 1911 5l and 10l Hermes overprinted Hellenic Administration (from set October 1912+)

 *15.13 Bulgarian 1911 Tsar Ferdinand overprinted Greek Administration and 10l (from set 1 July 1913)*

 *15.16 Samos 2d Scene of Turkish repulse and signature (from set January 1913)*

 *15.14 Ikaria 2d Hermes (from set 8 October 1912)*

 *15.17 Limnos 1911 Greek 1d Hermes and Arcas overprinted (from set 1912+)*

 *15.15 Turkey 2pa overprinted Greek Possession Mytilene (from set 9 November 1912)*

  *15.18 3l eagle over Mount Olympus and 50l vision of Constantine (from set 16 April 1913+)*

 *15.19 25l Hoisting the flag at Suda Bay (15 November 1913)*

Around this time several Aegean islands wrested themselves completely free of Ottoman control. Prior to formal union with Greece in May 1913 Ikaria declared itself a 'Free state' and issued its own stamps, and Mytilene (Lesbos) used Turkish stamps overprinted *Greek Possession Mytilene*.(15.14/15.15) And until formal annexation in 1914 Samos used its own issues – first a crudely drawn set with a map of the island, then a set featuring Hermes, and then the Hermes set overprinted *Greece*. In 1913 Samos added a design picturing the castle where a Turkish force had been repulsed in 1824; it was signed by the Samian president Themistoklis Sophoulis.(15.16) After Limnos was occupied by Greece in October 1912 overprinted Greek stamps announced the annexation.(15.17)

At the end of the First Balkan War in 1913 the Treaty of London created an independent Albania and formally ceded Crete to Greece, but left League members to share out Kosovo, Macedonia and Thrace. The erstwhile allies fell out, primarily over Macedonia, and Bulgaria attacked Greece and Serbia. Soundly defeated, Bulgaria had to agree to Greece annexing southern Macedonia and southern Epirus. The Treaty also finally confirmed Greece's ownership of most Aegean Islands except the Dodecanese that Italy had occupied in 1911. Greece nearly doubled in size and population, and celebrated its success with a set of sixteen stamps inscribed *1912 CAMPAIGN* for use in the newly acquired mainland territories.(15.18) Powerful Christian and secular images were used. Some values featured the Cross and message *by this sign you will conquer* that the Emperor Constantine claimed he saw shining in the sky before his victory at Milvian Bridge in AD312 and conversion to Christianity. Others showed a victorious eagle flying over Mount Olympus clutching a writhing serpent in its mouth and claws. 1913 also saw a special stamp for use in Crete featuring the Greek flag being hoisted at Suda Bay on 1 May that year.(15.19)

By then Constantine I was King of Greece; his father had been assassinated in Thessaloniki in March. The outbreak of the First World War witnessed a progressive breakdown in the relations between Constantine and Prime Minister Venizelos that resulted in the violent National Schism lasting until 1922. Although Constantine's marriage to Princess Sophie of Prussia led many to see him as a German sympathizer, he preferred Greece to stay neutral and blocked the attempts by Venizelos to join the Allies, especially when the Allies were under severe Turkish pressure at Gallipoli. When Venizelos allowed Allied forces to disembark at Thessaloniki, and Constantine refused to honour Greece's alliance with Serbia as it reeled under Bulgarian attacks, the confrontation resulted in Venizelos resigning. Unrest mounted when the king made no move against the Bulgarians occupying part of eastern Macedonia, and by August 1916 Greece was politically split in two. That summer Greek forces that had occupied northern Epirus since December 1914 when Albania collapsed were ignominiously ejected by the Italians. Some overprinted stamps were the only Greek legacy.(15.20)

Venizolos established himself in Thessaloniki with Anglo-French support and most of Greece's newly acquired lands supporting him. Ignoring all constitutional niceties he declared war alongside the Allies against Bulgaria, Austria-Hungary and Turkey. The Nation Schism between the liberal republican Venizelist Government of National Defence based in Thessaloniki and the monarchist anti-Venizelists in Athens was to far outlast the war.

15.20   1913 eagle over Olympus overprinted (doubly in error) Northern Epirus (from set 8 December 1914+)

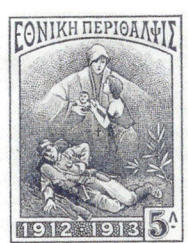

15.21   5l dying soldier and family (pair 31 March 1914+)

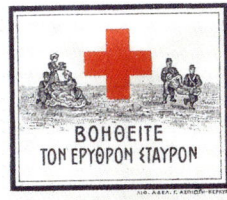

15.22   (5l) Red Cross and (5l) Greek Women's Patriotic League (September 1915)

15.23   1911 1l Hermes and 2l Iris overprinted E T and crown (from set 1 November 1916)

15.24   10l Iris with Provisional Government inscription (from Venizelos set 5 February 1917)

Worried about Constantine's intentions the French occupied the port of Piraeus, bombarded Athens and forced the Greek fleet to surrender. Constantine bowed to popular and Allied pressure and left for Switzerland in June 1917. Alexander, his second son, became king as the Allies opposed George, his eldest son, succeeding as he had served in the German army before the war. Alexander, though, only ruled in 'old' Greece, the southern pre-1913 lands, while Venizelos, basking in Allied approval, ordered his own Greek forces into battle against the Turks and Bulgarians.

Some time prior to the National Schism the purchase of charity stamps in addition to normal postage stamps was made mandatory for limited periods. The first two appeared on 31 March 1914, priced 2l and 5l, on behalf of the National Welfare Foundation and pictured a cloaked figure, possibly an allegory for the charity, hovering over a dying soldier and his wife and child.(15.21)

In September 1915 a 5l Red Cross stamp picturing nurses and wounded soldiers and a 5l Greek Women's Patriotic League stamp in the form of an inscribed label and a badge were introduced.(15.22) These were voluntary, and supplied to selected post offices that kept ten percent of the sale money and passed the rest to the charities.

In November 1916 Greece's deep divisions were reflected in its stamps. To ensure Venizelos could not use existing stocks of the on-going 1911 Hermes issues the royalists in Athens ordered them to be overprinted with the crown and letters E T (for Greek Post).(15.23) In February 1917 Venizelos responded with a set for northern Greece and the Greek islands featuring the goddess Iris inscribed *Provisional Government*.(15.24)

In April 1917 Athens reissued several values of the older 1901 Hermes stamps overprinted with surcharges and the Greek initials for *Kolnonike Pronea* (Social Providence).(15.25) The profits went to help those

15.25 1901 3l and 1d Hermes with Social Providence and surcharge overprint (from set April 1917)

15.26 Fiscal angel with Social Providence and new value overprint (from set 1917)

15.27 5l Red Cross with Patriotic Charity League overprint (Summer 1918)

monkey bite in October 1920 led the November elections to centre upon the return of King Constantine or the creation of a republic. Venizelos lost heavily, probably because of national war-weariness and accusations of his abuse of power. A plebiscite led to Constantine's recall, and the ambitious royalists continued the war against Turkey. It proved a disastrous mistake as the formally moribund Ottoman Empire had rejuvenated itself under the charismatic leadership of Kemal Pasha, better known under his later name of Kemal Ataturk. He had masterminded a nationalist army revolt against Sultan Mehmed VI who had been reduced to a humiliated puppet in the hands of the victorious Allies. While the Allies, who disliked Constantine, looked on, the Greeks were routed near Smyrna on 26 August 1922 and lost the newly acquired Turkish province soon afterwards.

Another revolution struck Greece. Dissatisfied army officers led a coup, Constantine was dethroned again, and several key royalists executed. Venizelos returned to power and reluctantly accepted Constantine's son, George II, as King. The 1915 Women's Patriotic League stamps were reintroduced in 1922 with higher values – a sure sign of the continuing suffering across the country.

In May 1923 the pair of 1913 Victory stamp appeared overprinted 'Revolution 1922' in Greek with surcharges.(15.30) During the disruption redundant stocks of superannuated Cretan stamps, including suffering as a result of the wartime blockade. Later the two Victory stamps from 1913 were similarly overprinted, as was a Winged Angel fiscal stamp.(15.26) Evidence of the haste in all these printings lies in the many inverted, double and shifted overprints.

In June 1918 a new Red Cross design picturing a wounded soldier was issued, and some stocks were earmarked through an overprint (P.I.P.) for the Patriotic Charity League.(15.27)

In May 1918 Greek forces defeated the Bulgarians at the Battle of Skra-di-Legen to the north-east of Thessaloniki, and in September a combined Greek, Serbian, Italian, French and British force finally broke through Austro-Hungarian and Bulgarian lines on the Macedonian Front. A few months later Venizelos hurried to the Paris Peace Conference. Here his force of personality and powers of persuasion secured for Greece not only western Thrace in the Treaty of Neuilly in November 1919, but also in the Treaty of Sevres in August 1920 eastern Thrace and the region around Smyrna in western Turkey inhabited by many Greeks. Overprinted Turkish and Greek stamps marked the occupation and subsequent acquisition of Thrace.(15.28/15.29)

Although initially popular, this successful expansion did little to bring the two Greek factions together. The death of King Alexander of blood poisoning after a

15.28 1911 Hermes overprinted with ET and crown (1916) and Administration of Western Thrace (set June 1920)

15.29 Turkish 20pa overprinted High Commission of Thrace and new value (for occupation of Adrianople) (from set August 1920)

15.30 1913 25l eagle over Mount Olympus overprinted Revolution 1922 and 10l (from series 8 May 1923)

15.31 Crete 1905 Europa overprinted Greece in September 1908 and overprinted again Revolution 1922 and 5l (from series 8 May 1923)

15.32 Red Cross (12 June 1924)

15.33 2d Savoia Marchetti flying boat (from set 21 October 1926)

15.34 80l Lord Byron and 2d (E) Byron at Missolonghi (16 April 1924)

15.35 (E) 25l tomb of Marco Botzaris (24 April 1926)

Postage Dues, also received the overprints and were used up for ordinary postage throughout the country.(15.31)

At the ensuing peace treaty in August 1923 Greek troops left Turkey, and Greece returned eastern Thrace. A huge exchange of population was agreed under which one and a half million Christians moved from Turkey to Greece and around half a million Muslims from Greece to Turkey. The historic 'Great Idea' was over, and Greece was demoralized, heavily in debt, isolated and still perilously unstable. A botched royalist coup and a landslide victory for the liberal-republicans led to George II being forced into exile on 1 April 1924 after just eighteen months as king.

A plebiscite led to the Hellenic Republic which was beset by coup and counter-coup, and quarrels with Italy and Bulgaria, until Venizelos returned to power in 1928 and in a rare full four year term of office as prime minister he introduced welfare reforms and improved relations with Turkey. However in 1932 the world-wide depression, extensive unemployment and ensuing unrest led to his replacement by a monarchist government which suppressed two Venizelist attempted coups in 1933 and 1935 and then restored King George II. With the support of Ionnis Metaxas, a retired royalist general, George established an authoritarian regime that lasted until the Second World War.

After the 1923 'Revolution' issue Greek stamp issues ignored the dramatic internal swings of political fortunes and concentrated upon the fund raising capacity of a series of sets celebrating the country's Classical past and more recent struggle for independence. However the single Red Cross Fund stamp in 1924, reissued in 1926, picturing a wounded soldier, his wife and child, marked the need for continuing support for the constant stream of casualties.(15.32)

In 1926 the first Air set comprised four attractive pastel views of a Savoia Marchetti S-55C flying boat.(15.33) The stamp shows the innovative triple hulls, the outside two for passengers or cargo and the centre one for pilot and crew. Equally unusual were the back-to-back engines above the hulls with contra-rotating propellors. Just eight 'C' variants were built, and they were highly successful for inter-island contact.

Fortuitously several important centenaries occurred during this period of political instability to facilitate stamp issues calculated to fortify national pride as well as raise revenue. In April 1924 the romantic figure of Lord Byron and his celebrated arrival at Missolonghi adorned two stamps marking the centenary of his death.(15.34)

In April 1926 a stamp commemorating the centenary of the eventual fall of Missolonghi to the Ottoman Turks featured the Greek clan leader and general, Marco Botzaris.

15.36 (E) 5l Corinth Canal, 10l Dodecanese costume, 20l Macedonian costume, 25l Simon Peter Monastery, and 3d battlecruiser Georgios Averoff 2d Acropolis, (from set 1 April 1927+)

The image was taken from the sculpture on his tomb.(15.35) He was killed in August 1823 leading a counter attack on the encroaching Ottoman army, and his life and death were celebrated in many poems and paintings.

Starting in April 1927 a long set of fifteen stamps embraced several patriotic themes. They included famous Athenian sites including the Temple of Theseus, the Acropolis, and the Academy of Sciences. Others ranged across the country, and featured provincial Dodecanese and Macedonian costumes, the Corinth Canal, the White Tower in Salonika, the cathedral at Mystras, and the spectacular Monastery of Simon Peter that seems to hang from a cliff top at Mount Athos.(15.36) The 3d featured the battlecruiser *Georgios Averoff* named after the benefactor of the 1896 Olympic Games. Completed in 1910, and armed with four 9.2" and several 7.5"guns, in 1912 it was instrumental in imposing two defeats on Turkish squadrons and securing the Aegean Sea for Greece.

In August 1927 three stamps honoured the French General Charles Favier who led the determined Greek defence of the Acropolis against the besieging Ottoman army.(15.37) He was forced to surrender in April 1827,

but Athens was finally liberated that August.

That October six stamps marked the centenary of the Battle of Navarino with pictures of the battle off the south-western tip of Greece and portraits of the Allied commanders, Admiral Sir Edward Codrington, the French Admiral Marie Henri de Rigny, and Admiral Lodewijk Gustaaf van der Heiden, the Dutch born commander of the Russian Mediterranean fleet.(15.38)

April 1930 saw no less than eighteen stamps commemorating the centenary of independence (15.39). The date referred to Britain, France and Russia initially agreeing the independence of Greece and guaranteeing its protection in the protocol they signed in February 1830. The majority of stamps portrayed leaders of Greek forces who had attained heroic status (despite their frequent feuding), including Marco Botzaris (1d 50). Among the others were the Eastern Orthodox Patriarch Gregory V (20l) of Constantinople who was hung on Easter Sunday 1821 by Sultan Mahumd II for failing to suppress the Greek insurrection, the poet Dionysios Solomos (15d) who wrote the *Hymn of Liberty* that, set to music, became the National Anthem, and the writer Adamantios Korais whose works were inspired by Revolutionary France and Ancient Greece and in turn inspired the Greek revolution. The 25d featured Bishop Germanos III blessing the banner of revolt at Agia Lavra on 25 March 1821 (and not as some suppose the National Assembly's Declaration of Independence), the 50d contains a famous painting of a sortie from the besieged town of Missolonghi, and the 4d proudly showed a map highlighting the expansion of Greece since 1830.

15.37 6d General Favier (from set 1 August 1927)

GREECE

15.38 (E) 4d Battle of Navarino, and 5d Admirals Sir Edward Codrington, de Rigny and van der Heiden (or Heyden) (set 20 October 1927+)

15.39 15d Dionysios Solomos, 1d 50 Marco Botzaris, 20l Patriarch Gregory V, 50d sortie from Missolonghi, 25d (E) Bishop Germanos blessing the banner, and 4d the expansion of Greece (from set 1 April 1930)

Bibliography

The key works informing this book along with Stanley Gibbons and Michel catalogues were:

Arblaster, Paul (2006), *A History of the Low Countries*, Palgrave

Clark, Christopher (2013), *The Sleepwalkers: How Europe Went to War in 1914*, Penguin

Cornwall, Mark (2005), *The Last Years of Austria-Hungary*, Exeter University Press

Duggan, Christopher (2007), *The Force of Destiny: A History of Italy since 1796*, Allen Lane

Fenby, Jonathan (2015), *The History of Modern France*, Simon & Schuster

Figes, Orlando (1996), *A People's Tragedy: The Russian Revolution*, Penguin

Gallant, Thomas (2001), *Modern Greece: from the War of Independence to the Present*, Bloomsbury

Gilbert, Martin (1995), *First World War*, Weidenfeld & Nicolson

Glenny, Misha (2012), *The Balkans 1804-2012*, Granta

Hastings, Max (2013), *Catastrophe: Europe goes to War 1914*, William Collins

Jackson, Julian (2002), *Europe 1900-1945*, Oxford University Press

Lee, Stephen J. (3rd ed 2008), *The European Dictatorships 1918-45*, Routledge

MacMillan, Margaret (2002), *Peacemakers: Six Months that Changed the World*, John Murray

MacMillan, Margaret (2013), *The War that Ended the Peace: How Europe abandoned Peace for the First World War*, Profile

Massie, Robert K. (2004), *Dreadnought: Britain, Germany and the coming of the Great War*, Pimlico

Mazower, Mark (2002), *The Balkans: from the end of Byzantium to the present day*, Phoenix

Roberts, J.M. (1996), *A History of Europe*, Helicon

Stevenson, David (2004), *The History of the First World War*, Penguin

Zamoyski, Adam (2009), *Poland: A History*, William Collins

Index

Emboldened page numbers indicate sections centred on that country

Adriatic Sea/Dalmatia 7, 127, 151
   Adriatic Ports (Fiume, Pola, Ragusa, Trieste), 90, 113, 117, 118, 134
   Dalmatia/Dalmatian Islands, 118, 134
   Gabriele D'Annunzio & Fiume, 118-121
   Venezia Tridentina/Giulia, 117, 118, 121
Aeroplanes/National Companies, 26-27, 37, 39, 75, 81, 99, 104-105, 116-117, 156, 163
Aisne, River/Battle of, 30, 43
Albania, 7, 113, 128, 129, 145, **151-156**, 160
   Independence, 139, 151
   Relations with Italy, 123-124, 153, 161

Wartime occupation, 152-153
Rise of Ahmed Muthar Zogolli, 154-156
Albert I, King, 18, 30, 32, 35, 36, 37
Alexander, King (of Greece), 161, 162
Alexander, King (of the Serbs, Croats & Slovenes), 129, 132, 135
Allenstein (Olsztyn) plebiscite, 21, 57
Antwerp, 30, 32
Alsace-Lorraine, 7, 8, 13, 17, 30, 44
Art Deco, 47-48, 49
Austria, 34, **95-99**,
   Barred union with Germany, 95-96

Loss of territory, 96
Establishment of Republic, 95-96
Austria-Hungary (see also Austria and Hungary) 6, 7, 8, 12, 13, 51, 54, 55, **84-95**, 116, 138, 139
And Albania, 152, 153
And Bosnia-Hercegovina, 88, 91-94
And Montenegro, 93, 129, 131
And Romania, 93, 139, 153
And Serbia, 92, 93, 127-128
Army/campaigns 14, 51, 64, 90, 131, 145, 146, 162
Becomes Dual Monarchy, 84

INDEX

Collapse of, 15, 107, 146
Past Hapsburg rulers, 86-87
Pre-war defeats by France and Germany, 84

Balkan Wars, First and Second (1912-13), 88-89, 128, 131, 138-139, 144-145, 151
Bavaria/People's Republic/Free State 8, 15-17
Belgium, 6, 13, 14, 18, 25, **29-37**, 44, 48, 50, 57
Arts and Culture, 29, 35
Covets Luxembourg, 34, 38
Eupen and Malmedy, 17, 34
Flemings and Walloons, 29, 32
Invasion and occupation, 30-33, 35
National Redoubt (Antwerp, Liege, Namur), 30
Belorussia, 14, 15, 64
Benes, Edvard, 106
Berlin, 11, 15
Berthelot, Pierre Marcellin, 48
Bessarabia, 87, 141
Bismark, Prince Otto von, 8, 87
Blanc, Paul Joseph, 42, 50
Bonaparte, Napoleon, 25, 29, 42, 48, 49
Boris III, King, 147-148, 149, 150
Bosnia/Bosnia-Herzegovina, 6, 12, 87-88, 89, 92, 93, 94, 127, 128, 131, 132
Bourchier, James, 149
Brest-Litovsk, Treaty of (see also Soviet Russia), 15, 54, 65, 74, 77
Brussels, 29, 31, 32, 35
Bulgaria/Bulgarians, 6, 34, 87, 88-89, 116, 127, **143-150**
And 1912-13 Balkan Wars, 128, 138-139, 146, 151, 159, 160
Achieves independence/kingdom, 143
Army/campaigns, 14, 129, 131, 145, 146, 161, 162
1916 occupies part of Romania, 139, 153
1918 defeat; territorial losses, 147, 162
Post war Balkan relations, 148-149
Post war internal tensions, 147-149
Byron, Lord, 157, 163

Carinthia, plebiscite in, 96, 131, 134
Carol I, King, 136-139, 142
Cavour, Count Camillo di, 112, 122
Charities and Social Welfare (featured on stamps)
Anti-TB, 20-21, 35, 36, 41, 104
Artists and Musicians, 9, 97
Famine relief, 66-67
Flood relief, 36, 72, 86, 97
Orphans and elderly, 21, 24, 25-26, 44-45, 66, 93, 98, 109
Red Cross, 30, 31-32, 44, 45, 60, 75, 78-79, 110, 116, 146, 156, 161-162, 163
Returning prisoners of war, 104, 148
Ruhr strikers' families, 24
War widows and wounded, 16, 18, 56, 89, 90, 93, 99, 135, 161
Welfare Funds, 137, 140, 142
Charleroi, 29, 30
Charles I, Emperor,, 55, 90, 94, 95, 100, 103, 117, 134, 141
Charlotte, Grand Duchess, 38-41
Cologne, 24-25, 26
Congress of Berlin, 87, 88, 143
Constantine I, King, 160, 162
Copernicus, Nicolaus, 60
Corfu, 123-124, 129, 153
Cossacks/Cossack Republics, 63, 67, 68, 76
Courland, 54, 67, 76, 77, 79
Crete, 157-158, 159
Croats/Croatia (see also Kingdom of the Serbs, Croats & Slovenes), 84, 87, 118, 128, 131, 132, 133, 134, 135

Czechoslovakia, 6, 25, 34, 54, 57, 59, 95, 97, 98, **106-112**
And Austria and Hungary, 101, 102, 107, 112
Pre-war Austro-Hungarian rule, 86, 87, 106
Czech Legions, 67, 90, 106, 107, 109, 117, 146
Establishment of, 96, 107

Dalmatia/Dalmatian coast (see Adriatic Sea)
Dante Alighieri, 121
Danzig, 19-21, 54, 57
Daugavpils, 76, 77, 79
Denmark, 8, 18-19
Dinant, 32, 34
Dmowski, Roman, 51, 54, 57
Dobruja, 136, 139, 140, 142, 143, 145, 146, 147
Dozsa, Gyorgy, 102

Eastern Rumelia, 87, 127
Ebert, Freidrich, 15, 28
Elisabeth, Queen (of the Belgians), 35
Elisabeth, Queen (Romania), 136-137, 138,
Elizabeth of Thuringia, Saint, 25
Epirus, 151, 152, 153, 157, 159, 160, 161
Essad Pasha, 152, 153
Estonia, 6, 34, 54, 67, **74-76**,
Eyschen, Paul, 38

Ferdinand I, Tsar, 143-147, 148, 149
Ferdinand and Marie (King and Queen of Romania), 14, 101, 137, 141, 142
Fiume, 118-121
France, 6, 34, 36, 38, **42-50**, 89, 97, 118, 134, 138, 152, 157
French Empire, 50
French army/campaigns, 12, 22, 32, 101, 117, 131, 146, 149, 153, 162
Invasion/Occupation, 13, 14, 31, 32, 43, 44-45, 48
Pre-war relations with Germany, 8, 12, 13
Post-war relations with Germany, 17, 18, 22, 25
Sinking Fund, 48-49
Francis of Assisi, Saint, 126
Franz Ferdinand, Archduke, 6, 12, 87, 89, 94, 105, 128
Franz Joseph, Emperor, 6, 12, 55, 84-90, 117, 129, 132
Frederick III, Emperor, 8
Fuhring, Anna (model for *Germania*), 8

Galicia, 14, 51, 55, 56, 57, 64, 70, 107, 145
Garibadli, Guiseppe, 113, 115, 122
Gediminas, Grand Duke, 80, 81
George I, King, 157, 160
George II, King, 162, 163
Germany, 6, 7, **8-28**, 41, 46, 99, 112,145, 157
And Baltic provinces, 76, 80
And Weimar Republic, 16, 17, 23-28, 67
Freikorps, 15, 16, 23, 67, 77
German army/campaigns, 13-15, 30, 51, 53, 54, 74, 76, 131, 139, 145, 146
Pre-war situation/attitude, 8-12
Territory lost/disputed after 1918, 17-23, 107
War and collapse, 12-16, 34, 36, 89, 116
Ghent, 32, 35
Great Britain, 6, 8, 18, 32, 34, 43, 48, 50, 67, 89, 118, 134, 138, 152, 157
British army/campaigns 22, 32, 117, 145, 146, 162
Greece, 7, 87, 88-89, 123-124, 128, **157-165**
And 1912-13 Balkan Wars, 159-160
And Albania, 151, 152, 153, 160

And Crete and other island, 157-158, 160
And Romania, 138-139, 144-145, 147, 149
Allied advance north from, 129, 139, 140, 145, 146, 162
Classical heritage highlighted, 158-159, 164
Occupation of Smyrna, 162-163
Political instability, 159, 160, 161
Wars of independence; *Megali Idea*, 157, 163-164

Hainisch, Dr Michael, President 98
Hindenburg, Paul von, President, 28
Hitler, Adolf, 7, 16, 28, 34, 37, 50, 58, 83, 99, 105, 135, 150
Horthy, Miklos, Admiral/Regent, 103-105
Hungary, 7, 34, 84, 97, **99-105**, 132
Count Mihaly Karolyi, 100-101
Dissolution of Dual Monarchy, 95, 100
Regency, 103-105
Romanian and Serbian occupation, 101, 141
Soviet Republic, 101, 102-103, 107
Western Hungary, 103
Hus, Jan & Hussite Wars, 109-110, 112

Italy, 6, 7, 8, 12, 48, 57, **113-126**, 138, 157, 160
And Albania, 116, 123, 139, 152, 153-154, 156, 161
And Austria, 86, 96, 97, 98
And Fiume, 118-121
And Hungary, 101
And Kingdom of the Serbs, Croats & Slovenes, 118, 131, 132, 134, 135
Colonies/Imperial ambitions, 113-115, 124, 126
Enters First World War, 116
Establishment of Kingdom of Italy, 113
Italian army/campaigns, 22, 44, 51, 89, 90, 116, 117, 145, 162
Mussolini/Fascists take control, 123-126
Reaction to Peace Conference, 118
Reigning House of Savoy, 113, 116, 122
Relations with Papacy, 113, 124-126

Japan, 67, 69
Joan of Arc, Saint, 48
John III Sobieski, King, 51, 55, 61

Kaulbach, Wilhelm von, 17
Kerensky, Alexander, 64-65
Kingdom of the Serbs, Croats & Slovenes, 34, 97, 112, **131-135**, 149, 155
And Italy, 118, 120-121, 134
Establishment of, 94, 95, 96, 101-102, 129, 131-132
Internal stresses, 131, 134-135
Post-war territory acquired, 134
Konarski, Stanislaus, 60
Kosciuszko, Tadeusz, 59
Krakow, 51, 61
Kun, Bela, 101, 102-103, 107

Latvia, 6, 54, 67, 74, **76-79**
League of Nations, 18, 19, 20, 21, 22, 23, 25, 49, 57, 75, 79, 81, 82-83, 97, 123, 153
Le Havre, 30, 31, 49
Lenin, Vladimir, 15, 65, 69, 72, 77, 140
Leopold 1, King, 29, 32, 35, 37
Leopold II, King, 30, 32, 37
Levski, Vasil, 143, 144, 150
Liege, 30, 33-34, 36
Lindbergh, Charles, 49
Lithuania, 6, 14, 57, **80-83**
And defeat of the Teutonic Knights, 81
And Memel, 22, 82-83
And Poland, 58-59, 80, 81

167

And Russia, 64, 67, 80, 81
Livonia, 54, 74, 77
Louvain, 32, 34, 35
Lublin, 52, 55
Ludwig III, King, 16,
Luxembourg, 13, 18, 34, **38-41,**

Macedonia, battles for, 87, 139, 144, 145, 146, 149, 150, 153, 157, 159, 160, 161
    Allied breakout from, 129, 139, 140, 145, 146, 153, 162
Manzoni, Alessandro, 125
Marie Adelaide, Grand Duchess, 38
Marienburg, 26
Marienwerder (Kwidzyn) plebiscite, 21-22, 57
Marne, River, Battle of, 13, 30
Martin of Tours, Saint, 29-30, 36,
Martinovics, Ignac, 102
Masaryk, Tomas, President, 106, 107, 110-111
Max, Prince, of Baden, 15
Mazzini, Guiseppe, 122
Memel (Klaipeda), 22, 82-83
Mercier, Desire-Joseph, Cardinal, 32
Merode, Count Louis Frederic de, 31
Merson, Nicholas Luc-Olivier, 22, 43, 45, 50
Mikiewicz, Adam, 59
Milo of Croton, 46-47
Minin, Kuzma, 63
Montenegro, 87, 88, 89, 127, **129-131**, 132, 152, 153,
    And 1912-13 Balkan Wars, 131, 138-139, 144, 151, 159
    Petrovic Njegos dynasty and Prince/King Nicholas, 130-131, 134
    Defeated and occupied 1916, 131
Moscicki, Ignacy, 61
Moscow, 55, 67, 72
Mouchon, Louis-Eugene, 42, 45, 50
Mucha, Alphonse, 109
Munich, 15-16, 24, 26
Muromets, Ilya, 63
Mussolini, Benito, 7, 57, 120-121, 122-126, 156

Napoleon III, Emperor, 42, 113,
Netherlands, The, 18, 28, 32, 36, 38, 50
Nevski, Alexander/Nevski Cathedral, 148-149
Nibelung legends, 98
Nicholas II, Tsar, 12, 62, 63, 64, 106, 107, 130
Nivelle, Robert, General, 43-44
Noli, Fan, 155

Olympic Games, (1896) 158-159, (1906) 159, (1920) 34-35, (1924) 46
Orval Abbey (Belgium), 36
Ottoman Turks/Ottoman Empire, 7, 34, 106, 116, 129
    And Albania, 113, 151, 152
    And 1877-78 Balkan War, 87, 127, 130, 136, 138, 144-145
    And 1912-13 Balkan Wars, 88-89, 146
    And Greece, 157-158, 159, 161
    Army/campaigns, 14, 87, 151

Paderewski, Ignacy, 54, 56
Paderewska, Helena, 56, 60
Paris/Paris Peace Conference (1919), 6, 7, 13, 34, 45, 46, 57, 118, 132, 134, 153, 162
    Inter-Allied Commissions, 21, 57
    Treaty of Versailles, 15, 17, 19, 21, 26, 27, 34, 49, 57, 75, 103, 107, 141
Pasic, Nikola, 132
Pasteur, Louis, 45-46, 48

Pats, Konstantin, President, 76
Petain, Philippe, Marshal, 44
Peter I, King, 129, 132, 134
Petofi, Sandor, 102, 104
Philatelic Exhibitions, 39, 41 (Luxembourg), 45 (France), 56 (Poland), 122 (Trieste)
Philibert, Emmanuel, Duke, 126
Pilsudski, Jozef, Marshal, 51, 53-54, 56, 57, 58, 61
Poland, 6, 7, 17, 25, **51-61**, 63
    Congress Poland, 51, 54, 55, 80
    Polish Corridor, 17, 19, 21, 22
    Polish Legion, 51, 54, 67
    Polish-Lithuanian Commonwealth, 51, 55, 57, 59, 80
    Puppet Kingdom of Poland, 15, 53
    Russian Poland (Vistula Land), 14, 15, 51, 54, 62, 64
    Republic of Central Lithuania, 58-59
    Silesian plebiscite, 22-23, 110
Pope/Papal States, 113, 124-126
Posen/Poznan, 19, 54, 56, 57, 61,
Pozharsky, Dmitry, 63
Prague/Prague Castle, 108-109, 111, 112
Prussia (see also Germany), 6, 22, 25, 34, 38, 42, 44, 51,
    East Prussia, 13-14, 57,

Reims Cathedral (smiling angel), 49
Rheinstein, Castle, 26
Rhine, River/Rhineland, 18, 26, 34
Riga, 14, 67, 76, 77, 79
Romania/Romanians, 6, 87, 89, 127, 128, **136-142**
    And Hungary, 101, 102, 139, 141
    Joins Allies 1916, 14, 139-140
    Post-war territorial expansion, 134, 141-142
    Pre-war territorial expansion, 139, 144, 147
Ronsard, Pierre de, 47
Ruhr, 18, 22, 24, 25
Russia, Imperial 6, 7, **62-64**, 157,
    Imperial Russian army/campaigns, 12, 13, 54, 63-64, 76, 90, 106, 129, 145
    Pre-war alliances/tensions, 8, 12, 13, 43, 51, 87, 127, 138, 139, 152
    Provisional Government, 64-65, 74, 76
    Russian Poland (see Poland)
Russia, Soviet, 57, **65-73**, 148-149
    Civil War (see also White Russian forces) 65, 67-70, 77
    Establishment of, 70-73, 80
    Exiting the war, 15, 54
    Red Army, 22, 65, 66, 67-70, 107, 150
    Revolution, 44, 64-65
Ruthenians, 59, 86, 101, 107

Saar, 18
St Petersburg/Petrograd, 63, 64, 65, 67, 73
Sarajevo, 6, 88, 89, 94, 128
Schleswig-Holstein, 8, 18-19
Serbia/Serbs, 6, 12, 48, 87, 94, 106, **127-129**
    And Albania, 151, 152, 153
    Balkan Wars (1912-13), 88-89, 59, 138-139, 144, 145, 160
    Black Hand secret society, 127, 128
    Establishment of monarchy, 127-128
    Role in Kingdom of the Serbs, Croats & Slovenes, 129, 132, 134,
    Serbia defeated/occupied, 129, 131, 146, 161
Shipka Pass, Battle of, 143, 144, 148, 149, 150
Ships/Shipping, 20, 32, 34, 36, 45, 49, 61, 66, 67, 90, 131, 136

Shkodra, 131, 151, 152, 153, 154, 155
Sigismund III Vasa, King, 55, 61
Silesia, partition of, 22, 57-58, 59, 110
Skanderberg, 151, 152, 153, 154
Slovaks, 87, 101
Slovenia/Slovenes (see also Kingdom of the Serbs, Croats & Slovenes), 96, 118, 128, 131, 133-134
Smetona, Antanas, President, 82, 83
Somme, River/Battles of the, 13, 43
Stalin, Joseph, 73, 83,
Stamboliyski, Alexander, 147, 148, 149
Stefanic, Milan, General 106, 107
Stephan, Heinrich von, 26

Tallinn, 75, 76
Tartu/Treaty of, 74, 75, 76
Teschen, 59, 110
Thrace, 144, 145, 147, 149, 150, 160, 162, 163
Transylvania, 14, 139, 142
Trumbic, Ante, 132, 134
Tyrol plebiscites, 96, 116

Ukraine, 7, 14, 15, 54, 57, 59, 62, 68, 86, 99
    War, independence, and defeat, **69-70**
United Baltic Duchy, 15, 77
United States of America, 18, 28, 34, 48, 72, 117

Vasov, Ivan, 148
Veliko Turnovo, 143, 144, 148
Venizelos, Eleftherios, 159, 160-161, 162-163
Verdun, 30, 43, 51
Versailles, Treaty of (see Paris Peace Conference)
Victor Emmanuel II, King, 113, 116, 122
Victor Emmanuel III, King,113, 122, 123, 124, 126
Vilna/Vilnius, 14, 54, 58-59, 61, 80, 81, 82
Vistula, River, Battles of the, 14
Vistula Land (see Poland)

War Memorials, 37, 41
Warsaw, 52, 54, 55, 59, 70
Wartburg Castle, 24-25
Washington, George, General/President), 49
Wembley Exhibition, 6
White Russian generals/armies, 65, 67-70, 107
    General Pavel Bermondt-Avolov, 67
    General Anton Denikin, 68
    General Mikhail Diterikhs, 69
    Admiral Alexander Kolchak, 67-68, 69,
    General Lavr Kornilov, 68
    Spiridon and Nikolai Merkulov, 69
    General Alexander Rodzianko, 67
    General Pyotr Wrangel, 68, 70
    General Nikolai Yudenich, 67
Wilhelm I, King/Emperor 8, 11
Wilhelm II, Emperor, 8, 11, 12, 26, 32, 43, 74, 89
William of Wied, Prince, 152, 154
Wilson, Woodrow, President, 54, 57, 94, 118, 153
Wurttemberg, 8, 17

Ypres/Battle of, 13, 32, 34, 43
Yser, River/ Yser Pocket, 13, 30, 32
Yugoslavia (see Kingdom of the Serbs, Croats & Slovenes)

Zogolli, Ahmet Muhtar, President/King, 153, 154-155